Serving
God's Words

To Peter, as a mark of our respect,
on the occasion of your sixty-fifth birthday.

2 Timothy 2:1–2

Serving God's Words

Windows on preaching and ministry

Edited by Paul A. Barker, Richard J. Condie & Andrew S. Malone

INTER-VARSITY PRESS
Norton Street, Nottingham NG7 3HR, England
Website: www.ivpbooks.com
Email: ivp@ivpbooks.com

First published 2011

British Library Cataloguing in Publication Data
A catalogue record for this book is available from the British Library.

ISBN: 978-1-84474-547-0

Set in Monotype Garamond 11/13pt
Typeset in Great Britain by Servis Filmsetting Ltd, Stockport, Cheshire

Inter-Varsity Press publishes Christian books that are true to the Bible and that communicate the gospel, develop discipleship and strengthen the church for its mission in the world.

Inter-Varsity Press is closely linked with the Universities and Colleges Christian Fellowship, a student movement connecting Christian Unions in universities and colleges throughout Great Britain, and a member movement of the International Fellowship of Evangelical Students. Website: www.uccf.org.uk.

CONTENTS

CONTRIBUTORS

Paul Barker was Vicar of Holy Trinity Doncaster for nearly fourteen years. He is now Visiting Scholar at Seminari Theoloji Malaysia, and Adjunct Professor of Old Testament at the Myanmar Evangelical Graduate School of Theology.

Gerald Bray is Director of Research for the Latimer Trust in London, and Research Professor of Divinity at Beeson Divinity School in Alabama.

D. A. Carson is Research Professor of New Testament at Trinity Evangelical Divinity School in Illinois, where he has taught since 1978.

Allan Chapple has served with the Australian Fellowship of Evangelical Students, as a pastor both in Western Australia and the UK, and as a lecturer at Seminari Theoloji Malaysia. He was the founding Principal of Trinity Theological College in Perth, where he continues to serve as Senior Lecturer in New Testament.

Graham Cole preceded Peter Adam as Principal of Ridley. He has since served as Professor of Biblical and Systematic Theology at Trinity Evangelical Divinity School in Illinois, before moving in 2011 to take up the Anglican Chair of Divinity at Beeson Divinity School in Alabama.

Richard Condie moved from lecturing at Ridley to succeed Peter Adam as Vicar of St Jude's Carlton.

David Jackman is the past President of the Proclamation Trust and the founding Director of the Cornhill Training Course, having also spent fifteen years in pastoral ministry. He now preaches, writes and works with church leaders internationally.

Peter Jensen was Principal of Moore Theological College for sixteen years, before becoming the Anglican Archbishop of Sydney in 2001.

Andrew Malone teaches biblical studies at Ridley, where he is also completing postgraduate research under Peter Adam's supervision.

David Peterson, after eleven years as Principal of Oak Hill College in London, has returned to Moore Theological College in Sydney as Senior Research Fellow and Lecturer in New Testament.

Michael Raiter taught theology in Pakistan and at Moore Theological College in Sydney, before becoming Principal of Melbourne School of Theology (formerly the Bible College of Victoria) in 2006.

Vaughan Roberts is Rector of St Ebbe's Church in Oxford, and President of the Proclamation Trust.

William Taylor has been Rector of St Helen's Church, Bishopsgate, in London since 1998.

PREFACE

'And in these restless times, my dear Wooster', he said, 'I fear that brevity in the pulpit is becoming more and more desiderated by even the bucolic churchgoer, who one might have supposed would be less afflicted with the spirit of hurry and impatience than his metropolitan brother. I have had many arguments on the subject with my nephew, young Bates, who is taking my old friend Spettigue's cure over at Gandle-by-the-Hill. His view is that a sermon nowadays should be a bright, brisk, straight-from-the shoulder address, never lasting more than ten or twelve minutes.'

Thus spoke the Reverend Heppenstall in P. G. Wodehouse's wonderful short story *The Great Sermon Handicap*. In these restless times, several decades later, preaching still comes in for mockery and attack. In Australia, at least, one of those who has both defended and modelled great expository preaching that is bright, brisk, straight from the shoulder (but seldom under twelve minutes, and often more than double that length) is the inimitable Peter Adam.

It is a joy and privilege to honour Peter on the occasion of his sixty-fifth birthday on 20 September 2011 with this Festschrift on the topic of preaching and ministry. For many years, Peter has not only been a faithful expositor but an able and thought-provoking trainer, a warm encourager by word and example, and a stimulating writer.

It was some years ago that Richard Condie and Paul Barker first discussed putting together this volume under the title of *Serving God's Words*, building on and complementing the titles of some of Peter's books. Andrew Malone was later recruited from a rival endeavour for much of the fastidious editorial work. From the start the venture was codenamed *Project Poodle*, honouring Peter's love of and tradition of having poodles, notably Poppy, George and Bella (and now the less purebred Bertie). More than that, his poodles have played a very significant role in his preaching, appearing frequently as illustrations, and thus breaking every homiletical rule about using family members in sermons.

The chapters in this volume reflect Peter's priorities and interests in the ministry of serving God's words: exposition of the Bible, systematic and historical theology, church history, and the practice of pastoral ministry. There are chapters on preaching and ministry arising from the Scriptures themselves: Richard Condie on the Ten Commandments, Paul Barker on Moses, David Peterson on Acts, David Jackman on 1 Corinthians, Allan Chapple on 1 Thessalonians, and William Taylor on 1 Timothy. Further chapters reflect on theological and devotional issues in preaching and ministry: Don Carson on devotional Bible reading, Graham Cole on ethics, Peter Jensen on judgment, and Mike Raiter on unction. Concluding chapters consider significant examples of preaching and ministry in church history: Gerald Bray on the Anglican *Homilies*, and Vaughan Roberts on Charles Simeon.

The authors are a combination of academics and pastoral ministers, a combination that Peter Adam has himself so ably embodied throughout his ministry. Indeed, such a union is not as common as it ought to be, and Peter's example of fusing wise pastoral ministry with rigorous scholarship is a significant one.

We express our thanks to Philip Duce of IVP for his gracious and warm acceptance and encouragement of this project. We thank the authors for fine and timely contributions; we have been encouraged by each contributor's enthusiasm and delight to honour Peter. Ruth Millard, longstanding librarian at Ridley's Leon Morris Library, graciously compiled the bibliography of Peter's writings.

For many years Peter has been an exemplar of serving God's words. We editors join the authors of this book – along with Peter's many friends throughout the world, so many of whom have sat eagerly under his teaching and preaching – not only to wish him a happy sixty-fifth birthday but to anticipate the 'Well done, good and faithful servant' that our Master will surely utter to Peter one day.

It is our prayer that this volume will encourage and challenge many to be, and to keep striving to be, better servants of God's words.

Paul Barker
Richard Condie
Andrew Malone

ABBREVIATIONS

AB	Anchor (Yale) Bible
AOTC	Apollos Old Testament Commentary
AV	Authorized (King James) Version
BDAG	W. Bauer, F. W. Danker, W. F. Arndt and F. W. Gingrich, *Greek-English Lexicon of the New Testament and Other Early Christian Literature*, 3rd ed., rev. and ed. F. W. Danker (Chicago: University of Chicago Press, 2000)
BNTC	Black's New Testament Commentaries
BriefCACE	Newsletter of the Centre for Applied Christian Ethics
BST	The Bible Speaks Today
ChrCent	*Christian Century*
CNT	Commentaire du Nouveau Testament
ConBNT	Coniectanea biblica: New Testament series
EB	Études bibliques
EKKNT	Evangelisch-katholischer Kommentar zum Neuen Testament
ICC	International Critical Commentary
ITC	International Theological Commentary
JSNT	*Journal for the Study of the New Testament*
JSNTSup	Journal for the Study of the New Testament, Supplement Series
JSOT	*Journal for the Study of the Old Testament*
JSOTSup	Journal for the Study of the Old Testament, Supplement Series

LCC	Library of Christian Classics
LD	Lectio divina
LXX	Septuagint
MNTC	Moffatt New Testament Commentary
NCB	New Century Bible
NIBC	New International Biblical Commentary
NICNT	New International Commentary on the New Testament
NICOT	New International Commentary on the Old Testament
NIGTC	New International Greek Testament Commentary
NovTSup	Novum Testamentum Supplements
NSBT	New Studies in Biblical Theology
NT	New Testament
NTS	*New Testament Studies*
OT	Old Testament
PNTC	Pillar New Testament Commentary
SJT	*Scottish Journal of Theology*
SNTSMS	Society for New Testament Studies Monograph Series
SP	Sacra pagina
s.v.	*sub verbo* (under the word)
TDNT	*Theological Dictionary of the New Testament*, ed. G. Kittel and G. Friedrich, tr. G. W. Bromiley, 10 vols. (Grand Rapids: Eerdmans, 1964–76)
ThTo	*Theology Today*
TLNT	C. Spicq, *Theological Lexicon of the New Testament*, tr. and ed. J. D. Ernest, 3 vols. (Peabody: Hendrickson, 1994)
TrinJ	*Trinity Journal*
VE	*Vox evangelica*
WBC	Word Biblical Commentary
WTJ	*Westminster Theological Journal*
WUNT	Wissenschaftliche Untersuchungen zum Neuen Testament

1. WORDS OF LIFE OR TABLETS OF STONE? PREACHING THE TEN COMMANDMENTS TODAY

Richard J. Condie

During Peter Adam's incumbency at St Jude's Carlton, two historic plaques were reaffixed to the walls of the sanctuary after some time in storage. One displayed the Lord's Prayer and the Apostles' Creed and the other the Ten Commandments. When the church interior was repainted in 2009, there was some discussion about the relocation of these plaques. Eventually, we settled on placing them in the main entry of the church. The first thing you see when you enter St Jude's is a plaque depicting the Ten Commandments, and the last thing you see as you exit is the Lord's Prayer and the Creed. The new placement elicited a couple of comments about the appropriateness of having a statement of the law as your first experience of church. Some were very troubled that we might be sending a message that we were more interested in law than in grace.

So what is the right place for the Ten Commandments today? In some ways, in the Australian context at least, they have fallen out of fashion.[1] I remember as young boy listening to the solemn reading of the Commandments and

---

1. I understand that the situation in the USA is very different, where the place of the Ten Commandments in the political and cultural scene is quite prominent. See Thomas G. Long, 'Dancing the Decalogue', *ChrCent* 123.5 (2006), p. 17, and Patrick D. Miller, 'Is There a Place for the Ten Commandments?', *ThTo* 60.4

making my response – 'Lord, have mercy upon us, and incline our hearts to keep this law' – in our monthly services of the Lord's Supper in an erstwhile Methodist church. Yet it is quite uncommon today to recite them in most Anglican services I go to. We are much more likely simply to use the Two Great Commandments in the Lord's Supper. In addition, the relative disuse of the catechism in evangelical Anglican circles in Australia means that few young people are taught to memorize the Commandments today.

Others have gone even further to sideline the Commandments intentionally. A prominent Melbourne city church undertook a A$120,000 advertising campaign in 2008 to promote 'a new faith for the 21st Century'. Among many things, they posted several large billboards across major freeways in Melbourne with the words 'The Ten Commandments: one of the most negative documents ever written' as a ploy to entice people to their church to hear an obligation-free exposition of the 'Christian' faith.[2]

It is not altogether surprising that this has happened. After all, evangelicals have tended to cling to the chorus 'you are not under law but under grace' (Rom. 6:14)[3] as their song in trying to avoid justification by works. Liberal Christians have tried to free people from the strict moral demands of the faith, and to provide a new approach less rooted in restrictive authoritarian texts. But both miss the point that Jesus himself made, that 'not one letter, not one stroke of a letter, will pass from the law until all is accomplished' (Matt. 5:18). On the surface of it, this seems to imply that Jesus thought they still had some relevance to his followers.

So is there a case for bringing the Ten Commandments back into the life and ministry of the church? What is their function in the Christian life? Specifically, is there a case for preaching on them? And, if so, how do we treat them as Christian Scripture, as life-giving words of grace, without falling into preaching law that condemns? This chapter seeks to address these questions and reclaim the Ten Commandments for our pulpits, for our catechesis, and for our memorization and use.

Footnote 1 *(cont.)*

    (2004), pp. 473–477, for a discussion about the Chief Justice in the Alabama Supreme Court and his monument to the Ten Commandments.

2. Barney Zwartz, 'New Faith Throws out the Ten Commandments', *The Age* (16 Sept. 2008).

3. Bible quotations in this chapter are from the NRSV.

The role of the Ten Commandments in the Christian life

There is a popular temptation to treat the Ten Commandments simply as a list of laws to keep, which produces legalism, where trying harder and harder to keep the moral code leads to despair, or to the pride of praying, 'God, I thank you that I am not like other people: thieves, rogues, adulterers, or even like this tax-collector' (Luke 18:11). However, the Ten Commandments do not necessarily function that way in the Christian life.

Speaking generally about the law, Calvin suggests that it serves three main functions. First, it points out the perfect demands of God in the lives of believers, underscores their inability to keep it, and thereby directs them to Christ. Its function is to put a burden of sin on people so that they can unreservedly accept the free offer of salvation in Christ, who brings relief from its demands.

> [R]ighteousness is taught in vain by the commandments until Christ confers it by free imputation and by the Spirit of regeneration . . . it would be of no value to know what God demands of us if Christ did not succour those labouring and oppressed under its intolerable yoke and burden.[4]

The law outlines the holiness of God and his demands, giving clarity and insight and naming the sin that holds the sinner back, of which he or she is otherwise unaware.

> [I]t shows God's righteousness, that is, the righteousness alone acceptable to God, it warns, informs, convicts, and lastly condemns, every man of his own unrighteousness . . . he is compelled to weigh his life in the scales of the law, laying aside all that presumption of fictitious righteousness, he discovers that he is a long way from holiness, and is in fact teeming with a multitude of vices, with which he previously thought himself undefiled . . . For if by the law covetousness is not dragged from its lair, it destroys wretched man so secretly that he does not even feel its fatal stab.[5]

When preaching the Commandments at St Jude's recently, this principle was vividly illustrated when we came to the eighth commandment. A number of members of the congregation confessed to me after the sermon that they

---

4. John Calvin, *Institutes of the Christian Religion*, ed. John T. McNeill, tr. Ford Lewis Battles, LCC 20–21 (London: SCM, 1961), 2.7.2.

5. Ibid. 2.7.6.

had come to church not thinking that this commandment really applied to them because they had never committed a major crime of theft. But when we looked at the application of the commandment to plagiarism, and the thieving of copyrighted music from the Internet, the conviction of the Spirit fell on many in the congregation that they needed to repent of their sin. One strong young Christian woman confided in me that the week following the sermon was the first time she had ever paid for music that she downloaded from the Internet. She had finally felt the 'fatal stab' of her sin.

In addition, Calvin cites St Augustine to make his case, that in pointing out sin, the law stirs a need to seek grace:

> Augustine often speaks of the value of calling upon the grace of His help . . . 'The law bids us, as we try to fulfil its requirements, and become wearied in our weakness under it, to know how to ask the help of grace' . . . Again: 'The law was given to accuse you; that accused you might fear; that fearing you might beg forgiveness; and that you might not presume on your own strength.'[6]

The second function of the law that Calvin notes is its role in restraining the behaviour of people even if they are not regenerate. Fear brought about by having the public sanctions of the law made known helps evil people to keep their sinfulness in check even when their hearts are not predisposed towards God:

> [T]hey are restrained, not because their inner mind is stirred or affected, but because, being bridled, so to speak, they keep their hands from outward activity, and hold inside the depravity that otherwise they would wantonly have indulged.[7]

Thirdly, Calvin argues that the law has a positive role for believers in instructing them in the ways of God, 'to learn more thoroughly each day the nature of the Lord's will to which they aspire, and to confirm them in the understanding of it'.[8] This not only increases the believers' knowledge of divine will, but also motivates their obedience:

> [B]y frequent meditation upon it to be aroused to obedience, to be strengthened in it, and be drawn back from the slippery path of transgression . . . The law is to the flesh

---

6. Ibid. 2.7.9.
7. Ibid. 2.7.10.
8. Ibid. 2.7.12.

like a whip to an idle and balky ass, to arouse it to work. Even for a spiritual man not yet free of the weight of the flesh the law remains a constant sting that will not let him stand still.[9]

Augustine offered the same idea, arguing that the true significance of the Decalogue was that it 'maps the character of holiness'.[10] He emphasized that the Commandments were given to Israel and not to the nations, to instruct them in God's will. In the power of the Holy Spirit, the appetite and will of the disciple is turned towards true obedience and righteousness as defined in the Ten Commandments.

By way of contrast, Luther saw them as 'both a form of natural law manifesting God's moral will for fallen humanity, but also . . . the practice of God's love command by the Christian'.[11] In the preface to the Large Catechism he famously said that 'anyone who knows the Ten Commandments perfectly, knows the entire scripture'.[12]

It is true that some of the Ten Commandments (murder, adultery, theft) are common to other ancient moral codes, while other commandments (proper worship of the Lord, the sabbath) are unique to the people of Israel. This fact suggests that rather than being just a list of requirements, the Commandments function as a kind of 'moral vision' for the people of God, 'to give us a picture of the character of God and God's people, rather than to give us a list of rules to live by'.[13]

So the Ten Commandments will by their nature point out and identify sins in the life of the believer; as Paul said, 'Yet, if it had not been for the law, I would not have known sin. I would not have known what it is to covet if the law had not said, "You shall not covet"' (Rom. 7:7). Believers find conviction and warning and even condemnation by them, which drives them to despair that leads them to seek grace. We should not be afraid of this function of

---

9. Ibid.

10. Philip Turner, 'The Ten Commandments in the Church in a Postmodern World', in Carl E. Braaten and Christopher R. Seitz (eds.), *I Am the Lord Your God: Christian Reflections on the Ten Commandments* (Grand Rapids: Eerdmans, 2005), pp. 3–17, quote p. 12.

11. Patrick D. Miller, 'Preaching the Ten Commandments', *Journal for Preachers* 25.2 (2002), pp. 3–10, quote p. 5.

12. Ibid.

13. Andrew Sloane, *At Home in a Strange Land: Using the Old Testament in Christian Ethics* (Peabody: Hendrickson, 2008), p. 170.

procuring right guilt in the heart of the believer. It is here that the salve and succour of the cross finds its target, bringing consolation and encouragement to the sin-sick soul.

But also we see the role of the Commandments in setting out the map or the guide for the process of sanctification in the believer's heart. Motivated by the Spirit who gives us a desire for the things of God, the Commandments show us the nature of holiness or, as one preacher has defined them, 'the disciplines of grace'.[14]

The case for preaching the Ten Commandments

But why *preach* them today? Why not simply resurrect them to the liturgy Sunday by Sunday, whereby we call our people to reflect on them for their lives, to help them in confession of sin and in the training of their righteousness?

First, it is interesting to note (and we will return to this below) that Jesus preached from the Commandments and used them in his instruction. He used them in his encounter with the rich young ruler in Luke 18, he used several of the Commandments as the basis for his monumental ethical treatise in the Sermon on the Mount in Matthew 5 and 6. The point for us here is that if Jesus expounded them, then so must we.

Secondly, they are part of the Holy Scripture, which we believe in its entirety is 'inspired by God and is useful for teaching, for reproof, for correction, and for training in righteousness, so that everyone who belongs to God may be proficient, equipped for every good work' (2 Tim. 3:16–17). This seems obvious and a little unnecessary to say, but the rarity of preaching on the Commandments in any detailed way would suggest we need to be reminded of it.

The point is that each commandment lends itself to an exposition about how it plays out in a biblical-theological context. That is, we ought not to be just expounding the Commandments as a whole in a series on Exodus or Deuteronomy, but be demonstrating to the congregation how the Bible as a whole treats each one, and specifically how each might be applied in a NT context in the life of Christian believers.

If that were not sufficient reason in itself, then the relevance of the material in the Commandments for contemporary life in the twenty-first century might

---

14. R. Kent Hughes, *Disciplines of Grace* (Wheaton: Crossway, 1993).

be. In 2002 the *New York Times* ran a series of articles on how the themes of the Ten Commandments and their teaching came up in contemporary issues of the day.[15] There was no shortage of material for the ten-week series. Our world is full of issues addressed by the Commandments: atheism, materialism, workaholism and other contemporary gods and idols, work–life balance, the place of the family, wars and violence, street crime, marriage and sexuality, poverty, greed, injustice; and the list goes on. It sounds like the topic areas of daily newspapers, but each area is addressed in some way by the Ten Commandments. The reaction of members of St Jude's to our series on the Commandments was quite remarkable. People counted this as one of the most practical and relevant sermon series they had heard in a long time.

Issues for interpretation

There are several issues of interpretation that need to be either resolved or borne in mind when preparing to preach on the Commandments. Following are a few of these issues.

Context

The first and most obvious point to make is that the Commandments must be preached in the context in which we find them. This is worth stating explicitly so that they are not expounded as universal aphorisms, but commands within a specific context.

In Exodus the Commandments come in the context of God's saving activity among his people. It is only when we grasp the entirety of the story that we get the real sense of the place of the Commandments in the life of the people of Israel.

The Israelites were the descendants of Abraham, Isaac and Jacob. Jacob's sons were the ancestors of the twelve tribes of Israel, who had travelled to Egypt during a famine in Canaan. Their descendants settled in Egypt, and came under oppression and the yoke of slavery there. The book of Exodus tells the story of how God commissions Moses to lead the people out of slavery and bondage in Egypt to be his people. They endure the plagues, and experience the Passover where the Lord strikes down all the firstborn in Egypt but passes over the Israelite firstborn. They come out of Egypt through

---

15. The series by Chris Hedges began with 'Unending Journey Through Faith and Heartbreak', *New York Times* (15 Dec. 2002).

the Red Sea, and enter the desert. Here God makes the bitter waters sweet, provides quail and daily manna for them to eat, provides water from the rock for them to drink, gives them victory over Amalek, and brings them to Mount Sinai as a new and rescued nation. Then, and only then, he says with resounding clarity, 'I am the LORD your God, who brought you out of the land of Egypt, out of the house of slavery' (Exod. 20:2), a phrase that, with the reminder of the context, drips with rich meaning and poignancy.

How easy, then, to read the Commandments as words about the covenant relationship with a God who has acted in mercy and kindness and grace towards his people. How hard with this context to find a legalistic list of rules to keep.

In line with this context in Exodus, the Commandments can be seen as the expression of worship or service, the very purpose for which the Israelites were brought out of Egypt. As Moses seeks to convince Pharaoh to let his people go, on four occasions he reminds him that the Lord said, 'that they may worship/serve me' (7:16; 8:1; 9:1; 10:3).[16] The Ten Commandments, then, express the true worship and service of the Lord.

In Deuteronomy the Commandments are placed prominently at the beginning of Moses' second speech in the book, in which he lays a foundation for the place of the law in Israel's life. The context recalls the salvation story from Exodus, but the content of the Commandments changes ever so slightly, as it performs a function of readying the people to enter the land. So, for example, the reason for keeping the sabbath command is more focused on redemption than on creation, as it is in Exodus (Deut. 5:15; cf. Exod. 20:11). Also the tenth commandment mentions land explicitly as a temptation for coveting as the people prepare to have land.

In addition, the particular context of Deuteronomy helps us in our own interpretation of the Commandments. In Deuteronomy 5:3 Moses says, 'Not with our ancestors did the LORD make this covenant, but with us, who are all of us here alive today.' Here Moses ensures that the people know that the Commandments are of enduring force and value in their lives as they head into the land. These commandments are no historical curiosity, but the living and active and contemporary word of God.

It is very important to work hard at keeping the context at the front of one's mind when preparing expositions of the particular commandments and in preaching them. It is worth reflecting on such context for each exposition, and regularly reminding the congregation of it in each sermon.

---

16. Miller, 'Preaching the Ten Commandments', p. 7.

All of grace

The context and indeed the opening line of the Commandments in both Exodus and Deuteronomy remind us that they are a response to divine grace. The Commandments do not begin with the words 'I am the LORD your God, who requires you to keep these rules', but an expression of grace, of salvation: 'I am the LORD your God, who brought you out of the land of Egypt, out of the house of slavery', and as such they carry a very self-conscious grace framework. That is, the Commandments themselves are in response to the gracious activity of God.

We see this pattern often throughout the Bible, where the statement of God's grace is followed by a command for humanity's obedience. For example, 1 John 4:10–11: 'In this is love, not that we loved God but that he loved us and sent his Son to be the atoning sacrifice for our sins. Beloved, since God loved us so much, we also ought to love one another.' God's saving act leads to our loving response, which in itself is a grace and freedom to us. David Wells describes it like this:

> Freedom is a gift from God, not something that can be earned by years of striving. The commandments are not a prison in which God places his people, a straitjacket to prevent them from getting above themselves. God has done what Israel could not do for itself – he has given it freedom in the crossing of the Red Sea. He now gives his people a second gift – the means of keeping that freedom. In the process he shows them who he is and what freedom is.[17]

We can also think of the Commandments as descriptions of the life that prevails in the zone of God's liberation:

> 'Because the Lord is your God,' the Decalogue affirms, 'you are free not to need any other gods. You are free to rest on the seventh day; free from the tyranny of lifeless idols; free from murder, stealing and covetousness as ways to establish yourself in the land.'[18]

It is a call to a radically God-directed freedom and grace.

Again this is a principle that needs repeating over and over again in both preparation and preaching. In preparing expositions on each commandment,

---

17. David F. Wells, 'God Spoke These Words', *ChrCent* 117.9 (2000), p. 301. Wells is not here implying that keeping the law is the means to retaining one's salvation, but is defining how the freedom of salvation looks.

18. Long, 'Dancing the Decalogue', p. 17.

it has been my habit to read aloud the entire text every time, to drum into my mind this grace framework.

The biblical trajectory of meaning

Both Luther and Calvin saw that the Commandments could best be under-stood not just by the things they prohibited (commandments 1–3 and 6–10) or expected (commandments 4 and 5), but also by the converse of these things. That is, the prohibitions, by implication, also speak of an opposite positive moral vision for how God's people are to live. So Calvin writes:

> In each commandment we must investigate what it is concerned with; then we must seek out its purpose, until we find what the Lawgiver testifies there to be pleasing or displeasing to himself. Finally from this same thing, we must derive an argument on the other side, in this manner; if this pleases God, the opposite displeases him; if this displeases, the opposite pleases him; if he commands this, he forbids the opposite; if he forbids this, he enjoins the opposite.[19]

He offers this example:

> In [the] commandment, 'You shall not kill', men's common sense will see only that we must abstain from wronging anyone or desiring to do so. Besides this, it contains, I say, the requirement that we give our neighbour's life all the help we can . . . So at the same time he requires those duties of love which can apply to its preservation. And thus we see how the purpose of the commandment always discloses to us whatever it there enjoins or forbids us to do.[20]

Calvin advocates three steps to identify the larger whole from the smaller part: First, to work out the subject of the commandment, 'what it is talking about'. Secondly, to determine the end of the commandment, 'what it indicates to us is pleasing or displeasing to God'. And thirdly, to develop an opposite argument, 'what the negative commandment affirms and the positive commandment forbids'. This 'opens them up and moves from reductionistic and negative interpretations to rich and complex ways in which the commandments create an ethic of love for the Christian'.[21]

---

19. Calvin, *Institutes* 2.8.8.
20. Ibid. 2.8.9.
21. Miller, 'Preaching the Ten Commandments', p. 5. Of course, we need to be alert to the pitfalls that can attend our estimation of positive equivalents. To what extent

Miller develops this idea to speak of a 'trajectory of meaning flowing out of the particular commandment'.[22] Tracing the key texts throughout the canon that expound this trajectory of the moral vision gives a 'whole Bible' perspective on the teaching of the particular commandment.

For example, in his exposition of the sixth commandment, Miller unpacks the meaning of the words 'you shall not murder', then looks at how the trajectory of murder, killing and the honouring of life is treated in the rest of the Bible. He examines the cities of refuge in Numbers 35, where those who kill accidentally are provided protection. Then he examines the elaboration of the sixth commandment in Exodus 20:22 – 23:19, and its underpinning that life is to be protected and honoured in the community. There follows Deuteronomy 19 – 22 and Leviticus 24:10–23, the so-called *lex talionis* texts ('life for life', 'eye for eye', etc.), which, he argues, teach the fundamental value of human life that the commandment is trying to protect, and its corollary: the prohibition of taking life. He then examines the commandment in the context of Israel's story: Cain and Abel (Gen. 4), the covenant with Noah (Gen. 9), the Joseph Narrative (Gen. 37), the sin of Gibeah (Judg. 19 – 20), and so on. He ends by looking at Jesus' teaching in the Sermon on the Mount, and the call for his followers to deal with the motivations of murder and to seek rather to be peacemakers.[23]

Thus Miller advocates for biblical theology, in the context of the whole Bible, to be the hermeneutic for the Commandments and their trajectory of meaning.

How the Bible uses the Commandments

The best method of understanding the Commandments is to see how the Bible itself uses them.[24] There are two main steps to do this in the OT context: through how the Commandments are picked up in the OT law codes, and then how the Commandments are picked up in OT narrative, which we see demonstrated in the example above.[25]

---

should we construe the opposite of 'you shall not murder' to be 'you must preserve life at all costs'? This example resurfaces below.

22. Ibid.

23. Patrick D. Miller, *The Ten Commandments*, Interpretation (Louisville: Westminster John Knox, 2009), pp. 221–269.

24. Peter Adam, *Written for Us: Receiving God's Words in the Bible* (Nottingham: IVP, 2008).

25. Miller, 'Preaching the Ten Commandments', p. 7.

The book of the covenant (Exod. 21 – 23), the Deuteronomic code (Deut. 12 – 26) and the Holiness Code (Lev. 17 – 26) are of particular value in providing case law pertaining to the Commandments.[26] These texts show how ancient Israel worked out the parameters and details of the Commandments and their specific applications in daily life. For example, Deuteronomy 15 seems to apply the sabbath principle more widely than being simply a weekly rest, extending its application to the remission of debts every seventh year and thereby expressing compassion on the needy. In fact, a number of scholars have argued that Deuteronomy 12 – 26 is a sustained commentary on the Commandments, almost following them in order.[27]

Narrative texts dealing with the subject matter of the Commandments provide 'food for the homiletical enterprise of preaching the commandments'.[28] They are not simply examples, but show context, colour and the real-life struggles of the people of God in living out this moral vision. So, for example, David's coveting and adultery with Bathsheba (2 Sam. 11 – 12), and Ahab's coveting Naboth's vineyard and subsequent murder plus the false witness of the two scoundrels selected by Jezebel (1 Kgs 21) all show clear narrative illustrations of the Commandments.

And of course the biblical picture is complete when the Commandments are picked up in the NT. Jesus' exposition of various commandments in the Sermon on the Mount and Paul's summing up in Romans 13 help us make the transition to the new-covenant understanding of their application to the lives of our hearers.

The meaning and application of the Commandments change through the Bible, depending on the context and position in revelation history. Walter Brueggemann reflects on this question:

> [T]he ten commandments are absolute and non-negotiable, taken as God's
> sure decree. It is, however, equally clear in the Bible itself that Israel and the
> church maintained and practiced amazing *interpretive openness* in order to keep the
> commandments pertinent to ongoing ethical burdens of the community in various
> changing circumstances.[29]

---

26. Ibid. See also Paul A. Barker, *Deuteronomy: The God Who Keeps Promises* (Brunswick East: Acorn, 1998), p. 27.

27. E.g. ibid.

28. Miller, 'Preaching the Ten Commandments', p. 8.

29. Walter Brueggemann, 'The Commandments and Liberated, Liberating Bonding', *Journal for Preachers* 10.2 (1987), pp. 15–24, quote p. 20, emphasis original.

Brueggemann demonstrates his thesis with reference to the sabbath commandment, showing how it morphs and changes in application (with what he calls an 'interpretive openness') in different contexts. He notes how it is interpreted in Exodus as a reminder of creation, in Deuteronomy as a reminder of redemption, in Amos as a protection of the poor, in Isaiah as a marker of covenant community membership, in Mark with Jesus using the sabbath to care for humanity and rejecting its use in 'social control'.

Brueggemann uses this example to make the point that 'interpretive openness' should be applied to each commandment by preachers today, both to treat the Commandments with serious respect and also to apply them to the specifics of our time. He concludes that 'serious evangelical faith understands the commandments as guides for God's liberating activity, and when they work against that liberating activity, they must be reconsidered, as Jesus does with the Sabbath commandment'.[30]

While I agree with his observations about the trajectory of the fourth commandment, where we see its application change in the course of the development of the canon, it would seem more difficult to sustain an argument for 'interpretive openness' in the canon for any of the other commandments. He has chosen the commandment with the most fluid of applications to build a case for the interpretation of the others. One simply does not see the same fluidity or openness of interpretation in the applications of the other commandments.

For example, in his encounter with the rich young ruler, Jesus quotes (in this order) commandments seven (adultery), six (murder), eight (stealing), nine (false witness) and five (honouring parents) as a kind of summary of his expectations of the man's obedience. There is an assumption here of the enduring nature of these commandments into the new-covenant era without any interpretative reconsideration. Similarly, Jesus affirms at least commandments six, seven and nine in the Sermon on the Mount. Here he not only assumes them, but intensifies them and calls his hearers to deal with the motivations behind them.

The issue Brueggemann struggles with is an important one. While I agree that we should not lay restrictive sabbath practice on people today, I conclude this not because of an interpretative openness with the Commandments in general or because I treat them as mere 'guides for God's liberating activity', but because this is the trajectory of the biblical theology of sabbath. Yes, Brueggemann is right that we want to avoid moralism in our preaching, that

---

30. Ibid.

we should see the transformative nature of the Commandments, but asserting the absolute nature of the other commandments as the Scriptures themselves hold them must be part of the answer.

Following the careful biblical trajectory of each commandment through Scripture allows us to interpret them, holding to both their absolute, non-negotiable status and their contemporary applicability. It allows us to acknowledge the interpretative openness when it exists within Scripture, without imposing it on the text. It also allows us to keep the absolute nature of the Commandments firm, avoiding the slippery ground of suggesting that the Commandments are mere guides to living, while at the same time appreciating the nuances of Scripture.

Preaching the Ten Commandments

There are several challenges for preaching the Ten Commandments. Chief among them is the challenge to preach the Commandments from a grace framework, and related to this is dealing with their polarity and ambiguity.

Woe to the preacher who heaps up burdens from the Commandments on the congregation that may lead to either boasting or despair. Paul's view was this:

> Therefore the law was our disciplinarian until Christ came, so that we might be justified by faith. But now that faith has come, we are no longer subject to a disciplinarian, for in Christ Jesus you are all children of God through faith. (Gal. 3:24–26)

Here Paul underscores the glorious freedom of the children of God, not to have to strive for the perfection of the law, but to trust in Christ. Now this is always a challenge for the preacher, but particularly so in the middle of the Ten Commandments.

Yet the Commandments, as we have seen from Luther and Calvin above, provide necessary instruction for the believer to understand the shape and pattern of holiness. In our preaching it will be of paramount importance to keep this balance right. Acknowledging the presence of the Spirit in the life of the believer who is saved by grace alone is the pathway to living this holy life.

In addition, regularly reminding the congregation of the context of the Commandments in their own redemptive setting will be vital to stave off discouragement. In our series we made sure we read the entire passage each week, to emphasize the grace setting of the Commandments.

Important as well is our readiness to preach the consolation of the gospel in each sermon, to point people to the finished work of Jesus for their redemption. There are many ways to do this without boring repetition and the same ending to every sermon. But do it we must, to provide the ready remedy, because the Commandments rightly expounded will no doubt convict people of their sin. Only then can we boldly call people to the radical freedom of serving God his way.

A related issue arises for the preacher, given the nature of the Commandments as polarity literature.[31] That is, like wisdom literature and much of the teaching of Jesus, the Commandments portray the life of the people of God in strict 'either/or' polarities. One either follows the Commandment or not. Take these polarized texts, for example:

Happy are those
   who do not follow the advice of the wicked,
or take the path that sinners tread,
   or sit in the seat of scoffers;
but their delight is in the law of the LORD,
   and on his law they meditate day and night . . .

The wicked are not so,
   but are like chaff that the wind drives away.
(Ps. 1:1–2, 4)

The memory of the righteous is a blessing,
   but the name of the wicked will rot.
(Prov. 10:7)

You will know them by their fruits. Are grapes gathered from thorns, or figs from thistles? In the same way, every good tree bears good fruit, but the bad tree bears bad fruit. A good tree cannot bear bad fruit, nor can a bad tree bear good fruit. Every tree that does not bear good fruit is cut down and thrown into the fire. Thus you will know them by their fruits. (Matt. 7:16–20)

You shall not make wrongful use of the name of the LORD your God, for the LORD will not acquit anyone who misuses his name. (Exod. 20:7)

---

31. I am indebted to a sermon by Don Carson on Ps. 1 for these ideas (Ridley Melbourne Preachers' Conference, 16 Aug. 2010).

If preached on its own as a simple matter of polarized obedience or not, such a polarity may lead to despair in the hearers of the sermon, as much as if we preached without grace. It is also a problem because it sets up a disconnection with reality. After all, our hearers' own lives are not this crisply defined. It will never be the case that the believer will live the Commandments perfectly one day and not at all the next. In addition, the Bible itself is filled with examples of the faithful people of God who have not kept the Commandments in their entirety yet are still numbered among the saints: Abraham, Moses, Gideon, Samson, Jephthah and David are all listed among the heroes of the faith in Hebrews 11.

An example of this disconnect occurred when I was preaching on the sixth commandment, 'you shall not murder'. I had expounded the Hebrew *rāṣaḥ* not simply as 'kill' or 'murder', but as the intentional taking of life. 'Kill' seemed too broad and does not seem to be in view in the commandment, as accidental killing and killing in war are elsewhere excused from the application of the commandment. 'Murder' seemed too narrow by attributing intent in *rāṣaḥ* to 'malice aforethought'. So I settled on the definition of 'the premeditated taking of a life, or the taking of life on the basis of your own will or desire'. I then applied this to murder, suicide, euthanasia and abortion.

After the sermon, a member of the congregation who works as a physician came to speak to me, with tears in his eyes. His work has taken him frequently to teeter on the grey and blurry edge of this polarity. When he prescribes a certain sedative for a person close to the end of life, does he somehow fall foul of the definition 'taking of life, on the basis of your own will and desire'? He knows that without the drug the patient will linger on for days, but with the drug their life will be shortened. The polarity of the sixth commandment well serves the person who is 'breathing murderous threats under their breath' at an enemy (cf. Matt. 5:21–22) or considering elective abortion for birth control, but is not so clear for the palliative care doctor. This is an example of the ambiguity of the life experience of our people.

Or take the example of the ninth commandment, which, among other things, sets up a polarity around truthful speech. One young member of the congregation rightly asked me about Rahab's barefaced lie to the King of Jericho's men in Joshua 2 and her subsequent commendation in Hebrews 11:31 and James 2:25. This led to a reflection on the rightness or wrongness of the actions of people like Corrie ten Boom, lying to the authorities to hide Jews in their houses during the Second World War.

How should the preacher confidently and boldly preach the polarities of the Commandments and, at the same time, recognize that the narrative of Scripture and the experience of those in the congregation are often much more laced with ambiguity? Here we are helped once again by taking the biblical-theological view of the Commandments. We need to preach the relevant narrative texts alongside the moral code, to ground the application in real life. What assuring grace there is for the repentant adulterer, faced with the wretchedness of his sin, to know that even an adulterer like David could still be used to bring about God's eternal purpose. What a joy for the convicted liar to see Rahab commended in Hebrews, when she beats her breast in repentance.

The twin strands of polarity and ambiguity that run through the Commandments as they are played out in law and narrative are bold biblical strands that, if taken seriously in tension, will prevent us from preaching crushing law or cheap grace.

Conclusion

Preaching the Ten Commandments at St Jude's was a great journey in wrestling with a difficult OT text, but in it much to challenge a contemporary congregation. One devotional commentary commends the preacher to urge the congregation to memorize and recite the Commandments throughout the series.[32] What a joy to internalize and, like our Puritan forebears, chew the cud of the Scriptures and extract from them the nourishment therein. As mentioned above, there was great appreciation for real practical learning, more than any series in a long time, especially among younger folk in the congregation, as people grappled with these words of life.

One response is reproduced here. Will Mackerras is a bush poet who uses the metrical settings of some famous Australian poets, such as Banjo Paterson, to retell the Bible stories.[33] He is a member of St Jude's and offered this poem in response to the series. I thought it appropriate to reproduce his work here as he is also a student at Ridley under the tutelage of Peter Adam. Enjoy!

I find my delight in your commandments,
    because I love them.
(Ps. 119:47)

© Richard J. Condie, 2011

---

32. Hughes, *Disciplines of Grace.*

33. See <http://banjobible.wordpress.com>; the cited poem was posted 17 Aug. 2010.

Clancy of the Overflow
Will Mackerras

He had written them a letter which he had, upon his better
Knowledge, chiselled with his finger on some very heavy stone.
They were loyal when he knew them so perhaps he sent it to them
With an introduction saying: 'To a people all my own.'

'Now you know that I have saved you from a nation that enslaved you:
You were living down in Egypt and were getting very low.
So I put some simple posers through my humble servant Moses
To the King along the lines of "Would you let my people go?"'

'But the King was quite resistant, so I had to be persistent
With some methods only those of us divine have ever used.
It was wonder and disaster 'til your very stubborn master
Came at last to say (exasperated) "People you're excused!"'

'Then I parted up the ocean with a stiff and breezy motion
To enable you to leave the place for good, and with a cheer.
And I led you in a fire ('til the sun was getting higher)
And I led you in a cloud until you came at last to here.'

'And a place for some reviving, not to mention happy thriving,
Lies a little further on and we can go there in a trice.
But this high and rocky mountain with its running water fountain
Seems an excellent location for a bit of stern advice.'

'Now you know that I am holy and I'm also meek and lowly –
Well I've chosen to reside among you – right within your view.
But you'll only be my treasures if you follow all the measures
I have fashioned for the purpose that you all be holy too.'

'So I've written ten instructions with some obvious constructions,
and I've put them on some tablets so you have them ever near.
And my very strong advising is you all be memorizing
Them until they're well cemented in the spot from ear to ear.'

All of this the Lord unending may have added to his sending
of his letter with its regulations, rules, and caveats.
Prob'ly different in expression but a similar impression
To the record in the Bible of his mountaineering chats.

And the laws he legislated for the nation he created
Could be summarized as follows 'Love the Lord with all your heart,
And you need to love the fellas in your neighbourhood as well as
All the women and the children: every human counterpart.'

Now the things he was commanding you would think were quite demanding,
After all the Lord is perfect and he wished them be the same.
But he knew that they were wayward and without assistance they would
Do whatever came a-naturally and put themselves to shame.

So he made them special offers from the never-ending coffers
Of his mercy – he would give them second natures to obey.
With a broken-hearted pleading they would find what they were needing
And would suddenly be wanting to be sticking to the way.

And he had another blessing for the willingly confessing:
He would pardon them a temporary punishment of sin.
With a solemn sacrificing of some animals sufficing,
They could stay a little longer at the Lord Almighty's inn.

Now the matters more eternal would remain inside his journal,
But the promised land was waiting so he told them to proceed.
With the 'letter' in their keeping and the little kiddies leaping,
They began the happy journey to wherever he would lead.

2. MOSES THE PREACHER: DEUTERONOMY 1 – 4

Paul A. Barker

Introduction

Deuteronomy 1 – 30 is Moses' final sermon, a sustained exhortation to the second generation of Israelites following the exodus from Egypt. We should not underestimate the importance of this sermon because the task ahead for Israel is immense, namely the conquest of the land first promised to Abram in Genesis 12. Moses himself is soon to die, prohibited from entry into the land (1:37; 3:27; 4:21–22; 32:48–52). Israel is poised at the border of the land, on the Plains of Moab overlooking the Jordan River (1:1, 5). To compound the challenge ahead, the previous generation of Israelites had failed dismally when at a different border nearly forty years before.

While many commentaries on Deuteronomy regard it as consisting of three speeches or sermons by Moses (1:6 – 4:40; 5:1 – 26:19; 27:1 – 30:20), it appears better to consider it as one sermon, even if broken into three sections. The content of the three sections makes sense as one sermon. The second section develops the argument from the end of the first section and the final section is clearly a conclusion to the whole.

The opening paragraph of the book introduces this sermon, three times mentioning that Moses speaks (1:1, 3, 5). In particular, 1:5 describes Moses' speaking as 'expounding' the law.[1] The word suggests explaining, making clear God's law. This is more than simply teaching what the law says. That has already been done, in effect, in Exodus and Leviticus. Now the thrust in Deuteronomy is not 'this is the law' but rather 'do it'!

When 1:5 says that Moses 'undertook to expound this law', we must remember that law (*tôrâ*) has a wider semantic field than the English word 'law'. Torah is about how to live, direction for life. It is thus broader than legislation. After all, the first five books of the OT are designated the Torah, and yet a significant portion of these books is narrative. So Moses' exposition of the law involves both expounding narrative, as in Deuteronomy 1 – 3, as well as legal texts, as in Deuteronomy 5 – 28. In addition, there is general exhortation, as in chapters 4 and 29 – 30.

This chapter considers the purpose, content and style of Moses' preaching in Deuteronomy 1:6 – 4:40, the opening section of the book-long sermon. Canonically, this is the first expository sermon in the Bible, as Moses expounds several texts from earlier in the Pentateuch. In particular, we will look at Moses' use of the Bible, and secondly at his use of language and rhetoric. In so doing, we anticipate that preachers can learn from Moses the preacher.

Preaching historical narrative

Deuteronomy 1:6 – 3:29 is preached historical narrative. The history narrated in these chapters is recorded not merely for information. Moses is not giving a history lesson. The history Moses preaches here is already recorded in Genesis, Exodus and Numbers. That history is recorded not merely for information is far from unusual in the Bible. Recorded history anywhere in the Bible serves the purpose not only of informing but also of training in righteousness. Narrative, or story, is *tôrâ*.[2] In Deuteronomy this *tôrâ* is preached.

The assumption in Moses' preaching is that these events are known by his audience, as we will see further below. In particular, the history of Deuteronomy 2:1 – 3:29 is in the immediate past, within months of this sermon, and had been personally experienced by the generation listening to Moses. However, even the events of 1:19–46 occurred only a generation earlier and many in Moses' audience would have memory of those events,

---

1. Bible quotations in this chapter are from the NRSV.
2. E.g. Gordon J. Wenham, *Story as Torah: Reading Old Testament Narratives Ethically* (Grand Rapids: Baker, 2000).

though they were then just children. Apart from Caleb and Joshua, the rest of Moses' audience had been born subsequently in the wilderness.

One of the functions of preaching is to remind congregations about God's word and action. 'Remind' implies existing knowledge with the danger of forgetfulness. That is the role of the Spirit (John 14:26) and Paul often reminds his readers of something they already know (e.g. 1 Cor. 15:1; 2 Tim. 1:6; 2:14), as does Jude (Jude 5). Moses makes no apology for reminding Israel of its history, even though that would be well known. His aim is to teach a lesson from that history. The language of 'do not forget' and 'remember' is relatively frequent in Deuteronomy. In the section we are reviewing, Israel is exhorted not 'to forget the things that your eyes have seen' (Deut. 4:9) and 'not to forget the covenant that the LORD your God made with you' (4:23).

Remembering and forgetfulness are matters of morality, not memory. So in 8:11, forgetfulness of what God has done in the wilderness is in parallelism with disobedience. The same association is seen in 4:23–24, where forgetfulness of the covenant is parallel with idolatry. Ancient Israel needed reminding, not because of bad memories but because they were prone to turn aside from God. That Israel was prone to turn aside is seen in the repeated exhortations in Deuteronomy to remember, the recounting of past sins, the pessimistic expectation for the future in chapters 29 – 32, the repeated strong warnings against idolatry, and the urgency and seriousness of 'take care' in 4:9 and elsewhere.

In a similar way, much Christian preaching is to remind congregations of what God has done and said. Christians today, like ancient Israel, are also prone to sin, and need repeated reminders of God and his past words and actions. Moses sets a good model for contemporary preaching.

With regard to any historical narrative in Scripture, the preacher today needs to work out the purpose of that history for the original readers or hearers. Why does Moses select the historical sections he does? All history is selective. Not everything or every incident is recorded. The process of selectivity is usually influenced by the speaker or writer's aims and argument. Moses could have begun with a rehearsal of the events of the exodus, but he chooses his own material, and within the chosen material makes his own abbreviations, selections and emphases.

I have argued elsewhere that the aim of Moses' preaching in Deuteronomy 1 – 3 is to motivate and urge the current generation of Israelites to conquer the land.[3] This exhortation is in the context of the failure of the previous

---

3. Paul A. Barker, *The Triumph of Grace in Deuteronomy* (Milton Keynes: Paternoster, 2004).

generation to do exactly that from the southern border of the land at Kadesh-barnea. The failure of the previous generation is an act of rebellion (1:26) that is a manifestation of an underlying lack of faith (1:32). So Moses seeks to instil faith that will produce the fruit of obedience. In particular, Moses is demonstrating that God is faithful to his promises made to Abraham and that he is powerful and able to keep those promises.

Moses' use of Scripture in preaching

In this sermon Moses preaches from several key texts: Genesis 15:5; Exodus 18:13–27; Numbers 13 – 14; Numbers 20 – 21; Numbers 32:28–42; Genesis 1:14–27; and Exodus 19 – 24. I will argue below, in the cases of Genesis 15:5 and Numbers 13 – 14 especially, that knowledge of these texts is assumed and in fact is part of the argument in Moses' sermon. In fact, the opening paragraph of the book implies that the audience knows of the spies incident at Kadesh-barnea, with the references to eleven days and fortieth year in 1:2–3. While we are not engaging in discussion about dating of either Deuteronomy or the preceding biblical books, the argument that Moses is preaching from Genesis, Exodus and Numbers makes sense canonically at least.[4]

Genesis 15:5
In Deuteronomy 1:10 Moses refers to Genesis 15:5 without naming the source: 'today you are as numerous as the stars of heaven'. He is assuming knowledge, not only of that verse, but also of its wider context in Genesis 15. This is not unusual, as many biblical references back to earlier Bible verses do the same. They quote a small part or verse but imply much more.[5] Nor is this reference surprising in Deuteronomy, as the book frequently refers by name

---

4. See John H. Sailhamer, *The Pentateuch as Narrative: A Biblical-Theological Approach* (Grand Rapids: Zondervan, 1992), p. 424: Moses preaches 'on the basis of the account of the past already written in the preceding narratives. Moses' view of the past is a "scriptural view." He does not recount events which were not recorded earlier. In other words, he does not assume knowledge of Israel's history that is independent of the biblical account itself. His focus is on those events already present in the mind of the readers of the Pentateuch.'

5. E.g. when Jesus quotes Ps. 22:1 on the cross, in my opinion he is probably implying the full psalm and its context, which ends not with God-forsakenness but with confident faith.

to Abraham, Isaac and Jacob as the recipients of Yahweh's promises (1:8; 6:10; 9:5, 27; 29:13; 30:20; 34:4).

The obvious point Moses is making in Deuteronomy is that God has fulfilled the promise to Abraham of numerous descendants. Certainly, the numbers of Israelites in the censuses of the book of Numbers, and the earlier remarkable growth of Israel in Egypt despite Pharaoh's attempts to curtail it in Exodus 1, back up Moses' claim. By referring to Genesis 15:5 Moses is not simply making a point about the size of the population of Israel; he is making the more significant point about the faithfulness of God. What God promised Abram in Genesis 12, and repeated in Genesis 15, has been fulfilled.

However, Moses is making yet a further point from Genesis 15. The issue in Deuteronomy is not descendants but land. The acknowledgment of the fulfilment of the descendants part of the Abrahamic promise package is for the purpose of leading the current generation of Israel to keep trusting in the land promise. Moses' point is that if God has been faithful to keep the promise of descendants, he can be trusted also to keep the promise of land.

That this is important to Moses can be seen in two ways. One is that Israel's sin in not entering the land in the previous generation, as noted above, is described as a lack of faith or unbelief (Deut. 1:32). Secondly, Moses keeps on saying throughout Deuteronomy that the land before Israel is the land God promised or swore on oath to give, a point I will return to below.

What is often not noticed in the reference to Genesis 15:5 is the implication of the wider context of Genesis 15. There Abram is doubting God's promise of descendants (Gen. 15:2). Showing Abram the night sky and its multitude of stars is an act of reassurance of promise to Abram by God. It is striking that the reference in Deuteronomy 1:10 functions in the same way for this generation of Israelites. Moses is reassuring a doubting people of God's faithfulness. Furthermore, Abram's response to such assurance was faith, described in the famous words of Genesis 15:6, 'he believed the LORD; and the LORD reckoned it to him as righteousness'. Moses is preaching Genesis 15 to elicit the same response from his audience. In fact, he is using Scripture accurately, seeking to apply it in a way consonant with its original purpose.

There is more from Genesis 15 that is striking. Genesis 15:1–6 deals with Abram's doubt regarding descendants. The second section of the chapter, verses 7–18, deals with the promise of land. Again Abram is reassured that God will keep this promise. As Moses preaches from 15:5, he intends to carry over the full argument of Genesis 15 to reassure the Israelites.[6] We see this in various ways.

In Genesis 15:7–12 God conducts a ceremony to enter into a covenant with Abram regarding the promises made in Genesis 12 (where the word 'covenant' does not occur). The reiterated promises in Genesis 15 are described as 'covenant' in verse 18.

In Genesis 15:13–16 God tells Abram that the land promise will be fulfilled only after a substantial period of time – over four hundred years (v. 13). Moses is alluding to the fact that this period of time is now complete. The Israelites had been aliens and slaves in a foreign land (v. 13). They have seen the great 'judgment' on this land and they have left it 'with great possessions' (v. 14). The timing is right, then, for the fulfilment of this land promise.

Further, Genesis 15:18 ends with a description of the borders of the Promised Land, a new addition to the land promise for Abram. This description is clearly echoed in Deuteronomy 1:7, which likewise refers to 'the great river, the river Euphrates' as the northern border. These are the only two occurrences of the same Hebrew expression in the OT. As in 1:10, so 1:7 alludes back to Genesis 15.

What is the homiletic purpose of Moses here? Abram, in Genesis 15, is doubting the promises of God regarding descendants and land. God reassures him of both and underscores his earlier promises with a covenant. Likewise, Israel had previously doubted the promise of land, seen in its failure to enter the land in the previous generation. So, by referring not only to Genesis 15:5 but by association to the whole of that chapter, Moses is now seeking to reassure his audience of God's faithfulness to the promise of descendants, and thus to instil faith that the promise of land still holds. The prerequisite events as told to Abram have now been completed. The borders of the Promised Land remain unchanged. God is faithful and can be trusted. As Genesis 15 associated the promises of descendants and land together, so Moses uses that chapter to make the same association. The strength of reassurance from Moses comes from the fact that one of those promises is already fulfilled; hence the quote of Genesis 15:5.

So Moses is preaching Genesis 15 in line with its original purpose for Abram, to reassure and instil faith. In effect he is expounding the main message of that chapter at least implicitly. He appears to be assuming

6. Cf. J. Gordon McConville, *Deuteronomy*, AOTC 5 (Leicester: Apollos; Downers Grove: IVP, 2002), p. 65, who regards this linking of land and descendants as 'incidental'.

knowledge of that text and knowledge of its wider context. This use of Genesis 15 helps us to be clear about the purpose of this whole opening section of Deuteronomy, as Moses draws out further arguments from other texts to argue the same point, that this current generation of Israel has good reason to trust in God's faithfulness.

Unfortunately, modern preachers may not always be in the position of being able to allude to biblical texts as Moses did with Genesis 15. Where congregations have less biblical literacy, such allusions would be lost. The subtlety of Moses' approach may more often in modern times need to be replaced by directness and fuller quotation and explication.

Exodus 18:13–27

The appointment of assistants for Moses, to judge cases and disputes among the people, is referred to in Deuteronomy 1:12–18.

On the surface 1:12–18 seems not to maintain the focus on the land that the rest of 1:6 – 3:29 does.[7] It raises the question about why Moses recounts this episode here in Deuteronomy. The primary reference in this paragraph is back to Exodus 18:13–27, though it also echoes Numbers 11:10–25 ('I am not able to carry all this people alone', Num. 11:14) and is not precise on the timing ('at that time', Deut. 1:9). Jethro is not named, though he was the initiator of the idea of the appointment of assistants in Exodus 18 so that Moses did not wear himself out. This combination of references, and abbreviation of the accounts, need not be a concern, as Moses' aim in this reference in Deuteronomy is not to give precise history.

The function of Moses' reference back to the episode in Exodus 18, along with the echo back to Numbers 11, is perhaps best described as evidence supporting the claim that Israel has been so numerous. Thus the context of a complaint in Numbers 11 is omitted and the context now is of the growth of Israel as a sign of blessing. In the verses leading up to this reference, Moses has been arguing that God's faithfulness is seen in the remarkable number of Israelites. Though his audience in Deuteronomy may not doubt this, the reference to the appointment of assistants emphasizes this growth in number and gives tangible evidence of God's faithfulness to the promise to Abram of descendants. This evidence adds to the argument already noted above, namely that Moses is linking the promises of descendants and land, in order to bolster Israel's faith in the yet-to-be-fulfilled land promise. As Sherwood notes, 'The fact that the promise to the ancestors [concerning descendants] has manifestly

---

7. Ibid., p. 58.

been fulfilled ought to give the people confidence in YHWH's ability to fulfill his other promises.'[8]

The theme of justice is addressed later in Deuteronomy (16:18–20; see also 10:17–18) and that theme is not the issue at this stage of Deuteronomy. However, Moses does not omit reference to justice here, though it does not directly contribute to his point at this stage. He includes the reference, knowing that the point about justice will be dealt with later and thus is anticipated by this reference in Deuteronomy 1.

Numbers 13 – 14

In Deuteronomy 1:19–46 Moses preaches from Numbers 13 – 14: the episode of the reconnaissance of the Promised Land by the spies, their report and the people's reaction. The purpose here is not to analyse the entire passage but to see how Moses preaches it.

There are several significant variations from the text of Numbers. In Numbers 13:1 it is Yahweh who suggests that spies be sent into the land. In Deuteronomy 1:22 it is the people of Israel who request spies, a request Moses accedes to. If any importance is given to this variation, it is possibly that, since the spies incident ended in failure, Moses is laying the blame squarely on Israel. The desire for sending spies is seen to be an expression of lack of faith. This is also supported by the contrast between 1:30, where Moses reassures Israel that Yahweh himself 'goes before you', and the people's desire in 1:22 to have spies sent 'ahead of us' (the same preposition each time in Hebrew). So the reworking of the Numbers account spotlights Israel's culpability.

A more significant variation between Deuteronomy 1 and Numbers 13 – 14 lies in the report from the spies, recorded in Deuteronomy 1:25. Here the spies' report is unequivocally positive. 'It is a good land that the LORD our God is giving us.' In the corresponding place in Numbers 13 the spies' report is longer and makes mention of the enemies inhabiting the land (13:27–29). How do we account for this emphasis that Moses places on the account in his sermon? Moses is not seeking to deceive his audience. He assumes they know the account. That is clear from his rehearsal of the people's response to the spies. In Deuteronomy 1:28 the people express their fear because 'our kindred have made our hearts fail' and continue with the negative aspect of the report from Numbers 13. If we did not know the account in Numbers, the people's fear seems peculiar and inexplicable. However, knowing the

---

8. Stephen K. Sherwood, *Leviticus, Numbers, Deuteronomy*, Berit Olam (Collegeville: Liturgical, 2002), p. 243.

account in Numbers, we can see that Moses is highlighting the people's sin, and seeking not to allow the possibility of blame being passed to the spies.[9]

Moses is therefore faithfully expounding the passage in Numbers 13, but selecting and emphasizing to make his point about the groundlessness and seriousness of Israel's sin. Remember, his reason for preaching this sermon is to instil faith in this next generation so that they will do what their parents failed to do: conquer the land.

In this context it is important to note Moses' use of the second person. Rather than say that his audience's parents sinned and failed, he says 'you' (e.g. 1:26). In 1:30 Moses says 'before your very eyes', though technically it was before their parents' eyes. This is a typical device Moses uses in Deuteronomy. For example, in 5:2–3 Moses makes the deliberate point that the covenant made at Sinai was not with the parents but with the current generation. Positively, this draws the current generation under God's word. When referring to past sin, it makes the current generation as culpable as its parents and unable to rely on its own ability.

This device of generational conflation serves a homiletical purpose. It identifies the current generation as being no different morally from its parents. Most children consider themselves better than their parents. So Moses' preaching technique draws his audience into the sin of their parents. The purpose of this is to prevent false pride and self-reliance with regard to the task ahead of conquering the land. Moses is thus applying the narrative in a very direct way to the children of the previous generation so that they properly learn from the mistakes of the past. In this way, the text of Numbers 13 – 14 serves as a negative example for the current generation. The decision facing the audience, and later readers, is in a sense existentialized by this conflation.

Generational conflation suggests a dynamic view of God's word. God's word still speaks, as if the current generation was there in the previous generation, both hearing God's word at Sinai and in sinning at Kadesh. The device takes away distance, along the lines of Paul in 1 Corinthians 10:1–6, thus bringing later generations directly under God's word. For Moses, as for the Bible as a whole, God's word is not limited to its original audience but still speaks, directly, to succeeding generations.[10] Such a strong view of God's

---

9. Ian Cairns, *Deuteronomy: Word and Presence*, ITC (Grand Rapids: Eerdmans; Edinburgh: Handsel, 1992), p. 35.

10. J. Gordon McConville and J. Gary Millar, *Time and Place in Deuteronomy*, JSOTSup 179 (Sheffield: Sheffield Academic Press, 1994), pp. 31–32. See also Paul R. House, 'Examining the Narratives of Old Testament Narrative: An Exploration in Biblical

word is part of the platform of Moses' preaching, and something preachers still can learn from and copy.[11]

That Moses assumes knowledge of Numbers 13 – 14 is seen also in his reference to Caleb and Joshua in Deuteronomy 1:36, 38. If the fuller account in Numbers is not known, then the reference to Caleb's 'complete fidelity to the LORD' makes no sense, as the reference to Caleb comes out of the blue. Likewise, the reference to Joshua in 1:38 has no background in Deuteronomy and assumes knowledge of the history recorded in Numbers 13.[12] By assuming knowledge of Numbers, Moses draws attention to Caleb as an example of 'complete fidelity' in contrast to the faithlessness of Israel in 1:32. Caleb becomes a role model not for being a spy but for faithfulness to Yahweh. Moses' way of referring to Caleb here, and by not recounting the full version of the spies' reconnoitre and report earlier, draws attention to his purpose in preaching. Namely, he is seeking to elicit a response of 'complete fidelity' from this generation of Israel as they confront the task of conquest. Moses is both faithful to his text, but also able to draw out its emphases through his selection of material.

Numbers 20 – 21

We need to pay careful attention to the people's words in 1:28. Moses has highlighted them by omitting the spies' words from Numbers 13 about the enemies. In particular, the people's fear derives from three related points. The enemies are 'stronger and taller', their 'cities are large and fortified up to heaven' and the enemies include 'the offspring of the Anakim!'

In order to address that sin of fear, and in anticipation that the current generation is likely to replicate it (see above on generational conflation), Moses turns to later sections of Numbers.

In Deuteronomy 2:1–23 he brings together the peaceful progress of Israel

---

Theology', *WTJ* 67.2 (2005), pp. 229–245; e.g. 'Moses recounts them [items of Israel's story] to incite the hearers to faith in Yahweh' (p. 234); such summaries that use 'you' language 'place readers in the story' (p. 245).

11. This does not mean that we ignore the historical distance between original readers and modern times, nor that the original purpose of a scriptural book is ignored. However, in my observation, modern preachers perhaps underemphasize the immediacy and directness of Scripture's speaking to contemporary congregations.

12. Often Numbers is accredited to JE, with the P source regarded as providing the names of the spies and the notion of one per tribe. However, it is clear here that Deuteronomy knows Num. 13. So McConville, *Deuteronomy*, p. 60.

through Edom, Moab and Ammon. Again, this is not a mere history lesson, as these events had occurred within months of Moses preaching this sermon. Rather, Moses seeks to address the particular issue of trusting God. While his sermon so far focuses on God's faithfulness to his promise, now his attention turns to God's ability to keep his promise. In particular, is God able to defeat strong, tall and fortified nations?

So the focus in 2:1–23 is not on the negotiations between Israel and the three nations for Israel to pass by without fighting. Thus there is no mention, for example, of Edom coming out against Israel as in Numbers 20:20. The focus is on God, using God's past activity on behalf of those three nations as a model, and thus a lesson for how he will act in a similar way for Israel in the near future. The aim is encouragement for this current generation of Israelites, to inculcate the obedience of faith.

Unlike in Numbers, Moses three times uses a relatively uncommon word to describe the way in which God has given to Edom, Moab and Ammon their land 'as a possession' (Deut. 2:5, 9, 19). In each case the emphasis is on God giving land to those three nations. In 2:12 the same expression occurs with respect to Israel. It refers to the giving of land for Israel as a past event, possibly to underscore the certainty of land possession. Moses is drawing out of Numbers the point that Yahweh is God over even other nations.

More than this, however, is the comment on the previous inhabitants of the lands of Edom, and especially Moab and Ammon. In verses usually bracketed in English translations we find a crucial theological and homiletical point. Both Moab and Ammon were given their lands by God, who dispossessed other nations of strong and tall people (2:10, 21). The language used directly recalls the Israelites' fear in 1:28. In addition, both 2:10 and 21 make explicit reference to the similarity of those previous inhabitants with the Anakim, the very people Israel was afraid of in 1:28. Sherwood is a rare commentator, noting this purpose of these verses, which he calls a 'sidebar'. 'The purpose of some of this sidebar seems to be to show that the people's fear of the land's (giant) inhabitants was groundless since in other lands that YHWH had given to other peoples the giants had been replaced by others (presumably not giants).'[13]

_____

13. Sherwood, *Leviticus, Numbers, Deuteronomy*, p. 246. He goes on to say, 'If the sidebars are regarded as part of the divine speech (rather than asides of the narrator) then they would be quite pointed reminders that the people's fear of the present inhabitants of Canaan was groundless.' There appears no reason to isolate these verses as a narrator's comment rather than as part of the speech of Moses and thus God's word. The theological value of the verses, though not necessarily their origin

Moses is thus drawing out from Numbers 20 – 21 an exhortation to complete fidelity, showing the groundlessness of the previous Israelite generation's fear at the spies incident. It is striking how few commentators understand the purpose of these historical references in Deuteronomy 2. Yet this history is in fact crucial to Moses' argument.[14]

Similarly in 2:24 – 3:11. Here Moses moves on to recount the recent victories of Israel over the two nations of Kings Sihon and Og, of Heshbon and Bashan respectively. These events are recounted in Numbers 21:21–35. The particular fear of Israel being addressed here is no longer giants, but fortified cities. So 2:36 and 3:4, referring to Sihon and Og's kingdoms respectively, say that 'there was no citadel too high for us' and 'there was no citadel that we did not take from them'. In both verses are echoes of the people's fear expressed back in 1:28, namely that 'the cities are large and fortified up to heaven'. Further direct allusions back to 1:28 include 3:5, with its mention of fortress towns and high walls, and the reference in 3:11 to Rephaim. The Rephaim are linked to the Anakim in 2:11.

These emphases on the fortified and strong towns and citadels are not found in Numbers 21. So Moses is making his own emphases from these recent victories, emphases that address specifically Israel's fear in 1:28. Further, in Numbers 21:21–31 there is no mention at all of God, whereas in Deuteronomy 2:24–37 Yahweh is mentioned several times (vv. 24, 25, 31, 33, 36, 37). A similar emphasis is found in 3:1–11 with the defeat of Og's kingdom of Bashan. Moses is drawing out from Numbers a new emphasis on the victory over Sihon coming from Yahweh. All this is to persuade the current generation that God is powerful to bring victory and worthy of complete fidelity.

Deuteronomy 3:11 is often regarded as an aside. There is debate over whether what the NRSV translates as 'bed' was a sarcophagus. However 'bed' is the more obvious and preferred translation and fits more easily here. Moses is returning to Israel's fear of giants in the land. Yes, it was an extraordinarily large bed. That is the point. Og must have been a giant. And, as Moses speaks,

---

with Moses, is also explored by Christopher J. H. Wright, *Deuteronomy*, NIBC 4 (Peabody: Hendrickson, 1996), pp. 35–37.

14. Peter Craigie dismisses these verses as 'brief comments of historical interest', which 'apparently have been inserted into the original text of the address of Moses' (*The Book of Deuteronomy*, NICOT [Grand Rapids: Eerdmans, 1976], pp. 110–111). A. D. H. Mayes judges that these additions actually obscure Moses' rhetorical point (*Deuteronomy*, NCB [London: Marshall, Morgan & Scott, 1979], p. 134).

Og is dead. That his bed is still on show in Rabbah is evidence to support
the claim, a device similar to the discussion of the assistants for Moses to
judge Israel in 1:12–18. No mention is found in Numbers of Og's bed or
that he was a giant. So Moses is making this a deliberate emphasis for the
purpose of exhorting his audience to trust in Yahweh's power to defeat strong
enemies.

It is important to note that Moses never downplays the strength of the
enemy. They are giants and their cities are heavily fortified. The whole point
is not to belittle the enemy and give Israel confidence that way. Such would
be false confidence. Rather, acknowledging the strength of the enemy enables
the spotlight to shine more sharply on the greater strength and ability of God
to bring victory.

The theme of God's faithfulness, emphasized especially in Deuteronomy
1, is not lost in Deuteronomy 3:1–11. The language Moses uses in 3:2–3
shows a clear understanding that what God promised he would do he
has done. He is faithful in giving over the land of Og. The implication is
that, for the major land conquest still ahead of Israel, God can be utterly
trusted.

Numbers 32:28–42 and 34:1–12

In Deuteronomy 3:12–17 Moses recounts the distribution of Transjordan
land to the tribes of Reuben, Gad and half of the tribe of Manasseh. This has
already been recounted in Numbers 32, and will be again in Joshua 13. The
function of the reference in Deuteronomy is to add evidential weight to
the point that Yahweh has already given land.

What is distinctive in Moses' sermon, compared to Numbers, is the
way the Transjordanian land is regarded as part of the Promised Land in
Deuteronomy. This is reflected in holy-war motifs applied to it, as well as this
land being part of Moses' vision before his death in Deuteronomy 34:1–4.
In Numbers 34:1–12 the impression gained is that Transjordan was not part
of the Promised Land. The rhetorical significance of this distinction is that
Moses is using the Transjordanian victories as encouragement and motivation
for Israel to cross the Jordan and conquer the remaining land. The reference
to the Rephaim in 3:13 alludes again to the issue of God's power to give the
land west of the Jordan to Israel.

In 3:18–22 Moses speaks to the tribes inheriting Transjordanian land.
Theirs is land Yahweh 'has given . . . to occupy'. They already have 'rest'
(3:20). Moses uses this language here as deliberate encouragement by example
for the conquest of the main Promised Land. Note the emphasis in 3:22, 'it is
the LORD your God who fights for you'. Again, this is expressed more strongly

than in the Numbers account, showing once more Moses' selective use of Numbers to support his exhortation.[15]

In 3:23–25 Moses records his prayer, which has no parallel in Numbers. The prayer continues the emphases already seen above in motivating Israel to conquer the land in obedient faith. So Moses' prayer mentions that God has 'only begun to show your servant your greatness and your might; what god in heaven or on earth can perform deeds and mighty acts like yours!' (3:24). The reference to 'only begun' points forward to what he will continue. Further, in 3:25 Moses twice uses the word 'good' to describe the land (see more on this below). In addition, his mention of 'hill country' and 'Lebanon' refers back to the description of the land in 1:7, a verse which we saw above is tied to the Abrahamic promise recounted in 1:8.

Genesis 1:14–27
Idolatry is the major sin in Deuteronomy and there are repeated references warning Israel against it. Deuteronomy 4:15–19 grounds its warning in Genesis 1:14–27, reversing the creation order. Such an allusion implies that idolatry is the polar opposite of the worship of the Creator and suggests its folly. Moses' creative use of Genesis 1 here is by allusion, rather than by direct quote or exposition. He assumes knowledge of the text so that his allusion carries rhetorical impact.

Exodus 19 – 24
Deuteronomy 4 is a transition between the preached narrative of chapters 1 – 3 and the preached legislation beginning in chapter 5. This chapter is not directly an exposition of a past text or narrative. It presupposes chapters 1 – 3,[16] and brings the opening section to a rhetorical and hortatory climax.

In 4:9–14 Moses expounds briefly on some points from Exodus 19 – 24. Moses here preaches as if his current audience actually heard God's voice at Horeb, conflating the generations as noted above, thus creating immediacy and ongoing validity of God's word. Further, verses 13–14 imply a distinction between the Ten Commandments, equated here with the Horeb covenant, and the rest of the laws. McConville argues that this difference from Exodus, where all the laws appear to be part of the covenant, suggests that in each generation the Horeb covenant is made new, adding to

---

15. McConville, *Deuteronomy*, p. 95; cf. Num. 32:6–15.

16. Mayes, *Deuteronomy*, p. 148.

the rhetorical aim of bringing the current audience directly under God's word.[17]

In chapter 4, with its general reference back to the Sinai event of Exodus 19 – 24, Deuteronomy emphasizes the hearing of God's word (4:1, 10, 12–13). While this is not in disagreement with Exodus, the emphasis in Deuteronomy on God's word continues the theme of the ongoing direct speech of God to Israel and the ongoing validity and authority of his word, spoken through Moses. Indeed, Deuteronomy emphasizes the presence of God via his word.[18] As Moses preaches God's word, God is present with his people – a high view of God's word and the authority of Moses the preacher.

The climax of chapter 4 is the assertion of the uniqueness of Yahweh (4:35, 39). Rhetorically, this emphasis continues to address the fear of Israel expressed in 1:28. Yahweh is supreme, incomparable and unrivalled. There is no need to fear anyone or anything else.

Moses' use of rhetoric in preaching

Though he pleaded a lack of eloquence and slowness of tongue and speech when first called by God to lead Israel (Exod. 4:10), Moses demonstrates a number of rhetorical techniques in his preaching in Deuteronomy. Commentators, at least since Driver, have remarked on Deuteronomy's hortatory style and rhetorical techniques, showing that the book is thoroughly sermonic in style. Driver's summary is both famous and, though overstated, worth reciting:

> In Deuteronomy, a new style of flowing and impressive *oratory* was introduced into Hebrew literature, by means of which the author strove to move and influence his readers. Hence (quite apart from the matter of his discourse) he differs from the most classical writers of historical narrative, by developing his thought into long and rolling periods, which have the effect of bearing the reader with them, and holding him enthralled by their oratorical power . . . The practical aims of the author, and the parenetic treatment, which as a rule his subject demands, oblige him naturally to expand and reiterate more than is usually the case with Hebrew writers; nevertheless, his discourse, while never (in the bad

---

17. McConville, *Deuteronomy*, p. 106.
18. See further ibid., p. 115.

sense of the term) rhetorical, always maintains its freshness, and is never monotonous or prolix.[19]

In essence, Deuteronomy is sermonic and, as numerous books on preaching argue, Deuteronomy models an oral style of sentence structure, use of language, repetition and other rhetorical devices.[20] What is the precise nature of the rhetoric in Deuteronomy 1 – 3?

We noted above Moses' use of 'you' to conflate the current generation with the parent generation. Rhetorically, this makes God's word immediate and direct to the audience. The same immediacy is brought about by the use of 'we'. For example, in 3:1–3, a passage that quite closely follows Numbers 21:33–35, Moses uses the first-person plural. Of course, since Moses is speaking here and was part of the victory, the first-person plural makes sense. In the Numbers account the unknown author uses 'they'. However, the rhetorical effect of the first person also draws the current generation into the account. God's word and actions are not distant or remote for this new generation at Moab. Indeed, in 4:23 the covenant at Sinai was made 'with you', the generation now at Moab.

Peter Adam comments briefly on the spirituality of the word in Deuteronomy. He says, 'These sermons were not only spoken but also written down, so that Israel could continue to hear God's words through Moses even after his death.'[21] McConville comments further that

> Deuteronomy's reflection on the capacity of the words once spoken to have continuing validity is part of its very theology . . . In theological terms, Deuteronomy makes a claim that God not only spoke, but goes on speaking by means of the teaching and interpretation of his word in believing communities.[22]

McConville makes this comment with regard to Deuteronomy's ongoing validity for Israel post-conquest. However, this observation is linked to the sermonic aim of the book for the second generation of Israel after the

---

19. S. R. Driver, *Deuteronomy*, 3rd ed., ICC (Edinburgh: T. & T. Clark, 1902), pp. lxxxvi–lxxxviii.
20. On orality in preaching, see e.g. Donald R. Sunukjian, *Invitation to Biblical Preaching: Proclaiming Truth with Clarity and Relevance* (Grand Rapids: Kregel, 2007), chs. 14–15.
21. Peter Adam, *Hearing God's Words: Exploring Biblical Spirituality*, NSBT 16 (Leicester: Apollos; Downers Grove: IVP, 2004), p. 53.
22. McConville, *Deuteronomy*, p. 41.

Exodus. If Deuteronomy has continuing validity, as it does, it does so in part because of its demonstration of the ongoing validity of God's words at Horeb to the Moab generation standing before Moses.

One rhetorical feature that assists this is the frequency of the word 'today'. It occurs many times throughout the whole book, referring to the day of Moses' preaching to Israel. In this context, in Deuteronomy 1 – 4 it is found in 1:10; 4:4, 8, 26, 38–40. Notice the frequency in chapter 4, especially with its more overt exhortation. The word impresses on the audience that 'today' is the day of God's speaking and the day of decision.[23] There is a directness and urgency of appeal in the frequency of this word. Moses' preaching is urgent. It is hardly a casual speech. His urgency is a good model, even for preachers today.

Another rhetorical device, common throughout Deuteronomy, is the way that the word 'land' is qualified. Moses rarely leaves the word standing alone. He almost always adds a motivational clause, as he seeks to stir up Israel to conquer the land. So in 1:8 it is 'the land that I swore to your ancestors, to Abraham, to Isaac, and to Jacob, to give to them and to their descendants after them'. The effect of this clause is assurance of God's faithfulness to his promise, a promise that still stands. A similar expression occurs in 1:21, 'take possession, as the LORD, the God of your ancestors, has promised you'.

As well as the emphasis on promise, Moses also uses motivational clauses focusing on God giving the land, as in 2:29 ('into the land that the LORD our God is giving us') in words spoken to Sihon but recounted here to encourage his hearers. The same occurs in 2:12, paralleling God's gift of the land to Israel with his past giving of land to Edom, Moab and Ammon ('in the land that the LORD gave them as a possession').

The third group of clauses focuses on the land itself as 'good', something noted above. This is the focus of the spies' report in 1:25, which also combines with the theme of giving: 'It is a good land that the LORD our God is giving us.' And God's own words in 1:35 echo those of the spies, 'the good land that I swore to give to your ancestors'.[24] Moses also twice uses the word 'good' in his qualification of the land in his prayer in 3:25.

---

23. See Simon J. DeVries, *Yesterday, Today and Tomorrow: Time and History in the Old Testament* (London: SPCK, 1975), pp. 164–186; McConville and Millar, *Time and Place in Deuteronomy*, pp. 41–44.

24. Moshe Weinfeld, *Deuteronomy and the Deuteronomic School* (Oxford: Oxford University Press, 1972), pp. 341–343, lists all the occurrences of these motivational clauses associated with land in Deuteronomy.

The repetition of these motivational clauses steps up in frequency in chapter 4, fitting the character of this chapter as heightened exhortation. So there is reference to the land promised to the ancestors (4:1), land that God is giving (4:1, 21, 38, 40) and the good land (4:21–22). There is also mention of 'the land that you are about to enter/cross the Jordan and occupy' (4:5, 14, 26).

Moses is using language deliberately to seek to persuade his hearers to enter the land. He uses repetition, with variety, to drip-feed the reminder that God is faithful, that God will give the land, and that the land itself is indeed good. Against this consistent pattern of using motivational clauses, it is striking that the people's words in requesting the spies include no such clause. They simply ask that spies go 'ahead of us to explore the land for us' (1:22). The implication is that Israel had neither trusted that God was giving the land, nor had promised the land, nor that the land was good.

Another rhetorical feature found in Deuteronomy 1 – 4 is a blurring between the voice of God and the voice of Moses. In 2:4–7 Moses recounts words God had given to him to say to Israel. Thus in 2:7 Moses speaks of the Lord in the third person. Yet in 2:5 the first-person speaker is obviously God. Moses' words and God's words come together from time to time, a device that adds authority to Moses' words. This ought not to surprise, since we are told in the opening paragraph that, in Deuteronomy, Moses is expounding the *tôrâ*, namely God's own words (1:5). Further, the role of the prophet of which Moses is the exemplar identifies his words with those of God in 18:15.[25] Millar argues that Deuteronomy 4 goes to lengths to integrate the Sinai theophany with the Mosaic preaching at Moab.[26]

Polzin notes how the rhetorical style of Deuteronomy 4 changes from that of chapters 1 – 3. In the earlier chapters, speech is recorded directly; in chapter 4 it is indirect. Thus now Moses appeals more directly to his current audience.[27]

Another technique Moses uses is the chiastic structure of the speeches in Deuteronomy 1. While modern readers may not use and be familiar with such structures, they are frequent in the OT. In Deuteronomy 1

---

25. Christopher Ash, *The Priority of Preaching* (Fearn: Christian Focus, 2009), pp. 15–43.

26. McConville and Millar, *Time and Place in Deuteronomy*, pp. 35–36.

27. Robert Polzin, *Moses and the Deuteronomist* (New York: Seabury, 1980), p. 40.

we have a chiastic pattern of speeches by God (1:6–8), Moses (1:20–21), Israel (1:22), the spies (1:25), Israel (1:27–28), Moses (1:29–33) and God (1:35–36). The links in vocabulary and theme tie together the words of Yahweh, Moses and the spies, isolating Israel's words but also rhetorically adding weight to Moses' words. Chiasms also draw attention to the central item, in this case the unequivocal report of the spies. So Moses uses a known structure as a rhetorical device to highlight the goodness of the land, at the same time associating his own words with those of Yahweh.[28]

Classical rhetoric from Aristotle argues for the importance of *logos, pathos* and *ethos*.[29] *Logos* is the appeal to the mind, and Moses exhibits this in arguing for Yahweh's faithfulness and power, appealing to historical evidence of the appointment of assistants in 1:12–18, Yahweh's past action for Edom, Moab and Ammon in 2:1–23, and the existence of Og's bed, for example. With regard to *pathos*, Deuteronomy 1 – 4 is not as strong on this as elsewhere in the book, especially the repeated appeal to the 'heart' as the organ of love and obedience (e.g. 6:5; 10:12–13). However, Moses' passing references to his own inability to enter the Promised Land may also create a sympathetic *pathos*. He comments in 1:37 that 'on your account' he is prevented from entering the land. While not blaming the people, he may be appealing for Israel to act obediently out of sympathy. With regard to *ethos*, Moses' alignment of his words with Yahweh's, as noted above, suggests an appeal to Moses' derived authority and credibility.

Moses is prepared to use some sarcasm as a rhetorical device, ridiculing idolatry by saying that idols are 'made by human hands, objects of wood and stone that neither see, nor hear, nor eat, nor smell' (4:28).

Rhetorical questions too are found in Deuteronomy 4, especially in verses 32–40 but also earlier in verses 7–8 on the lips of other nations. Rhetorical questions, with clear, implied answers, bring this section of the sermon to a climax. The questions invite the futile search through the full extent of time and space to find another god as great as Yahweh. They draw the audience

---

28. See further Barker, *Triumph of Grace*, pp. 17–22.

29. *The Rhetoric of Aristotle*, tr. Lane Cooper (New York: Appleton, 1932). See also Lester De Koster, 'The Preacher as Rhetorician', in Samuel T. Logan Jr. (ed.), *The Preacher and Preaching: Reviving the Art in the Twentieth Century* (Phillipsburg: Presbyterian & Reformed, 1986), pp. 303–330; Martin E. Marty, 'Preaching Rhetorically: Thanks Aristotle and Apostles', in Michael P. Knowles (ed.), *The Folly of Preaching* (Grand Rapids: Eerdmans, 2007), pp. 98–109.

to the firm conclusion that 'the LORD is God; there is no other besides him' (4:35). Then, to be absolutely certain, Moses answers the questions in verses 36–38 and comes to the same conclusion in verse 39: 'there is no other'. From the powerlessness and ridicule of idols to the grandeur and greatness of Yahweh, Moses invites his audience to an exclusive allegiance to Yahweh alone.

Conclusion

Moses' sermon demonstrates several important lessons for preachers. Not least is his recognition of, and dealing with, the relationship between faith and obedience. Moses recognizes that underneath rebellion is inadequate faith. So he addresses the tendency to rebel by preaching Yahweh, his power and faithfulness, in order to increase and stir up Israel's faith. Moses therefore holds together grace and law, neither turning to cheap grace nor to legalistic preaching.

It is a temptation for preachers addressing sinful tendencies either to preach personal ability to conquer sin (e.g. power of positive thinking, victorious Christian living) or to preach more and more legalistically. Instead Moses preaches God, as he seeks to produce the 'obedience of faith' (Rom. 1:5) in his audience.

To do this, Moses bases his sermon on the Bible, at least on the four preceding books of the OT. He shows both faithfulness to the text or tradition, but is able to draw out appropriate emphases to make his point. He assumes some knowledge of these texts and thus shows some subtlety in allusions, especially to Genesis 15 but also in his treatment of Numbers 13 – 14. However, Moses is always faithful to the original intentions of those texts as he reapplies them to a new generation.

Rhetorically, Moses uses a variety of techniques to persuade and convince his audience. His preaching shows appropriate urgency and clear authority, an authority that derives from God's words, not from Moses' own person. He brings the first section of his sermon to an appropriately high level of rhetorical climax in 4:32–40.

Moses exhibits a high view of the power of God's word, trusting that, as he preaches, God speaks directly to his audience. Though God's word spoken by a prophet (as Moses was, 18:15) did not often meet with the desired response from the audience, in Moses' case it did. Under Joshua, Israel did cross the Jordan into the Promised Land. Though there were stumbles of disobedience along the way, the book of Joshua shows that Moses' preaching in Deuteronomy was used by God to bring about an astonishing conquest.[30]

May the preaching of God's powerful word continue to bring people to the obedience of faith.

© Paul A. Barker, 2011

---

30. See e.g. Joshua's appeal to Moses' commands (Josh. 1:13; 8:35); the people's obedience to Moses' preaching (8:33); Joshua's own obedience to Moses' preaching (11:15); and Joshua's commendation of the tribes of Gad, Reuben and half of Manasseh for their obedience to Moses' preaching (22:1–5).

3. PROPHETIC PREACHING IN THE BOOK OF ACTS

David G. Peterson

Many of the prophets of Israel appear to have been preachers, proclaiming the words of God in public contexts and using a variety of methods to express what they received. Although they were delivering specific revelations from the Lord, their distinctive personalities, experiences and gifts seem to have played an important part in the process. Much can be learned from looking at the way they communicated, though there are cultural, linguistic and contextual reasons why we cannot simply copy what they said and did.

Most importantly, links between the ministry of OT prophets and what is called prophecy in the NT ought to be investigated. More precisely, we need to consider whether preaching can be considered as an aspect of NT prophecy and, if so, what that tells us about this ministry today. The Acts of the Apostles is the best starting point for such an exploration, since it provides evidence of Christian prophesying and gives a theological framework for understanding this ministry.

The nature of prophecy in Acts[1]

The prophetic Scriptures and apostolic preaching

The noun 'prophet' appears thirty times in Acts and the verb 'prophesy' four times.[2] By far the most common use of 'prophet' is with reference to prophetic figures in the OT such as Joel (2:16), David (2:30), Moses (3:22) or Isaiah (8:28; 28:25). God is said to have foretold certain events such as the suffering of his Christ 'through the mouth of all his prophets' (3:18, my tr.). The words were theirs, but God was directing their utterances, revealing his mind and will to his people through them.

In particular, 'all the prophets from Samuel on, as many as have spoken, have foretold these days' (3:24),[3] and all testify about Jesus, 'that everyone who believes in him receives forgiveness of sins through his name' (10:43). Many and varied strands of OT prophecy are regarded by the earliest Christian preachers as providing a united testimony to Christ and the situation of the early church. Their written words continue to give special insight into the person and work of the Lord Jesus and to challenge unbelievers to repentance and faith (3:22–23; 8:30–35; 13:32–41).

'The Law and the Prophets' (13:15; 24:14; 28:23; cf. 26:22, 'the prophets and Moses'), or more narrowly 'the prophets' (26:22), are regularly used in the record of Acts by those engaged in apologetic and evangelistic work with Jews or Gentile God-fearers (e.g. 17:2–3; 28:23). The assumption is that those who accept the divine inspiration and unique authority of these writings will respond to their appeal. The prophetic Scriptures are also used by Christians to interpret their own situation and to solve dilemmas in their community life (e.g. 1:20–22; 4:25–30; 13:47; 15:15–18).[4] Since the Holy Spirit was believed to

---

1. Much of the substance of these opening sections is drawn from my earlier reflections in 'Acts and the Spirit of Prophecy', in Barry G. Webb (ed.), *Spirit of the Living God, Part One*, Explorations 5 (Homebush West: Lancer, 1991), pp. 95–115, revised as *Prophecy and Preaching: Acts and the Church Today*, Orthos 16 (Buxton: Fellowship of Word and Spirit, 1997), further updated at <http:///davidgpeterson.com/acts/prophecy-and-preaching-in-acts>.

2. The verb *prophēteuō* is only ever used in Acts with reference to Christian prophesying (2:17–18; 19:6; 21:9). The noun *prophētēs* is used of OT and NT figures alike.

3. Unless stated otherwise, Bible quotations in this chapter are from the NIV.

4. Cf. Darrell L. Bock, 'Scripture and the Realisation of God's Promises', in I. Howard Marshall and David G. Peterson (eds.), *Witness to the Gospel: The Theology of Acts* (Grand Rapids: Eerdmans, 1998), pp. 41–62.

have spoken in a unique and distinctive way through Moses and the prophets (1:16; 4:25; 28:25), the earliest Christian preachers expected that those who were 'sons of the prophets' and heirs of the covenant (3:25) would recognize the fulfilment of God's promises in Jesus and turn to him.

Yet Stephen speaks about a 'stiff-necked people, with uncircumcised hearts and ears', always resisting the Holy Spirit, persecuting the prophets and then betraying and murdering the Messiah (7:51–53). Such apostasy continues in the opposition to Stephen and others who testify to Jesus on the basis of the prophetic Scriptures. By implication, the Holy Spirit who spoke through the prophets continues to speak through the witness of Christians.

Characteristics of prophecy in the last days

Given this emphasis on the special role and authority of OT prophets in the plan of God for his people, it is highly significant that the Pentecost sermon of Peter proclaims the fulfilment of Joel 2:28–32. A distinctive characteristic of 'the last days' is the pouring out of God's Spirit 'on all flesh', so that

> Your sons and daughters will prophesy,
>> your young men will see visions,
>> your old men will dream dreams.
> (Acts 2:17)

God promises through Joel:

> Even on my servants, both men and women,
>> I will pour out my Spirit in those days.

And Peter repeats the words 'and they will prophesy' from the previous verse to make the point absolutely clear (Acts 2:18). In other words, things will be revealed, which Israel's sons and daughters will then make known as the word of God.

Peter's sermon is clearly programmatic for Acts, alerting us in advance to look for signs of the Spirit's presence in the believing community, and especially for prophetic activity. Searching for such signs, however, one is initially struck by the paucity of explicit references to prophecy as a gift or ministry operating amongst Christians. Leaving aside for a moment the question of whether the disciples were actually prophesying on the day of Pentecost, the first mention of Christian prophets is in 11:27–28. There we are told that amongst some prophets who came down from Jerusalem to Antioch one of them (named Agabus) stood up and 'through the Spirit predicted that a severe

famine would spread over the entire Roman world'. The immediate result of
this prophecy was that the Christians at Antioch were encouraged to give gen-
erously to the needs of their fellow believers in Judea. Perhaps the prophetic
ministry of Agabus also included an exhortation to respond to his prediction
in this practical way.

The presence of prophets and teachers in the church at Antioch is mentioned in Acts 13:1 and their names are given. No specific indication of the
function of these prophets is supplied, and it is not clear whether some of
those mentioned were prophets and some teachers, or whether all five exercised both ministries. Paul certainly combined the role of teacher and prophet,
as Jesus did (cf. 1 Cor. 14:37–38). It seems likely from the context that, while
they were 'ministering to the Lord and fasting' (my tr.), the Holy Spirit spoke
through one or more of the prophets, saying, 'Set apart for me Barnabas and
Saul for the work to which I have called them' (Acts 13:2, my tr.). The fasting
and praying that followed may have been to test the validity of this revelation
or to intercede for those about to be sent off on this important mission.

Judas and Silas are mentioned in Acts 15:22 as leaders among the brothers
in the Jerusalem church. Sent by the apostles and elders to the Gentile believers in Antioch, Syria and Cilicia with the letter concerning the decision of the
so-called Jerusalem Council, their task was to 'confirm by word of mouth'
what was written (15:27). When Luke describes their ministry in Antioch,
he says that Judas and Silas, 'being themselves also prophets [*autoi prophētai
ontes*], exhorted [*parekalesan*] the brothers with many words and strengthened
them' (15:32, my tr.). Their ministry on this occasion was a distinctive feature
of their *prophetic* role, but not in the sense of giving new revelation. As they
explained the ruling that the apostles and elders believed to have come from
the Holy Spirit (15:28), and as they talked about its meaning and purpose, God
used them to encourage other believers. Perhaps they were chosen for this
task 'because they had already exercised an influential role in establishing (or
proclaiming) the biblical rationale upon which the provisions of the Decree
were justified'.[5] Their ministry of explaining and urging a positive response to
apostolic writings has obvious parallels with the work of preaching and teaching in our churches today.

Believers more generally are said to have engaged in prophesying in Acts

---

5. E. Earle Ellis, 'The Role of the Christian Prophet in Acts', in W. Ward Gasque and
   Ralph P. Martin (eds.), *Apostolic History and the Gospel* (Exeter: Paternoster, 1970),
   p. 62. Ellis rightly emphasizes the role of the prophet in interpreting Scripture and
   providing encouragement (*paraklēsis*) to believers (cf. 1 Cor. 14:3).

19:6. Paul had discovered a group of about twelve people in Ephesus who appeared to be true 'disciples', but who had received only John's baptism and were still looking forward to the Messiah's coming. Their situation is without parallel elsewhere in Acts. When Paul proclaimed Jesus as the Christ and they were baptized 'into the name of the Lord Jesus', Paul placed his hands on them and 'the Holy Spirit came on them, and they spoke in tongues and prophesied'.[6] The language here suggests that their experience was being compared, at least in some respects, with that of the original group of disciples on the day of Pentecost (2:4–11; cf. 11:15–17). John Stott concludes that 'they experienced a mini-Pentecost. Better, Pentecost caught up on them. Better still, they were caught up into it, as its promised blessings became theirs.'[7]

Acts 21 contains several references to prophesying. First, the disciples at Tyre were urging Paul 'through the Spirit' not to go on to Jerusalem (21:4). But Paul had already been warned 'in every city' by the Holy Spirit that prison and hardships were facing him (20:23). Perhaps such warnings came through the prophetic ministry of other believers. Even though the urging in 21:4 is not called prophecy, there seems no better way to identify what was taking place. Nevertheless Paul, who had earlier described himself as journeying to Jerusalem 'bound in/by the Spirit' (20:22), would not be deflected from reaching his goal (cf. 20:24).[8] The four unmarried daughters of Philip the evangelist

---

6. These 'disciples' can hardly have been Christians already since they had not received the gift of the Holy Spirit when they believed. Their ignorance of the Holy Spirit (19:2) can only mean that, although they had heard John's prophecy about the coming baptism of the Spirit, they had not discovered that it had been fulfilled in Jesus. Paul's next question (v. 3, 'Then what baptism did you receive?') suggests that it was anomalous for baptized persons not to have received the Spirit. Cf. David G. Peterson, *The Acts of the Apostles*, PNTC (Grand Rapids: Eerdmans; Nottingham: Apollos, 2009), pp. 527–533.

7. John R. W. Stott, *The Message of Acts: To the Ends of the Earth*, BST (Leicester: IVP, 1990), pp. 304–305. Max Turner suggests that 'to prophesy' here probably does not have the sense 'to report a revelation (word, vision or dream) received', but more simply 'to speak while under the external influence of the Spirit' ('Spiritual Gifts Then and Now', *VE* 15 [1985], pp. 7–64, quote p. 11).

8. Acts 20:22 probably alludes to Paul's decision to go to Jerusalem in 19:21, 'in/by the Spirit' (*en tō pneumati*). Although the compulsion of his own spirit could be on view, the influence of the Holy Spirit on his spirit in this decision is surely implied. For a helpful discussion of Paul's attitude to the guidance of the Spirit in Acts 19 – 21, see Stott, *Acts*, pp. 332–333.

are then described as those who regularly engaged in prophesying (21:9), though no details are given about what they said and did.

Finally, Agabus the prophet from Judea reappears (21:10–11). Like many of the OT prophets, he employs a symbolic action to reinforce the point of his prediction and speaks as the mouthpiece of God. Tying his own hands and feet with Paul's belt, he declares, 'The Holy Spirit says, "In this way the Jews of Jerusalem will bind the owner of this belt and will hand him over to the Gentiles."' Once again, Paul ignores the warning and refuses to be dissuaded by the pleas of his friends (21:12–14). But he is not rejecting a command of the Spirit: like Jesus before him, he sets his face steadfastly to fulfil his God-given ministry, despite clear predictions of suffering and arrest.[9]

David Aune suggests that 'the distinctive feature of prophetic speech was not so much its content or form, but its (direct) supernatural origin'.[10] But the prophetic ministry of Judas and Silas in Acts 15 does not easily fit into that framework. Moreover, although Luke restricts the term or title 'prophet' to a select few, prophetic-type activity is evidenced more widely in the early Christian communities.

Thus Stephen is introduced as 'a man full of faith and of the Holy Spirit' (6:5), who 'did great wonders and miraculous signs among the people' (6:8). His opponents could not resist 'his wisdom or the Spirit by whom he spoke' (6:10), as illustrated in his lengthy address in Acts 7, which expounds Scripture and proclaims Jesus as the exalted Son of Man. Philip too is presented as a prophetic figure (8:5–13), whose ministry includes an explanation of Scripture in the light of its fulfilment in Christ (8:26–38).

Even though Ananias is not designated as a prophet, he receives a prophetic revelation concerning Paul and his future (9:10–16). Again, Peter displays the marks of a prophet in his knowledge of people's hearts (5:3; 8:20–23; cf. Luke 7:39) and in his experience of revelations in visions and dreams (10:10). Paul similarly receives prophetic-type communications from the Lord (16:9; 18:9; 22:17–21; 27:23–24) and combines the roles of apostle, teacher and prophet.

In short, then, explicit Christian prophecy in Acts is rarely mentioned. Where it is, most obviously it involves prediction of future events, direction from God about the way in which the ministry of the gospel should proceed, interpretation of an apostolic letter and its significance, and exhortation or praise based on such insights.

---

9. Cf. Peterson, *Acts*, pp. 580–582.

10. David E. Aune, *Prophecy in Early Christianity and the Ancient Mediterranean World* (Grand Rapids: Eerdmans, 1983), p. 338.

Prophecy and preaching

Two significant manifestations of the outpouring of the Spirit at Pentecost are recorded in Acts 2. The first is the phenomenon of speaking 'in other tongues as the Spirit enabled them' (v. 4). This is further explained as 'declaring the wonders of God' in various expressions of foreign, but intelligible speech (vv. 6–11). Unlike the glossolalia evidenced in 1 Corinthians, this required no interpretation but appears to have been a form of ecstatic, but understandable, praise of God and his mighty works (cf. 19:6). Peter immediately describes it as a fulfilment of what Joel says regarding prophecy (vv. 14–21).

The second manifestation of the Spirit's outpouring is Peter's prophetic-type speech, which brings some three thousand people to repent and be baptized in the name of Jesus Christ (2:37–41). Luke does not explicitly attribute this event to the work of the Holy Spirit, though the context suggests that it is further evidence of what Joel predicts about prophesying 'in the last days'. The convicting activity of the Spirit (cf. John 16:7–11) is most obvious in the outcome, and the opponents of Peter and John soon draw attention to their remarkable courage in speaking out as 'unschooled, ordinary men', not trained as interpreters of Scripture and rabbinic tradition (4:13; cf. 15:32). For Luke, such courage (*parrēsia*) is evidence of a divine compulsion (4:20) and the Holy Spirit's enabling (4:29, 31).[11]

Acts contains a number of speeches, short and long, directed either to Jewish or Gentile audiences. The responses vary, but the prophetic nature of many of these discourses seems obvious once the significance of the primary speech in Acts 2 has been understood. Such speeches are outstanding examples of the ministry of 'the word', which is Luke's regular method of describing the gospel. This linguistic choice suggests the continuity of the Christian message with the prophetic Scriptures and with the ministry of prophets called to proclaim the word of the Lord to Israel. As 'the word of God', the gospel on the lips of apostles, of prophetic figures such as Stephen and Philip, and of ordinary believers (8:4; 11:19–21) has divine authority and power to transform lives.

However, the relationship between prophecy and preaching in the NT is disputed. Ernest Best began his treatment of the subject by observing that prophesying in the OT related to past, present and future: 'the prophet takes up the old revelation and applies it to the present

---

11. Cf. Peterson, *Acts*, p. 194.

situation; he gives under God something new; and by the incomplete-ness of his own revelation he implies that God has yet further "words" to speak'.[12]

Yet, since the redemptive action of God to which the OT prophets pointed has now taken place in Jesus Christ, we do not require further or supplemen-tary revelations. The NT preacher can be described as a prophet only in an attenuated sense. So the preacher

> will not expect the Spirit to lead him to utter new truths, nor can he bear witness to the incompleteness of the truth as already revealed; the Spirit can only lead him to the truth which is Jesus Christ; but he may still take up the Word of Scripture and apply it to his own day, finding perhaps new depths in it, but never anything uniquely new.[13]

Best rightly concedes that special prophetic status does extend to the authors of the NT and compares them with the canonical or writing prophets of the OT. This is signalled in various ways elsewhere in the NT. For example, Paul insists on the foundational and abiding authority of the message he received from the Lord (Gal. 1:6–16), his distinctive role in explaining and making known 'the mystery of Christ' (Eph. 3:1–9), and his status as one who can write 'a command of the Lord' (1 Cor. 14:37, my tr.).[14] Hebrews calls upon its readers to heed what the Holy Spirit is saying through the Scriptures (Heb. 3:7 – 4:13) and to give the same attention to the writer's own words of exhortation (5:11 – 6:12).

Non-writing prophets such as Agabus stand more in the tradition of non-canonical prophets in the OT, but are never regarded as being false prophets in opposition to apostolic teaching. Best rightly opposes a simplistic identifi-

---

12. Ernest Best, 'Prophets and Preachers', *SJT* 12 (1959), pp. 129–150, quote p. 136.

13. Ibid., pp. 136–137. He goes on to point out that the living Lord Jesus actually confronts people through authentic Christian preaching.

14. Wayne A. Grudem has similarly argued that the apostles and other NT writers truly inherit the mantle of the OT canonical prophets, since they claim absolute divine authority for their words and call upon believers to acknowledge that authority (*The Gift of Prophecy in 1 Corinthians* [Lanham: University Press of America, 1982], pp. 43–54). By contrast, the prophetic ministry given to certain members of the Corinthian church required assessment and evaluation, which implied the possibility of challenging and even rejecting such contributions (1 Cor. 14:29; cf. 1 Thess. 5:21–22).

cation of the prophet and the teacher, but does not explain how the two roles or functions might be shared by the one person.

The argument that inspired preaching, exegesis or teaching are actually (wholly or in part) what the NT means by prophecy has been asserted by writers such as David Hill and Earle Ellis.[15] However, since early Christian writers regularly distinguished the *charismata* of teaching and prophecy (e.g. Acts 13:1; Rom. 12:6–7; 1 Cor. 12:28–29; Eph. 4:11), it seems likely that the old and widespread difference between these functions in Judaism and in the Greco-Roman world was being maintained.

Max Turner notes manifestations of Spirit-given wisdom and discernment in passages such as Acts 5:3; 6:10; 10:27–29, 34–43. He argues that this phenomenon is closely associated with, and can result in, powerful preaching – as especially in the case of Stephen (7:55–56). Power in preaching is a major feature in Luke's record of the early church, but it is not to be confused with the essence of the Pentecost gift. According to Turner it is 'merely one aspect of the activity of the Spirit as the christocentric Spirit of prophecy'.[16] The Spirit may give to the speaker 'direct revelation where the content informs the preaching', 'charismatic wisdom', assurance and boldness.[17]

In Acts, prophesying is a ministry shared by all believers in different ways, though it is particularly manifested in those designated as prophets, either in prediction or in encouragement. Teaching was clearly an apostolic function in the first place (2:42), though it was soon carried out by others (11:26; 13:1; 15:1; 18:25) both formally and informally. Prophecy and teaching appear to overlap in the ministry of preaching or public proclamation of 'the word'.

---

15. David Hill, 'Christian Prophets as Teachers or Instructors in the Church', in Johannes Panagopoulos (ed.), *Prophetic Vocation in the New Testament and Today*, NovTSup 45 (Leiden: Brill, 1977), pp. 108–130; E. Earle Ellis, *Prophecy and Hermeneutic in Early Christianity*, WUNT 18 (Tübingen: Mohr [Siebeck], 1978), part 2.

16. Turner, 'Spiritual Gifts', p. 41.

17. Max Turner, 'The Spirit of Prophecy and the Power of Authoritative Preaching in Luke–Acts: A Question of Origins', *NTS* 38 (1992), pp. 66–88, esp. pp. 69–70. Turner goes on to speak of other *charismata*, which heighten the effect of preaching, and envisages the Spirit conveying 'the numinous sense of *God's presence and activity*' (emphasis original). However, it is better to view the convicting work of the Spirit in relation to the word proclaimed and the promise of John 16:8–11.

Characteristics of prophetic preaching

By way of example, four speeches will be examined briefly (2:14–41; 3:12–26; 13:16–41; 17:22–31) and three common features discussed. These 'sermons' might otherwise be classified as evangelistic, since they involve proclaiming Jesus as Lord and Christ (5:42; 8:5, 35; 9:20; 10:36; 11:20; 17:18; 19:13) and are examples of what Luke calls preaching 'the word' (8:4) or preaching 'the kingdom of God' (8:12; cf. 20:25; 28:31). However, if the preceding argument is correct, they are also significant manifestations of prophetic speech, and Luke means us to understand that in content, style and effect they are the result of the outpouring of the Holy Spirit by the ascended Lord Jesus.

Christocentric
Acts 2
Peter addresses a crowd of Jews in Jerusalem, drawn together by the phenomenon of Spirit-directed speech (vv. 4, 6–12). Peter's message essentially argues that Joel 2:28–32, which is his foundational text, has been fulfilled by the Lord Jesus Christ, who has been resurrected and exalted to the right hand of God. An inclusion is formed between the statement of God's intention in Acts 2:17 ('I will pour out my Spirit on all people') and the claim in 2:33 that the ascended Christ has brought this about ('he has received from the Father the promised Holy Spirit and has poured out what you now see and hear').

Although the sermon begins with an explanation of the events outlined in 2:1–13, it moves immediately to a recollection of the ministry of Jesus and the circumstances of his death (vv. 22–23). A resurrection apologetic follows (vv. 24–32), claiming from the Scriptures that it was impossible for death to keep its hold on the Messiah. The sermon climaxes with the proclamation of his ascension and pouring out of the Spirit (vv. 33–36), leading to the conclusion that 'God has made this Jesus, whom you crucified, both Lord and Christ.' In the final analysis, therefore, Jesus rather than the Spirit is the focus of this sermon. Yet the Spirit is at work in the testimony of the preacher, glorifying the Lord Jesus (cf. John 16:13–16).

Acts 3
Peter explains to a crowd gathered at the temple in Jerusalem how the healing of a lame man is evidence of the exaltation of Jesus as the Servant of the Lord. An inclusion is formed between the opening claim that God has 'glorified his servant Jesus' (v. 13; cf. Isa. 52:13) and the concluding assertion that 'When

God raised up his servant, he sent him first to you to bless you by turning each of you from your wicked ways' (v. 26; cf. Isa. 49:5–6). These servant allusions surround explicit teaching about the salvific effect of Jesus' death and resurrection (vv. 17–22), and an insistent appeal to fellow Israelites to recognize the enormity of disowning him (vv. 13–15) and continuing to resist him (vv. 21–26). As in the Gospels, the focus is on faith in Jesus as the means of physical healing (v. 16), but such healing is a sign of the complete restoration Jesus makes possible through forgiveness, of 'times of refreshing' from the Lord (probably a reference to the gift of the Spirit), and of the promised new creation (vv. 19–21).

Acts 13

Paul addresses a congregation of diaspora Jews and God-fearers in Pisidian Antioch. After the reading from the Law and the Prophets, he is invited to give 'a message of encouragement' to the synagogue (v. 15, *logos paraklēseōs*, 'word of exhortation'). He briefly recalls biblical teaching about God's choice of the people of Israel and his provision for them, culminating in the appointment of David as king (vv. 16–22). This leads immediately to the claim that 'from this man's descendants God has brought to Israel the Saviour Jesus, as he promised' (v. 23). The sermon then seeks to establish the truth of this claim by recounting what John the Baptist said about Jesus (vv. 24–25). It details the events leading up to the death of Jesus and proclaims his resurrection (vv. 26–31). A resurrection apologetic follows, similar to Peter's in 2:24–32, asserting from Scripture that it was impossible for the Messiah to be abandoned to death by God (vv. 32–37).

Paul then explains how Jesus is the Saviour of Israel (v. 23; cf. v. 26), focusing on the forgiveness of sins he makes possible and 'a justification you were not able to obtain under the law of Moses' (vv. 38–39 TNIV). Faith in Jesus Christ sets people free from the penalty and control of all those things from which it was impossible to find release in or by the law of Moses.[18] The sermon concludes with a warning not to scoff at these claims and perish (v. 41, citing Hab. 1:5). Although there are similarities to the messages in Acts 2 and 3, there is no mention of the gift of the Holy Spirit here and no explicit call to repent or be baptized. Instead, the controlling motifs are the messianic kingship of Jesus and salvation through the forgiveness of sins.

---

18. Cf. Peterson, *Acts*, p. 394.

Acts 17

At first glance, Paul's address to pagans in Athens appears to be entirely different in character from the messages examined so far. However, it should be remembered that Luke's account begins with a note about Paul's anger at the idolatry of the city and the culture it represented (v. 16). Paul's response was to proclaim 'Jesus and the resurrection' in the marketplace to anyone who happened to be there (vv. 17–18). For this he was called to account by representatives of two of the major schools of philosophy present in the city at that time, the Epicureans and the Stoics. They brought him to the Council of the Areopagus to discover the precise content and meaning of the new teaching he was presenting (vv. 19–21).[19]

Paul's defence is first to expose their ignorance of the one true God and to critique the theology underlying their idolatrous practices. Although he does not actually quote Scripture, he sets forth biblical teaching about the character of God and his purpose in creating human beings (vv. 22–29). The climax of the address is the call to repent in the light of imminent judgment 'by the man he has appointed', and the assertion that God has 'given proof of this to everyone by raising him from the dead' (vv. 30–31 TNIV). Although Jesus is not named at this point, Paul effectively returns to where he began in the marketplace, proclaiming Jesus and the resurrection as the fundamental challenge to pagan unbelief and idolatry. The intervening material shows why such a gospel proclamation is necessary. In this Gentile context, Jesus is not identified as Israel's Messiah, but his eschatological significance is nevertheless articulated.

There is no mention of the gift of the Holy Spirit here and the call to repent is not linked to baptism. Although there is no offer of forgiveness, this could be implied by the challenge to repent before the judgment comes.

Scripturally based

Acts 2

Joel 2:28–32 is the foundational text in Peter's Pentecost sermon. The opening promise in Acts 2:17 ('In the last days, God says, I will pour out my Spirit on all people') is repeated in 2:18, and declared to have been fulfilled by the ascended Christ in 2:33 ('he has received from the Father the promised

---

19. F. F. Bruce observes that the jurisdiction of the Council in religious matters made it 'the appropriate body to examine one who was charged with proclaiming "strange divinities"' (*The Acts of the Apostles: The Greek Text with Introduction and Commentary*, 3rd ed. [Grand Rapids: Eerdmans; Leicester: Apollos, 1990], p. 378).

Holy Spirit and has poured out what you now see and hear'). Peter uses the text to explain the phenomena of Pentecost, responding to the genuine questioning and the mocking in 2:12–13. At the same time, he uses the prophecy as part of his argument about the true identity of Jesus of Nazareth and his significance.

The citation from Joel includes several variations from the LXX and the Hebrew original. Most of these modifications serve to demonstrate the relevance of the text to the situation being addressed. Instead of Joel's introductory 'afterwards' (LXX, *meta tauta*), which points quite generally to future events, Acts has 'in the last days', signifying that this is part of God's final act of redemption. The coming of the Spirit means that God's purpose for humanity is about to be consummated.

Repetition of the words 'they will prophesy' make it clear that the Spirit has been poured out to enable all God's people to engage in this ministry (cf. Num. 11:29). In association with the gift of the Spirit, the Lord promises to give 'wonders in the heaven above and signs on the earth below'. Joel 2:30 has only 'wonders in the heavens and on the earth', but Peter identifies 'signs on the earth' as a separate, but related, category to 'wonders in the heavens' by introducing the contrasting words 'above' and 'below'. These could include all the events anticipating the arrival of the End – everything from Jesus' supernatural birth and miraculous activity to his resurrection and ascension, the outpouring of the Spirit at Pentecost and the miraculous events recorded in Acts.

Joel promised deliverance from the judgment of God for 'everyone who calls on the name of the Lord'. The rest of Peter's sermon is designed to show that *Jesus* is the Lord upon whom everyone should call (vv. 22–36; cf. Rom. 10:9–13). Furthermore, the explanation is given that calling on his name means submitting in repentance and faith to baptism in his name (vv. 37–39; cf. 22:16). Indeed, there are repeated references both to the name of Jesus and to the salvation available through him in Acts 3:6, 16; 4:7, 10, 12, 17–18, 30; 5:28, 40. Joel 2:32 appears to have had a profound influence on early Christian preaching to Jews and the related ministry of healing 'in the name of Jesus Christ'.[20]

The Christological portion of the sermon also relies upon two psalm quotations and an allusion. Psalm 16:8–11 is quoted in 2:25–28, and its

---

20. Note also in 2:39 that the final description of the people for whom the promise is made recalls the last clause of Joel 2:32 (not quoted in Acts 2:21): the blessings of salvation will be 'for all whom the Lord our God will call'.

implications are discussed in 2:29–31. Peter's aim is not to 'prove' the resurrection as a historical event – the apostles present themselves as witnesses in that particular respect (v. 32) – but to show how the resurrection testifies to Jesus' messiahship. An allusion is also made to Psalm 132:11 in 2:30. This reflects the promise of God to establish the throne of David's offspring for ever (cf. 2 Sam. 7:12–16; Ps. 89:3–4, 35–37). Together with the claim that David was a prophet, this certainty about God's promise explains how Psalm 16:8–11 predicts the resurrection of the Messiah. Psalm 110:1 is then quoted and used with reference to the claim that Jesus ascended into heaven to reach the climactic conclusion that 'God has made this Jesus, whom you crucified, both Lord and Christ.'

Acts 3

Biblical texts are cited only in the concluding part of this sermon, to encourage a right response to Jesus and the salvation offered in his name. The first quotation combines words from Deuteronomy 18:15, 19 and Leviticus 23:29. The plural 'for you' is inserted early in the citation, and another plural is inserted at the end of Acts 3:22 ('to you'), to emphasize the need for the audience to respond collectively to Jesus as the prophet like Moses.

When Moses said, 'The Lord your God will raise up for you a prophet like me from among your own people', it was in the context of warning Israel not to be like the nations. Instead of practising sorcery or divination, God's people were to 'listen to everything he tells you'. The warning is then individualized in verse 23 with the addition of words from Leviticus 23:29, 'Anyone who does not listen to him will be completely cut off from among his people.' A succession of prophets was raised up to follow Moses, but none was recognized as a prophet specifically like Moses himself (cf. Deut. 34:10). In time, Moses' words were interpreted as referring to one particular prophet who was yet to come and who would function as prophet-king and prophet-lawgiver in the last days. Moses' prophecy came to be regarded as messianic in its scope. Peter envisages Jesus as the eschatological prophet, because he brings the ultimate revelation of God's will and leads God's people to final salvation.

The second quotation comes in verse 25, after Peter addresses the crowd as 'heirs of the prophets and of the covenant God made with your fathers'. His audience ought to experience the ultimate blessing of the covenant made with the patriarchs and articulated in the predictions of the prophets. Genesis 12:3 ('and all peoples on earth will be blessed through you') is conflated with the promise of Genesis 22:18 ('and through your offspring all nations on earth will be blessed'). But this blessing can be experienced only if they recognize, through the apostolic preaching, that God has sent his exalted Servant first to Israel, 'to bless you by turning each of you from your wicked ways' (Acts 3:26). Israel needs to be blessed by the Messiah so as to become a blessing to the nations.

Use of the word 'first' implies the sort of sequence portrayed in Isaiah 49:5–6, where the Servant of the Lord is used to 'restore the tribes of Jacob' so that they can be 'a light for the Gentiles' and bring God's salvation 'to the ends of the earth' (cf. Acts 1:6; 13:46–48; 26:16–18). In other words, that significant 'Servant Song', which reveals the way in which God will ultimately fulfil his promise to Abraham, appears to lie behind the final challenge of Peter's sermon. In this sequence of thought the 'raising up' of Jesus most naturally refers to God's sending him as his Servant, to fulfil the divine plan for Israel and the nations.[21] The messianic blessing includes all the benefits of Jesus' saving work outlined in Acts 3:19–21, together with the gift of repentance ('by turning each of you from your wicked ways', v. 26).

Significantly, the opening words of the sermon also make the claim that 'The God of Abraham, Isaac and Jacob, the God of our fathers, has glorified his servant Jesus' (3:13, *edoxasen ton paida autou*). This is apparently an allusion to Isaiah 52:13 (LXX, *ho pais mou . . . doxasthēsetai sphodra*, 'my servant . . . will be . . . highly exalted'), a verse that introduces the so-called 'Fourth Servant Song' in Isaiah 52:13 – 53:12. The glorification of the Servant refers to his exaltation over the nations and their kings, after terrible humiliation and suffering. Peter's use of the title 'servant' here is more than an honorific way of describing Jesus as a faithful follower or child of God. He goes on to describe Jesus' rejection, death and exaltation by God (vv. 13–15) in a way that mirrors the portrait of the Servant in Isaiah 53. When Peter insists that God has fulfilled what the prophets said about the suffering of 'his Christ' (v. 18), it is logical to conclude that Isaiah 53 is a key text in his thinking. Jesus is the messianic Servant who accomplishes God's saving purposes for Israel and the nations by fulfilling the pattern set out in that prophecy. Isaiah 53 is not quoted by the preacher, but its influence can be seen in the way the argument of the sermon develops.

Acts 13

Scripture is first summarized, as Paul gives a brief overview of God's dealings with Israel from the moment he chose to enter into a relationship with

---

21. Cf. C. K. Barrett, *A Critical and Exegetical Commentary on the Acts of the Apostles*, vol. 1: *Acts I–XIV*, ICC (Edinburgh: T. & T. Clark, 1994), p. 213.

the patriarchs until the appointment of David as king (vv. 16–22). This first section of the sermon concludes with a conflation of words from 1 Samuel 13:14 ('the LORD has sought out a man after his own heart and appointed him leader of his people') and Psalm 89:20 ('I have found David my servant'). God's testimony about David is combined in this way: 'I have found David son of Jesse a man after my own heart; he will do everything I want him to do' (Acts 13:22).[22] Once David is mentioned, the rest of the message focuses on him and the promises made to him. However, Paul presents an immediate challenge to his audience with the words 'from this man's descendants God has brought to Israel the Saviour Jesus, as he promised' (v. 23; cf. 2 Sam. 7:12–16; Ps. 89:29; Isa. 11:1–16). The preacher speaks of the promised Son of David as having already come and identifies him with Jesus.

In the next portion of the sermon (vv. 24–30) Paul presents various testimonies to Jesus and claims that, even in condemning Jesus to death, the people of Jerusalem and their rulers 'fulfilled the words of the prophets that are read every Sabbath' (v. 27; cf. 'when they had carried out all that was written about him', v. 29). However, no Scripture is quoted until Paul embarks on an explanation of why it was necessary for the Messiah to be raised from death (vv. 32–37).

Paul first announces that 'What God promised our fathers, he has fulfilled for us, their children, by raising up Jesus.' He then cites one of the promises he has in mind:

As it is written in the second Psalm:

'You are my son;
today I have become your father [gegennēka se, 'I have begotten you'].' (TNIV)

'Begetting' in the context of this psalm is metaphorical, implying that when the Davidic king is installed on Zion, God's holy mountain (Ps. 2:6), the Lord in heaven acknowledges him as his own Son (2:7), promising to put down his enemies and make the nations his inheritance (2:8–9). Applied to Jesus and his resurrection, this psalm suggests that his resurrection-ascension brings him to

---

22. The words 'he will do everything I want him to do' reflect the Jewish Targum on the words 'after his own heart' in 1 Sam. 13:14; cf. Barrett, *Acts I–XIV*, p. 636. These words offer an implied contrast with Saul, whose disobedience is not mentioned by Paul, but which would have been well known to his synagogue audience.

the full experience of his messianic destiny in a heavenly enthronement and rule (cf. Rom. 1:3–4; Heb. 1:3–5).

The messianic significance of Jesus' resurrection is further explained by means of two scriptural quotations in Acts 13:34–37. The paragraph picks up the word 'decay' from Psalm 16:10, which lies at the centre of the argument. God raised Jesus from the dead so that he might never be subject to decay and could reign for ever at the Father's side. Before citing that text, Paul quotes from Isaiah 55:3 ('I will give you the holy and sure blessings promised to David'). The plural 'you' in this verse makes it clear that the promise of God is for Israel and so for Paul's listeners. Messiah's deliverance from death and decay is one of the blessings promised to David and this means salvation for Israel too. Israel's future is intimately connected with what happens to her Messiah, though there is no explicit mention of the return of Christ or eternal life here.

The salvation offered at the end of Paul's sermon is a comprehensive and definitive forgiveness of sins through Jesus (v. 38), possibly alluding to promises such as Jeremiah 31:34 and Ezekiel 36:25. The significance of this is explained in terms of being 'justified from everything you could not be justified from by the law of Moses' (v. 39). The ineffectiveness of the law to achieve a satisfactory atonement for sins and a way of moral transformation is implied. Such justification and renewal is now available for 'everyone who believes' and relies on the work of Christ that makes them possible.

Paul's appeal ends with a warning not to scoff at these claims and perish (vv. 40–41). Habakkuk 1:5 is cited without explanation, since the prophet's words speak so clearly of the wonderful things God intends to do for his people, but also predicts their unbelief. Paul's audience 'must choose which side of the prophetic cause they will embrace: that of the scornful opponents of Jesus, like those in Jerusalem, or that of believing disciples, like Paul and associates'.[23] If they do not believe, they will perish in the coming judgment of God (cf. 3:22–23; 4:11–12; 10:42; 17:30–31).

Acts 17

The external impulse for Paul's speech in 17:22–31 is the specific context in Athens and the challenge of Greek thought and practice more generally.[24]

---

23. F. Scott Spencer, *Acts* (Sheffield: Sheffield Academic Press, 1997), p. 146.

24. Robert C. Tannehill rightly suggests that 'there is an internal as well as an external impulse toward the viewpoint expressed by Paul in Athens' (*The Narrative Unity of Luke–Acts: A Literary Interpretation*, vol. 2: *The Acts of the Apostles* [Minneapolis: Fortress, 1990], p. 210).

More profoundly, however, Paul appears to be driven by an understanding of biblical theology that makes the gospel a message with universal relevance and appeal. This biblical-theological perspective is conveyed, without quotation, to an audience unfamiliar with the content and teaching of Israel's sacred Scriptures.

Paul's address is ultimately messianic and evangelistic, because it concludes with a proclamation of the resurrected man by whom God will judge the world and calls upon all people everywhere to repent in response to this (vv. 30–31). But the earlier part of the speech sounds more like a reflection on the opening chapters of Genesis (even though no text is actually cited), moving from a proclamation of the one true Creator to an assertion of his purpose for humanity, and concluding with a declaration of universal accountability before God as judge (cf. Gen. 1 – 11). Allusions to several ancillary texts can also be discerned in the progress of the argument.[25]

Summary of the use of Scripture
In three of these addresses Scripture is employed in a way that assumes some knowledge of its original context and the significance of citations in the unfolding plan of God for Israel and the nations. In other words, texts are used with reference to their biblical-theological context. Texts are not explained in full to Jewish audiences, but key words and themes are shown to be fulfilled in the person and work of the Lord Jesus Christ. Some texts are used as part of the appeal to repent and believe, offering the benefits and blessings of Christ's work or warning about the severe consequences of rejecting him.

The method of exposition is not exhaustive but selective. Scripture directs the progress of each sermon, but each message is also contextually and thematically driven. In the final analysis, the claims of the gospel and their implications for the hearers control the presentation. The preachers exercise a certain freedom in the way they use biblical material, though they share assumptions with Jewish audiences about the meaning and significance of texts and themes. The Spirit's ministry seems most obvious in the wise and discerning application of Scripture to the needs of those present.

---

25. Ancillary texts might include Exod. 20:11; 1 Kgs 8:27–30; Ps. 50:9–13; Isa. 42:5; 66:1–2. Paul cites pagan sources where they support his biblical argument, without endorsing their pantheistic assumptions. Cf. Peterson, *Acts*, pp. 495–503.

Situationally relevant

Peter's first sermon is driven by the need to explain the Pentecostal gift and to convict the Jerusalem crowd about God's exaltation of Jesus as Lord and Christ. Within that context, there is a special appeal to acknowledge their part in the crucifixion of Jesus (2:23), and to repent and be baptized to receive the benefits of his death, resurrection and ascension (2:38–40). The warning to 'Save yourselves from this corrupt generation' (2:40) calls upon the hearers to distance themselves from unbelieving Israel and to join the disciples of Jesus.

Peter's second sermon is driven by the need to explain that the healing of the lame man was achieved by the risen and exalted Lord Jesus, in response to faith. Within that context, Peter is keen to show the full significance of Jesus in the plan of God for Israel and the nations, to remind the crowd of their part in his crucifixion, and to offer again the chance to repent and receive the benefits of his saving work. The conclusion involves an explicit warning about being 'completely cut off from among his people' (3:23).

An invitation to bring 'a message of encouragement for the people' (13:15) in the synagogue at Pisidian Antioch gives Paul the opportunity to present Jesus as the promised Son of David and Saviour of Israel. The salvation Jesus has made possible is essentially the forgiveness of sins and a relationship with God surpassing the provisions of the Mosaic covenant. This salvation is necessary for Jews in the dispersion, even though they played no direct role in the crucifixion of Jesus, and for Gentiles attached to the synagogue (13:16, 26). Paul's conclusion involves a warning about missing out on the messianic salvation thus proclaimed.

The challenge for Paul to defend his preaching of Jesus and the resurrection in Athens gives him the opportunity to expose the ignorance and foolishness of pagan religiosity. His aim is to teach their culpability before 'the God who made the world and everything in it' (17:24). He wants to encourage Gentiles to repent and seek after the true God by acknowledging Jesus as the one whom he has raised from death (17:30–31).

Challenges for contemporary preachers

What are the benefits of viewing these sermons as examples of prophetic speech? What challenges do they pose to the style and content of our preaching today? What do they say about our preparation to speak?

The contributors to this volume – and Peter Adam himself – believe in the value of systematic expository preaching for the edification of the church. This method allows Scripture to set the agenda and confront us with its own questions. It forces us to look at topics and themes we might not otherwise consider. There is a built-in variety that is good for the preacher and also for the congregation. Preachers are forced to engage in serious Bible study as part of their preparation and are delivered from the uncertainty of knowing which text to choose each week. Congregations are taught how to handle the Bible for themselves and their general knowledge of Scripture and its themes is gradually built up. There is less chance of verses being expounded out of context. Each week in a series potentially brings a clearer understanding of the message of the book being studied.

However, there are potential dangers in this method of preaching. There is always the temptation to handle too much Scripture in one sermon, leaving little time to explain the text and apply it satisfactorily. The exposition may be too concerned about historical or literary features of the text and not move on to grasp the theological and practical import of what is written. People can be left wondering about the relevance of the exposition to their everyday lives. There are certainly occasions for preaching on large slabs of Scripture, but different methods of presentation may be required in a series so that a congregation is not inflicted with spiritual indigestion. Expository sermons can also become too predictable and heavy, sounding more like a lecture or Bible study than a sermon. The Bible is made to sound like a book of theological propositions rather than the story of God's involvement with his people in a vast array of circumstances. Preaching for too long on a particular section of Scripture can also lead to a feeling of boredom on the part of the congregation, unless the preacher is extremely skilled.

The prophetic sermons examined here show an interesting variety in the use of Scripture. They are clearly logical and thematically well structured. But, most significantly, they are consistently Christ-centred. Furthermore, they are distinctly motivated and directed by the situations they seek to address, and Luke regularly draws attention to their convicting power. None of the original hearers could accuse them of being irrelevant and boring!

It might be objected that these are evangelistic and apologetic sermons and not good models for the regular teaching of established congregations. Even Paul's address to the Ephesian elders (20:17–35) is not a normal congregational sermon, but an occasional message to a select group. In formal terms, these are topical or thematic addresses. Philip's conversation with the Ethiopian (8:30–35), explaining Isaiah 53 in terms of its fulfilment in Christ, comes closest to what is commonly regarded as expository preaching. However, as Greg Scharf has rightly observed, biblical exposition may be based on a very short passage or even part of a sentence. The practice reflected in Acts, though not always exposition as many define it, 'should nevertheless stretch our thinking and thus make our preaching more biblical instead of less so'.[26]

Nevertheless, I have not been arguing for a simple correspondence between contemporary congregational preaching and the sermons in Acts. Prophesying, as Luke presents it, includes evangelism, teaching and persuasion. It is a mode of communication applicable to a range of situations, structured and unstructured. Biblical exposition in various forms is absolutely fundamental to this ministry, although it is not the sum total of what is involved.

If we can classify the sermons in Acts as prophetic, the meaning will not be that they present new revelation or make predictions about the future. Rather, they demonstrate the wisdom of the Spirit given to understand the needs of the situation and how to apply Scripture appropriately. Although each one of these addresses appears to be spontaneous, they suggest much prior reflection on the meaning of biblical texts and a developed understanding of 'the whole will of God' (20:27), particularly as it relates to Jesus and God's kingdom plan (cf. Luke 24:44–49). So 'Spirit-led' is not to be simplistically equated with spontaneity: the Spirit must lead the preacher through a lifetime of biblical study and reflection, as well as careful preparation for each occasion! Likewise, 'Spirit-led' does not only mean discerning the needs of those addressed, but also discerning how to apply the Bible and glorify the Lord Jesus in the process.

It is significant that prophetic ministry in Acts is linked with exhortation or encouragement, both verbally and by way of example (e.g. 2:40; 11:23–24; 13:15; 14:22; 15:32; 16:40; 20:1–2).[27] Such exhortation or encouragement is enabled by the Holy Spirit (9:31). It is normally based on the application of Scripture or apostolic teaching to a given situation, though it may be motivated by a word of revelation about the future of an individual or group (e.g. 21:11–12; 27:33–36 [following 27:23–25]). So prophesying involves imparting

---

26. Greg Scharf, 'Were the Apostles Expository Preachers? Old Testament Exposition in the Book of Acts', *TrinJ* 31 (2010), pp. 65–93, esp. pp. 92–93. Scharf notes significant differences between apostolic preaching and contemporary situations, but argues that we must use Scripture for interpreting the Christ event much as the apostles did.

27. The verb *parakaleō* has a range of possible meanings, including 'call to, summon, invite, appeal to, urge, exhort, encourage, comfort' (cf. Otto Schmitz, '*parakaleō, paraklēsis*', *TDNT* 5:773–799). Context must determine the way it is translated in each case. This also applies to the noun *paraklēsis*.

spiritual wisdom, discernment or insight regarding God's character and purpose for his people. Prophetic preachers will give more space to what is commonly called application. They will see themselves as agents of the Spirit in ministering the Scriptures to the needs of those addressed. They will take the core message about Jesus and apply it with God-given insight to a whole range of contemporary situations.

The Holy Spirit's oversight and care for every local manifestation of 'the church of God' (20:28) reminds us to seek his guidance and enabling in preaching and teaching. As we study the Scriptures and analyse the context into which we must speak, we should pray for the Spirit to impart wisdom and revelation so that we might 'understand more fully God's saving plan and live in the light of it' (Eph. 1:17; cf. Col. 1:9).[28] Prophetic preachers will distinguish themselves by their prayerful approach to the ministry granted to them by God. We certainly need the Spirit-given courage the apostolic preachers had in applying the word of God to various contexts and we should pray also for the Spirit's convicting work in those to whom we minister.

© David G. Peterson, 2011

---

28. Peter T. O'Brien, *The Letter to the Ephesians*, PNTC (Grand Rapids: Eerdmans; Leicester: Apollos, 1999), p. 132.

4. PAUL'S PASTORAL METHOD: REFLECTIONS ON 1 CORINTHIANS

David Jackman

'It was he [Christ] who gave some to be . . . pastors and teachers, to prepare God's people for works of service, so that the body of Christ may be built up' (Eph. 4:11–12).[1] In this familiar list of the equipping gifts with which the ascended Lord Jesus has blessed his church, whether foundational (apostles and prophets) or continuing (evangelists and pastor-teachers), the apostle Paul brings together the two essential strands of church nurture in one identity. Pastors teach and teachers pastor. In fact, the two functions are inseparable in the one gifted practitioner, although the church still has great difficulty in holding them both together. All too often congregations focus on one or the other in making their ministry appointments and all too often ministers have become content to fill one but not both of these roles, according to temperament and personality. The blend of teaching excellence in its accurate exposition of God's Word and pastoral relevance, both in the pulpit and in the daily lives of the congregation, is difficult to find. And this is one reason, among many, why we salute our much loved brother Peter Adam and thank God for his many years of faithful service, both in the church and in the academy, as a teaching pastor and a pastoral teacher of the first rank. We rejoice that the Lord Jesus has given him to us, in our generation, as a gift of his grace.

---

1. Bible quotations in this chapter are from the NIV.

The contemporary challenge

This is all the more significant at a time when the church in the developed world is struggling to come to terms with the decline in its effectiveness and influence in the culture. Nations and communities once shaped by the gospel and its values are now largely ignorant of the true meaning of Christian faith and without any concept of the dynamic, life-changing power of the risen Lord Jesus to transform both individual lives and society. We all realize what a mountain there is to climb if the good news of Jesus is to reach the younger generation especially, many of whom have seldom been inside a church and never open a Bible. But there is a danger here that such an overwhelming need will panic the church into short-term measures, which in the end may prove to be counterproductive and even worsen the difficulties. The danger lies in thinking that the major problems are in the areas of communication and methodology, rather than in the idolatry of the human heart and our stubborn and studied human resistance to God's authority, as our creator.

If we follow the former path, we will find the church concentrating on the prevailing methodologies of our secular culture and seeking to imitate them. Large, 'exciting' events will dominate evangelistic presentation, but with minimal serious gospel proclamation. Celebrities become the focus of the Christian subculture, especially if their former lives have had some public notoriety. Preaching becomes salesmanship and marketing is king, so that spin becomes a way of life and substance is sacrificed to image. Reputations are built on great communication skills, irrespective of the content of what is being communicated.

More subtly, the focus of a local congregation's life can be dominated by the evangelistic-event mentality, so that its members are continually under pressure to corral their friends in to such occasions and then become valued only in proportion to their effectiveness in doing this. In view of the urgency of the situation this is understandable; but it is my contention that it is essentially wrong footed. It is notoriously difficult for pastors to find NT passages that major on exhortations to evangelism with which to challenge their hearers. The apostolic concern seems to have been much more with the transforming power of the gospel in the lives of the Christians, so that as the Word of God does this work, restoring the image of God in the believer, the world is made increasingly curious, and then even hungry, for the quality of spiritual reality it is witnessing:

> Live such good lives among the pagans that, though they accuse you of doing wrong,
> they may see your good deeds and glorify God on the day he visits us . . . Always be

prepared to give an answer to everyone who asks you to give the reason for the hope
that you have . . . with gentleness and respect. (1 Pet. 2:12; 3:15)

Interestingly, the latter exhortation follows on immediately from the command
to 'set apart Christ as Lord'. Clearly, verbal proclamation is demanded, but it is
the quality of life that opens the door of opportunity.

Our contemporary danger may well be that the nurture of godliness in
character is relegated down the list of church priorities, in favour of 'skill-
ing' a workforce of salesmen, whose task is to saturate the market with their
product. It has been well observed, however, that what is needed is not more
gospel salesmen, equipped with the latest techniques, but more free samples.
When Paul reminded the young pastor Timothy, in Ephesus, of the job
description of Scripture, within the church, 'useful for teaching, rebuking,
correcting and training in righteousness', it was because he knew there was no
other way in which the man of God could be 'thoroughly equipped for every
good work' (2 Tim. 3:16–17). The evangelization of any generation is directly
proportional, in its penetration and effect, to the Christlikeness of its propaga-
tors. The contact point with the watching world is not, in the first instance,
the pulpit. It is the lunch queue, the school gate, the water cooler, the office
meeting – wherever Christians are on view as salt and light, so that Christ's
truth and love have opportunity to make a connection. These are the contexts
where the majority of Christians inevitably spend the majority of their time,
so it is imperative that they are pastored and taught in ways that enable them
to do this graciously and confidently. This is where the integrity the gospel
brings to the inner life is demonstrated, or denied, because what we *are* shouts
so loudly that people don't hear what we *say*.

This introduces us to Paul's concerns in his correspondence with the
Christians in Corinth, in which these issues are never far away. The Corinthian
context has a number of clear similarities with our own, which means that it
can be particularly instructive for us to recognize Paul's priorities and concerns. We should also examine the way in which he deals with them, so as to
identify something of a template for our own contemporary ministries. That
Corinth was a challenging church, fraught with behavioural difficulties and
all sorts of potential division, is basic to our understanding of Paul's letters.
Founded as 'new Corinth' a hundred years earlier, this cosmopolitan, glitzy
city was proud of its diversity and desirability. Not surprisingly, the church
formed out of Paul's ministry there, first in the synagogue and then next
door in the house of Titius Justus, reflected the spirit of the city in which it
was planted (see Acts 18:1–18). The divisions soon surfaced, presented as
supporter groups for favourite leaders – Paul, Apollos, Cephas – but were

a denial, at the most fundamental level, of the unity the gospel alone could produce. After mentioning Christ by name in each of the first ten verses of the first letter, culminating in the last two with his full title, 'Jesus Christ our Lord', and demonstrating that everything they have is derived only from Christ through the gospel, Paul's razor-sharp question 'Is Christ divided?' (1 Cor. 1:13) opens up the whole epistle.

The primacy of the cross

The first four chapters of the letter then expound the gospel, which is not just the way in to their Christian experience, but the very fabric of the Christian life. The way in is also the way on. But clearly there was considerable dissatisfaction with Paul and the sort of Christian experience into which he had led them. The famous first chapter outlines the demands for both miraculous power and philosophical wisdom, which the congregation seems to have imagined to be essential, if they were to make real headway in trendy Corinth. Against this, Paul sets the essential ingredients of his gospel, which from the very beginning had characterized his preaching – 'Jesus Christ and him crucified' (2:2). To the unbeliever, the message of the cross will always appear weak and foolish, but Paul's point is that 'to us who are being saved it is the power of God' (1:18). That is to say, no one is or will be saved any other way. Whenever the Corinthian Christians looked around their house-church congregations and saw the diversity of background, temperament and social status represented, they had the most persuasive evidence of the saving power of the gospel. Not only had it brought them individually from death to life, but their commitment to Christ crucified united them in a common submission to his kingly rule, to walk the way of the cross.

If we take a bird's-eye view of the first letter, we see that this theme of the centrality of the cross, not only to Christian believing but also to Christian living, runs all the way through. The pastoral instruction Paul will give on a wide variety of issues, correcting, rebuking, instructing and training (see 2 Tim. 3:16), is all rooted entirely in the nature of the saving gospel of the cross. So, when we see Paul correcting the errors in Corinth, we always find the self-sacrificial love exemplified by the cross at the heart of his appeal. For example, the power many craved is demonstrated not in spectacular and dramatic spiritual gifts, but in the rescue of lost humanity from the wrath of God, through the incredible grace and mercy revealed in the death of the Son, on the cross. Preachers of such a gospel cannot be impressive, self-made, public performers, because lives of that sort deny the content of their message. Rather, they demonstrate that the authentic Christian lifestyle does not consist in superior knowledge, well-developed rhetorical skills or extraordinary manifestations of supernatural power, but in the self-sacrificing love that gives itself up in the service of others and keeps persevering in the way of the cross to the very end of the journey. Only that perspective can keep an Apollos or a Paul in their proper place, 'only servants, through whom you came to believe' (3:5), recognizing that 'only God . . . makes things grow' (3:7). Boasting about people, ourselves or others is always out of place, because the greatest human achievements are transitory and futile alongside God's eternal wisdom and power. God has given his Spirit to his believing people to grant understanding and develop a mature, Christlike mind as the foundation for a sacrificial Christlike life (2:12–16). But far from being lauded by the surrounding pagan culture, Paul knows that such a life leads to being made 'a spectacle to the whole universe', so that he can write about his apostolic ministry, 'we have become the scum of the earth, the refuse of the world' (4:9–13).

This explains why both letters have to contain so much rebuke, as an expression of Paul's pastoral care. The arrogant divisions and self-seeking behaviour, the elevation of knowledge above love and the desire for the manifestation of giftedness are all denials of the heart of the gospel. As chapter 13 memorably teaches, without love, all gifts, knowledge, faith and even martyrdom will be as empty and meaningless as the gongs and cymbals of the pagan temples. In the same vein, Paul's parting exhortation is, 'Do everything in love' (16:14). For although knowledge puffs up, only love builds up (8:1), which is what the body of Christ most needs and why the Lord of the church has given pastor-teachers to accomplish the task. Paradoxically, it is often by loving the congregation enough to warn, correct and rebuke them that pastor-teachers suffer most, in the double rejection of their teaching and of themselves, if the flock proves resistant and even hostile to their shepherds' care.

From chapters 5 to 10 in 1 Corinthians, Paul lovingly rebukes, corrects and teaches the Corinthians in the context of several issues that must be hindering true gospel progress in their city. The incident of the man who 'has his father's wife' in chapter 5 is followed by the issue of fellow Christians going to law against one another in chapter 6. Sexual morality and various contentious issues of marriage are the focus from 6:12 to the end of chapter 7. Food sacrificed to idols is the content of chapter 8, while idol feasts and the Lord's Supper are dealt with in chapters 10 and 11, also in the wider context of issues of Christian freedom. In between, in chapter 9, Paul introduces a detailed apologia for his own life and ministry, with his refusal to claim any of his rights 'rather than hinder the gospel of Christ'. The implicit rebuke to the Corinthians is strong, with his famous conclusion 'I have become all things to all men so that by all possible means I might save some. I do all this for the sake of the gospel' (9:22–23). Each passage repays the detailed study impossible in this present context, but a number of observations may help us to see the overall pastoral method Paul is exemplifying in this central section of the letter.

Correcting moral deviance

He begins each question with a clear, no-nonsense definition of the issue, which in its clarity, even starkness, is designed to undermine any attempts either to confuse or underplay what is really involved. We need to remember all the time that the applications here are congregational, since our own natural tendency is always to individualize them. This observation reminds us that an expository preaching ministry can address issues that affect the whole church in a way that no pastoral initiatives at a personal or group level can adequately replicate. So Paul's concern is to bring to light the realities of the situation and especially in a way that emphasizes how and where God's already revealed word in Scripture is being ignored or contradicted. It is a biblical function of the pastor-teacher to expose how the church has succumbed to the infection of the pagan world surrounding it, by accommodating to its norms. Paul's method is to be direct and completely uncompromising about things. There are expressions of outrage. 'A man has his father's wife. And you are proud!' (5:1–2). 'I say this to shame you' (6:5), and the repeated question 'Do you not know . . . ?' with its implications of culpable ignorance, or amnesia.

Next, the issue is related back to the gospel which the letter has been defining and which we now recognize to be the heart of the biblical revelation and enterprise. This is where the melodic line of the letter, with its emphasis on the cross-shaped, gospel spirituality of servant-hearted, self-sacrificing love is particularly strong. But it is always true in pastoral work with believers that sinful thoughts and actions are most effectively exposed when the way in which they deny the gospel of grace is clearly pointed out. To realize the inconsistency involved in affirming belief in the gospel and yet living in contradiction of it is always a powerful persuader and significant step on the road to repentance and recovery. This is also where the teaching element comes in more explicitly to the pastor's work. Just as in evangelism Paul reasoned, persuaded and proved the truth of the gospel, so in his pastoral care of his converts he uses the same methods. In dealing with the case of incest in chapter 5, the feast of unleavened bread is linked with Christ 'our Passover lamb' to illustrate and motivate his readers to get rid of the 'yeast of malice and wickedness' and to keep the feast with the 'bread of sincerity and truth'. An OT principle is being used to teach a predominantly Gentile church an ethical requirement, because it is a reflection of the character of God himself. Once again, it is the gospel of the sacrificial death of Jesus on the cross that is to be the controlling factor for the Corinthians' behaviour.

Correcting relational divisions

Similarly, in chapter 6 Paul exposes the shame involved in Christian believers' fighting one another in the pagan law courts. The repeated delineation of the 'unrighteous' from the 'saints', beginning in 6:1 and continued in terms of 'unbelievers' and 'brothers' (6:6), is itself a product of the gospel. The sad irony that 'the saints will judge the world', but cannot settle a dispute between themselves means, as Paul says, 'you have been completely defeated already' (6:7). The way of the cross, by contrast, is to be willing to be wronged and cheated, since the very means of their salvation and ours involved the Lord Jesus in just that sort of innocent suffering and sacrificial love. The victory of the cross is the product of this inextinguishable love, which is the very nature of God, the Trinity. So the section concludes with Paul's reminder of where the Corinthians were when God's grace rescued them, excluded from his kingdom (6:9–11). But now that they are washed, sanctified and justified, 'in the name of the Lord Jesus Christ and by the Spirit of our God', the values of that saving gospel must dictate the fabric of their daily lives.

Paul's point in both examples is that the gospel provides in itself the model for Christian ethical behaviour, as well as the motivation. Under the wise instruction of the pastor-teacher, the church is to be disciplining itself, which is a responsibility shared by the whole congregation. While no human pastor can claim infallibility in the application of God's truth, we must follow Christ's pattern in exposing and dealing with all that runs contrary to our humbling experience of total dependence on his grace. This is the heart of the gospel and the unique demonstration of its truth seen within the Christian community.

The concluding section of chapter 6 widens the discussion to more general issues of sexual morality, as an example of both gospel freedom and gospel discipline (6:12–20). Here the issue is stated in the form of a proposition or principle, which seems to have become something of a mantra to the libertarian Corinthians – 'Everything is permissible for me' (v. 12). The apostle's reaction is to introduce two controlling factors straight away. 'Not everything is beneficial' and 'I will not be mastered by anything'. The essence of the gospel is its unique ability to free human beings from the slavery inherent in our rebellion against God, and to bring the incalculable benefits of a right relationship with God into the very heart of our experience. Nothing can be allowed to threaten those gospel realities in the name of a spurious self-indulgent 'liberty'. Once again, Paul demands decisive action, 'Flee from sexual immorality' (v. 18a) and once again the argument is rooted in the gospel, in three specific ways.

First, Paul asserts that the redeemed body is 'for the Lord' (v. 13b); indeed, that 'your bodies are members of Christ himself' (v. 15). The cross and the resurrection are the essential theological link here (v. 14). Because the Lord Jesus died and was raised, our bodies too will be raised as his was. If this glorified body is the culmination of God's rescuing work in the believer, how can anyone who is united to Christ in this life use his body to be united to a prostitute? Secondly, 'he who sins sexually sins against his own body' (v. 18b), which is an offence against the indwelling Holy Spirit, the gift of God's grace to every believer, through the gospel (v. 19). Lastly, Paul appeals on the grounds of the redeeming work of Christ, whose blood was the purchase price of our salvation, so that we no longer belong to ourselves. 'Therefore honour God with your body' (v. 20).

Later in the letter, Paul returns to the slogan 'Everything is permissible' (10:23–24). Here he adds a third controlling factor, which is equally gospel based in its motivation – 'but not everything is constructive'. The love of the cross, which is the liberating dynamic from our self-indulgent, self-centred sinfulness, sets us free to love one another and so to build one another up (8:1). 'Nobody should seek his own good, but the good of others' (10:24). What an amazing difference that principle would make if applied to the issues ravaging the church in Corinth! Surely we need the same pastoral clarity in the contemporary church and the same commitment to do everything for the glory of God and for the upbuilding of our fellow Christians. Paul's concluding personal testimony is rooted in both Christ's saving work and his exemplary life, 'even as I try to please everybody in every way. For I am not seeking my own good but the good of many, so that they may be saved. Follow my example, as I follow the example of Christ' (10:33 – 11:1).

Remedial wisdom in action

This exercise could be followed through in a number of other specific examples, but even with this limited exploration, principles of apostolic pastoral care and methodology clearly emerge. Issues of behaviour that are contradic-

tory to the teaching of Scripture, and so to God's self-revelation of his character, have to be tackled if the church is to be able to function as the outcrop of
God's new community here in this world. The plausibility of the gospel itself
is at stake in the ethical quality of the lives of individuals and of the congregation as a whole. This is equally pressing for us in our contemporary context,
where the culture's curious ambivalence between political correctness and
tolerance makes confrontation of sin appear undesirable and perhaps unnecessary to many church leaders. Our inclination is to sweep things under the
carpet and hope that the 'problems' will resolve themselves, which of course
is almost never the outcome. It requires both courage and wise insight for the
pastor-teacher to discern and expose where the Word of God is being contradicted or undermined, in the present, but it is an essential part of the calling.

The more the gospel is seen to be at the heart of the individual Christian's
life and the controlling factor in the congregation's priorities, the more readily
its corrective to wrong thinking and action is likely to be received. Teaching
the Christian life biblically involves the widest of perspectives, focusing on the
progressive restoration of the image of God in the Christian, which was so
marred and distorted through the Fall. Too often holiness or sanctification is
understood as overcoming habitual temptations and experiencing deliverance
from certain sins. Of course, this is an essential part of the development of the
believer towards increasing godliness, but it cannot stand alone as the major
factor. Just as the sins we commit are symptoms of the disease of our broken
relationship with God and fundamental hostility to his creatorial rights as our
Lord, so the restoring power of the gospel achieves far more than an allevi-
ation of the symptoms. It is the cure. So while perfect spiritual health awaits
the heavenly fulfilment, when 'we shall be like him, for we shall see him as he
is' (1 John 3:2), the transforming power of the gospel has a 'now' dimension
potentially far greater than anything any of us has yet experienced. There is
always more grace. The specific emphasis in 1 Corinthians on the love of God
supremely revealed in the sacrifice of the cross provides both the foundation
and the shape of the building that is Christian discipleship. The maturity in
Christ, towards which Paul and all pastor-teachers aspire to bring themselves
and their flock (Col. 1:28), is defined for us as the cross-shaped spirituality of
1 Corinthians, characterized by serving sacrificial love, in order to build others
up, and energized by the Holy Spirit.

The other important ingredient concerns the repentant and remedial
actions that need to be taken. Specific and sometimes detailed instructions
are given about how obedience to the gospel will change behaviour. Concrete
examples are explained and nothing is left in the abstract. The application is
sharp in its focus, which in itself provides a motivation to act. It is arguable

that the weakness of much contemporary teaching ministry is its generality and practical vagueness. Too often the congregation hears expository truths and appreciates doctrinal propositions, but the point of connection with the hard realities of daily life never seems to be made. The exegesis is neatly laid out, the dogmatics impeccable, but the only application appears to be, 'He who has an ear, let him hear' (Rev. 2:7). Paul never leaves his hearers in any doubt as to what they are to do as a result of his teaching and neither must we. Dr Martyn Lloyd-Jones used to speak of the journey of biblical truth in the hearer, during preaching, in terms of progress through the mind, to the heart (the control centre of the personality) in order to activate and energize the will (in obedience). That is clearly the apostle Paul's pastoral method, involving all three aspects of the hearer's perception and experience.

The pastor-teacher is committed to the long haul, because life transformation takes time, being often resisted and impeded. But God is far more committed to bringing every one of his redeemed people home to glory, and by his Word and through his Spirit he has all the resources needed to accomplish his purposes. The marathon course involves the whole counsel of God applied to the whole of the human condition and every aspect of life. No wonder then that in his second letter, reflecting on the nature of this ministry, Paul asks, 'Who is equal to such a task?', only to reply a few verses later, 'Not that we are competent in ourselves to claim anything for ourselves, but our competence comes from God. He has made us competent as ministers of a new covenant' (2 Cor. 2:16; 3:5–6). The continuance of the church in Corinth, in spite of its many aberrations, is eloquent testimony to these truths and a never-failing stimulus to the twenty-first century's pastor-teachers to follow in the apostolic footsteps.

© David Jackman, 2011

5. PAUL'S MINISTRY OF THE WORD ACCORDING TO 1 THESSALONIANS

Allan Chapple

> [T]he Bible is a great God-given resource and guide . . . One of the wonderful gifts of the Bible in every area of Christian life and practice is to clarify what is godly and what is not.
>
> (Peter Adam, *Hearing God's Words*)

Peter Adam wrote these words in relation to Christian spirituality, but they are equally applicable to Christian ministry. He points out how regrettable it is that we are inclined to look anywhere and everywhere but to the Bible for guidance about spirituality. It is equally regrettable that we are willing to look in a great many places but the most important one of all for guidance about Christian ministry and leadership. In this regard, the apostolic letters are of particular importance, for they do not simply teach apostolic doctrine; they show apostolic ministry in process. Hence this case study in apostolic ministry of the word, which is carried out in the conviction that the fundamental elements of authentic ministry are to be learned from the apostolic letters. How, then, did Paul go about 'serving God's words'? What we learn about this from 1 Thessalonians can be summarized in eight points.

1. The emphases of the letter

The first emerges before we begin our investigation of the letter's contents, in the existence of the letter itself. Paul's ministry of the word is being continued at a distance by means of this letter; along with his other letters, 1 Thessalonians is an instrument of apostolic ministry. Accordingly, the nature of this ministry as it bears upon Thessalonica is reflected in the contents of the letter. Its keynotes are conveyed by the verbs with which Paul opens each of its major sections – thanksgiving (*eucharistoumen*, 1:2) and exhortation (*parakaloumen*, 4:1).

The introductory thanksgiving that is a common feature of the Pauline letters is spread throughout the first half of this letter (chs. 1–3), reflecting the particular circumstances of its composition (3:6).[1] Paul's thanksgiving centres on the character of the Thessalonians' response to the gospel – a response that is both fruitful (1:3, 8; 2:13) and faithful (1:6–7; 3:6–9). As with all of Paul's thanksgivings, this one has a variety of functions within the context of the letter.[2] Amongst other things, it makes it clear that he continues his ministry toward them by means of his prayers. It functions also as an implicit exhortation to continue the response to the gospel that has elicited his gratitude to God.

The second half of the letter begins with an explicit exhortation to continue and increase their loyal response to the teaching they have received (4:1, 10). The remainder of the letter deals with matters about which Paul exhorts them (5:12, 14), or about which they are to continue exhorting each other (4:18; 5:11).[3]

---

1. Thanksgiving features occur in 1:2–10; 2:13; 3:6–9. On Paul's regular practice, see Peter T. O'Brien, *Introductory Thanksgivings in the Letters of Paul*, NovTSup 49 (Leiden: Brill, 1977). On the first thanksgiving here extending from 1:2 to 1:10, see Ernest Best, *The First and Second Epistles to the Thessalonians*, BNTC (London: A. & C. Black, 1972), p. 65; Traugott Holtz, *Der Erste Brief an die Thessalonicher*, EKKNT, 3rd ed. (Zürich: Benziger; Neukirchen-Vluyn: Neukirchener, 1998), pp. 41–42; Simon Légasse, *Les Épîtres de Paul aux Thessaloniciens*, LD (Paris: Cerf, 1999), pp. 70–74; Abraham J. Malherbe, *The Letters to the Thessalonians*, AB 32B (New York: Doubleday, 2000), pp. 105–106; Earl J. Richard, *First and Second Thessalonians*, SP 11 (Collegeville: Liturgical, 1995/2007), pp. 58–60.

2. See O'Brien, *Introductory Thanksgivings*, pp. 165, 261–263.

3. In this context, 'we ask' (*erōtōmen*, 5:12; cf. 4:1) means much the same as 'we exhort' (*parakaloumen*, 5:14); see Best, *Thessalonians*, p. 223; Malherbe, *Letters*

This combination of thanksgiving and exhortation is a recognition that the health and progress of the church are dependent both on God's work in the believers and on their own fitting response to God's work. The contents of the letter thus continue the ministry Paul exercised in Thessalonica, which (as we shall see) revolved around the same twin foci: proclaiming God's word and teaching God's will, declaring God's saving work and giving instructions about the right response to that work.

2. An example of team ministry

We will consider the remaining seven points in the order that we meet them in the text. The second is that Paul's ministry of the word was a shared ministry. The use of the first-person plural throughout the first half of the letter indicates that Silvanus and Timothy were his colleagues during his church-planting stay in Thessalonica. The teamwork they displayed then is ongoing, as shown by both the letter's prescript and the first-person plurals throughout the letter.[4] Yet Paul is clearly the leader of this team. He sent Timothy to Thessalonica as an expression of his own deep commitment to and concern for them (3:1–2, 5). His leadership is also reflected in the occasional emphatic change from the first-person plural to the first-person singular (2:18; 3:5; 5:27). (As a result, this chapter usually refers only to Paul, even though the relevant passages generally include his two colleagues.)

3. The centrality of prayer

Paul's ministry of the word was accompanied by constant prayer. The letter reveals both that he prays regularly for the Thessalonian believers (1:2; 3:10)

---

to the Thessalonians, pp. 218–219, 316; Richard, First and Second Thessalonians, pp. 179, 267.

4. On the first-person plurals as denoting Silvanus and Timothy as both co-senders of the letter and as having some role in its composition, see Légasse, Thessaloniciens, pp. 57–58; Gordon D. Fee, The First and Second Letters to the Thessalonians, NICNT (Grand Rapids: Eerdmans, 2009), p. 4; E. Randolph Richards, Paul and First-Century Letter Writing: Secretaries, Composition and Collection (Downers Grove: IVP, 2004), pp. 33–36, 105.

and also what he prays for them – both what he thanks God for and also what he asks God for.[5] His prayers make it clear that he relies upon God to make his ministry of the word effective. Accordingly, he not only prays for the Thessalonians but also wants them to pray for him (5:25). He can safely assume that what he prays for them (as revealed in the letter) will enable them to see how best to pray for him.[6]

4. The results of ministry

Paul's ministry of the word had a decided impact. We see this at two different levels. At the most general level, Paul refers in 2:16 to what happens everywhere, not just in Thessalonica. The gospel he proclaims – God's gospel, the gospel of Christ – is the gospel of salvation. Wherever this gospel is declared and received it has a saving impact: it brings people to participate in God's salvation. Paul also refers in 1:5–6 to what happened in Thessalonica. He mentions first the manner in which the gospel came to the Thessalonians, namely 'not only by word but also by power, that is, by the Holy Spirit and with full impact' (*ouk . . . en logō monon alla kai en dynamei kai en pneumati hagiō kai plērophoria pollē*).[7] The best way of dealing with the interpretative questions raised here is to 'unpack' the statement methodically.

Our first step is to note that the beginning of verse 5b ('just as you know') implies that what Paul says in verse 5a was also known to the Thessalonians. As a result, Paul is unlikely to be referring merely to the subjective condition of himself and his colleagues. Instead, he is referring to the objective impact made by the gospel when they brought it to Thessalonica.

Our next step is to analyse the structure of the statement. We note first Paul's use of 'not only . . . but also'. In distinction from the somewhat similar statement in 1 Corinthians 2:4, he is not contrasting mere words with the demonstration of the Spirit's power. Rather, he is characterizing his ministry

---

5. For Paul's thanksgiving, see n. 1 above. For his intercession, see 3:10 and the 'wish prayers' in 3:11–13 and 5:23, on which see Gordon P. Wiles, *Paul's Intercessory Prayers: The Significance of the Intercessory Prayer Passages in the Letters of St Paul*, SNTSMS 24 (Cambridge: Cambridge University Press, 1974), pp. 52–68.

6. See Wiles, *Paul's Intercessory Prayers*, pp. 262–263.

7. Translations in this chapter are my own.

of the word as powerful.[8] Secondly, we note that no separate preposition (no additional *en*) should be read before *plērophoria pollē*.[9] As a result, we are not dealing with three parallel terms of which this is the last. Rather, the second *kai* is best taken as epexegetical: 'by the Holy Spirit and with full impact' specifies the sense of 'by power'.[10] The power attending the evangelists' proclamation was that of the Spirit, and the Spirit's presence and work meant *plērophoria pollē*.

What does Paul mean by this rather rare word (*plērophoria* occurs only four times in the NT and not at all in classical Greek or the LXX)? Most commentators take it as a reference to the conviction and assurance with which the evangelists spoke, but Paul is more likely to have used *parrēsia* to make such a point.[11] It is thus more likely to mean 'fullness, abundance'[12] – but 'fullness' of what? The most likely answer is that Paul is referring to a 'fullness of divine working'.[13] He means that in this church-founding period the Spirit's power was displayed in an overwhelming manner. When we ask where and how this power was displayed, several answers suggest themselves. It is possible that with the arrival of the gospel, miracles occurred. If so, then they are indicated

---

8. The use of 'not only . . . but also' is for intensification, not contrast; so Charles A. Wanamaker, *The Epistles to the Thessalonians*, NIGTC (Grand Rapids: Eerdmans; Carlisle: Paternoster, 1990), p. 79.

9. So Fee, *Thessalonians*, p. 33, n. 24; James Everett Frame, *The Epistles of St Paul to the Thessalonians*, ICC (Edinburgh: T. & T. Clark, 1912), p. 81.

10. So Fee, *Thessalonians*, p. 33, n. 24; Charles Masson, *Les Deux Épîtres de Saint Paul aux Thessaloniciens*, CNT 11a (Neuchâtel: Delachaux & Niestlé, 1957), p. 20, n. 4. This means that 'by power' (*en dynamei*) does not refer to the occurrence of miracles as accompaniments of the proclamation of the gospel, *pace* I. Howard Marshall, *1 and 2 Thessalonians*, NCB (Grand Rapids: Eerdmans; London: Marshall, Morgan & Scott, 1983), pp. 53–54; Wanamaker, *Epistles to the Thessalonians*, p. 79; Walter Grundmann, '*dynamai*', *TDNT* 2:311. By *dynamis* in a context like this, Paul is just as likely to mean the saving, converting impact of the gospel as distinct from signs and wonders (cf. Rom. 1:16; 15:19).

11. Ceslas Spicq, '*plērophoreō*', *TLNT* 3:120. The noun *parrēsia* is used eight times (and its cognate verb twice) in the Pauline corpus, as opposed to only two occurrences of *plērophoria* (Col. 2:2; 1 Thess. 1:5).

12. Gerhard Delling, '*plērophoria*', *TDNT* 6:310–311; Spicq, '*plērophoreō*', *TLNT* 3:120; Béda Rigaux, *Saint Paul: Les Épîtres aux Thessaloniciens*, EB (Paris: Gabalda, 1956), pp. 377–379.

13. Delling, '*plērophoria*', *TDNT* 6:311.

by the word *plērophoria* rather than by *dynamis*. Also likely to be involved was the evangelists' *parrēsia* as they proclaimed the gospel. Most of all, however, the reference will be to the drama of the Thessalonians' conversion, which was striking in two ways in particular. First, their conversion meant abandoning their idolatrous way of life in order to turn to God and serve him (1:9). Secondly, as Paul goes on to say in verse 6, their embracing the gospel meant facing hostile opposition. Yet they not only received it anyway, but have continued to hold it fast – and have done so with Spirit-inspired joy (1:6; 3:6–9). So when the Spirit worked powerfully in the evangelists, he also worked powerfully in the hearers; and the gospel has shown itself to be 'the power of God for salvation' (Rom. 1:16) through its effect upon the Thessalonians. In fact, the way the gospel impacted them made their election evident (1 Thess. 1:4, 6, 9–10).

So the principal result of Paul's ministry is that the Thessalonians have 'received' the gospel.[14] The fundamental mode of reception, the essential response to the gospel, is their faith. Although faith appears at first to be only one of a trio of key responses (1:3; 5:8), the following considerations make it clear that Paul sees it as more basic than either love or hope:

1. Paul denotes those who have received the gospel as 'those who believe' (*hoi pisteuontes*, 1:7, 2:10, 13).[15]
2. He refers to the widespread reports of their conversion in terms of their faith in God (1:8).
3. Upon being prematurely separated from the Thessalonians, Paul was greatly exercised as to the continuance of their faith (2:17; 3:7).
4. Timothy's return to Thessalonica was intended to shore up their faith (3:2, 5).
5. Paul hopes to see them again so that he can make good what is lacking in their faith (3:10).
6. Their love is displayed within the family of believers (4:9–10), and is thus

---

14. Paul uses both the ordinary word for receiving (*dechomai*, 1:6, 2:13) and the more technical word for receiving tradition (*paralambanō*, 2:13).

15. The present tense of the participle points to faith as a continuing response to God-in-Christ and the gospel; so Légasse, *Thessaloniciens*, p. 95; Richard, *First and Second Thessalonians*, p. 113; Daniel B. Wallace, *Greek Grammar Beyond the Basics: An Exegetical Syntax of the New Testament* (Grand Rapids: Zondervan, 1996), p. 621, n. 22. Greek uses a single family of words (*pist-*) in contrast to English, which has both 'believing' and 'having faith'.

to be seen as a fruit and expression of their faith (cf. Gal. 5:6; 6:10).

7. Their hope is directed to the Lord Jesus and to the eschatological salvation he will establish at his coming (1 Thess. 1:3, 10; 5:8–9). It is thus best seen as one dimension of the faith with which they have responded to the gospel of salvation.

Paul's ministry of the word thus seeks above all to win the response of loyal faith. This is where the Spirit's power was demonstrated: both in the conversion of the Thessalonians, where idolaters came to faith in the living God and his resurrected, returning Son (1:9–10), and in the continuance of their faith despite hardship.

5. The cost of ministry

Paul's ministry of the word was costly. In the first place, it meant that both he and the Thessalonians faced significant suffering. For the Thessalonians, like the believers in Judea before them, this took the form of hostile opposition from their fellow citizens (1:6; 2:14; 3:3–4).[16] For Paul and his colleagues, this hostility was directed against them not only in Thessalonica, but both beforehand in Philippi and also more generally (1:6; 2:2, 15–16).[17] The second way

---

16. On the causes and character of their suffering, see Todd D. Still, *Conflict at Thessalonica: A Pauline Church and Its Neighbours*, JSNTSup 183 (Sheffield: Sheffield Academic Press, 1999), pp. 208–267; Mikael Tellbe, *Paul Between Synagogue and State: Christians, Jews, and Civic Authorities in 1 Thessalonians, Romans, and Philippians*, ConBNT 34 (Stockholm: Almqvist & Wiksell International, 2001), pp. 94–115.

17. There is considerable debate as to whether 2:1–12 is apologetic; see Karl P. Donfried and Johannes Beutler (eds.), *The Thessalonians Debate: Methodological Discord or Methodological Synthesis?* (Grand Rapids: Eerdmans, 2000), pp. 31–131. There are good reasons for taking it this way, however; see Fee, *Thessalonians*, pp. 51–56; Holtz, *Der Erste Brief*, pp. 92–95; Légasse, *Thessaloniciens*, pp. 108–109, -137–138; Still, *Conflict at Thessalonica*, pp. 137–149. The most likely explanation of this section is that Paul is rebutting accusations against the integrity of his message and ministry, accusations that are designed by their opponents to undermine the Thessalonians' confidence in Paul and thus their commitment to his gospel; see Seyoon Kim, 'Paul's Entry (εἴσοδος) and the Thessalonians' Faith (1 Thessalonians 1–3)', *NTS* 51.4 (2005), pp. 519–542; Tellbe, *Paul*, pp. 98–99, 109–110; Jeffrey A.

in which Paul paid a price for his ministry was in his self-giving commitment to the Thessalonians. This meant choosing to work hard for long hours so as to be self-supporting rather than putting demands on the church and being dependent on its support (2:6–9). It also meant enduring the anguish that came from being separated from the Thessalonians without knowing how they were coping with the pressures they faced (2:17–20; 3:6–9).

6. The importance of character

Paul's ministry of the word was backed up by his example. Paul was careful to see that how he lived amongst them matched what he taught them. This is clear when he points out that he was a model for them of faithfulness in the face of suffering (1:5b–6; 2:1–2; cf. 2:14–16). That his conduct was consciously exemplary is seen in his use of 'for your sake': what he proved to be was intentionally for their benefit (1:5b).

His commitment to being an example to the believers is also made clear by the way terminology that applies to his ministry in the first half of the letter is applied to the believers' lives in the second half. Paul's gospel appeal does not spring from impurity; God has not called the Thessalonians for impurity (*akatharsia*, 2:3, 4:7).[18] Paul has been tested and approved by God; the Thessalonians are to test all things (*dokimazō*, 2:4, 5:21). Paul speaks the gospel to please God; he instructs believers as to how they can please God (*areskō*, 2:4, 4:1). Paul worked hard so as not to burden them; believers are to work with their hands so that they are not dependent on others (2:9; 4:11–12).[19] Paul's conduct was blameless; the Thessalonians are to be blameless before God on the last day (*amemptōs*, 2:10, 3:13, 5:23). Paul exhorted them; they are to exhort each other (*parakaleō*, 2:12, 4:18, 5:11). He comforted them; they are to comfort the fainthearted (*paramytheomai*, 2:12, 5:14). He overflows with love for them; they are to overflow with love for each other and for all (3:12; 4:10).

Footnote 17 (*cont.*)

    D. Weima, 'An Apology for the Apologetic Function of 1 Thessalonians 2.1–12', *JSNT* 68 (1997), pp. 73–99.

18. Note however that the sexual connotation of 4:7 is not present in 2:3; see Fee, *Thessalonians*, p. 60; Holtz, *Der Erste Brief*, p. 71; Légasse, *Thessaloniciens*, p. 116, n. 3.

19. Note also that, just as his 'labour' reflected his love for them (*kopos*, 2:8–9, 3:5), their love is expressed by their 'labour' (*kopos*, 1:3).

So Paul not only taught the Thessalonians how to live a new life in Christ but also modelled this life for them.

7. The content of Paul's ministry

Paul's ministry of the word had definite content. We learn from the letter that it had two fundamental elements: he brought them the word of God and then he taught them the will of God.

In the first place, then, Paul brought the word of God, the gospel, to Thessalonica.[20] He speaks of the gospel as his (1:5) in that he is its proclaimer, but also as God's (2:8–9) in that God is its originator and dispenser (2:4).[21] Paul speaks the gospel, shares it and heralds it.[22] He does so intent upon pleasing God, who has entrusted him with his gospel (2:4). As an evangelist he is thus, respectively, like a herald with significant news to proclaim, a nursing mother with infants to nourish and care for, and a steward who has received a trust.[23]

We discover the focus of Paul's gospel from his account of the results of his *eisodos*, his coming to Thessalonica with the gospel (1:5, 9–10). Those to whom he is writing are former idolaters who now serve the God to whom

---

20. On 'word', see 2:13; cf. 1:6, 8; on 'gospel', 1:5; 2:2, 4, 8–9; 3:2.

21. For this sense of the distinction between these two ways of referring to the gospel, see Best, *Thessalonians*, p. 74; F. F. Bruce, *1 & 2 Thessalonians*, WBC 45 (Waco: Word, 1982), p. 14; Frame, *Thessalonians*, p. 79; Légasse, *Thessaloniciens*, p. 85; Leon Morris, *The First and Second Epistles to the Thessalonians*, rev. ed., NICNT (Grand Rapids: Eerdmans, 1991), pp. 45–46; Gerhard Friedrich, '*euangelion*', *TDNT* 2:733.

22. For these verbs, see 2:2, 4, 16 (*laleō*); 2:8 (*metadidōmi*); 2:9 (*kēryssō*).

23. Although *trophos* in 2:7 could refer to a wet nurse, 'her own children' (*ta heautēs tekna*) most naturally implies that Paul is thinking of a mother; see Ben Witherington III, *1 and 2 Thessalonians: A Socio-Rhetorical Commentary* (Grand Rapids: Eerdmans, 2006), p. 80; Trevor J. Burke, *Family Matters: A Socio-Historical Study of Kinship Metaphors in 1 Thessalonians*, JSNTSup 247 (London: T. & T. Clark International, 2003), pp. 151–154. Further support for this interpretation is the fact that it has Paul comparing himself to all the members of the nuclear family: the children (reading *nēpioi* [infants] rather than *ēpioi* [gentle] in v. 7b; see Fee, *Thessalonians*, pp. 68–71; Jeffrey A. D. Weima, '"But We Became Infants Among You": The Case for NHΠΙΟΙ in 1 Thess 2.7', *NTS* 46.4 [2000], pp. 547–564), the mother (v. 7c) and the father (v. 11).

they have turned in repentance and faith.[24] They are now waiting for the return from heaven of the risen Jesus, the Son of God, who is their rescuer from God's eschatological wrath. This tells us that the gospel of God proclaims the living and true God as the One whom all should serve and who is to be the Judge of all (hence the reference to his coming *orgē*, 'wrath'). The gospel of God is also the gospel of Christ (3:2): it proclaims Jesus as Son of God, Messiah and Lord.[25] It is also the gospel of salvation: it proclaims the saving events and the eschatological salvation that stems from them, depending on Jesus' death and resurrection on the one hand and his final coming on the other hand.[26] All of these things Paul can mention only briefly here and there throughout the letter because he knows that the Thessalonians already know and believe them. They do not need to be elaborated or argued, as they are well-established convictions about which there is no dispute in the church.

Secondly, Paul not only brought the word of God to Thessalonica; he also taught the will of God to the Thessalonian believers. This aspect of his ministry involved giving both instructions and exhortations.

The instructions he gave taught the new believers how to live a God-pleasing life, a life lived according to God's will (4:1–3).[27] The letter makes it clear that Paul had previously instructed them about the following aspects of their new life:

1. It is the destiny of believers to suffer (3:3–4).
2. God's will for their holiness requires them to avoid sexual immorality and impurity (*porneia, akatharsia,* 4:3–8). Moral purity involves sexual purity.
3. They are to live responsibly by working to support themselves (4:11–12).

---

24. Paul's use of *epistrephō* (1:9) refers to both dimensions of conversion: the turning away (here, from idolatry) that is repentance, and the turning to God that is faith; see Malherbe, *Letters to the Thessalonians*, pp. 118–120; Morris, *Thessalonians*, p. 53.

25. For these titles, see 1:1, 3, 10; 2:14–15, 19; 3:11, 13; 4:1–2, 14; 5:9, 18, 23, 28.

26. Jesus' return, with attendant judgment, is prominent in this letter; e.g. 1:10; 2:19; 3:13; 4:14; 5:8–10.

27. Paul uses the noun *parangelia* and its cognate verb *parangellō* (4:2, 11), words that denote authoritative directives, like the orders given by a military officer or monarch, or like the summons issued by a court; see Otto Schmitz, '*parangellō*', *TDNT* 5:761–765; Ceslas Spicq, '*parangelia*', *TLNT* 3:9–11; Holtz, *Der Erste Brief*, pp. 153–154; Légasse, *Thessaloniciens*, p. 206; Witherington, *Thessalonians*, p. 111.

PAUL'S MINISTRY OF THE WORD

4. The Day of the Lord will come like a thief, suddenly and (for some)
   unexpectedly (5:1–3).

Paul had undoubtedly instructed them about other aspects of their life in
Christ as well; he raises these four only because there is a situational need for
them to be reiterated and elaborated.

It is significant that all but the third of these can be connected with Jesus'
teaching.[28] It is therefore worth considering the possibility that by saying they
were given 'through the Lord Jesus' (4:2), Paul was indicating that the teachings of Jesus were the basic source from which his instructions were derived.[29]
Although most commentators take the preposition *dia* here as a marker of
causal agency or efficient cause, it can be seen as an indicator of author or
origin.[30]

While scholars tend to be reluctant to find references in Paul to the teaching of Jesus, there are several pointers that lead us in this direction here.[31] One
is 1 Corinthians 7:10, one of only three uses of *parangellō* that Paul makes of
his own ministry outside the Thessalonian letters. In that passage Paul makes
it clear that he is citing the teaching of 'the Lord'. In addition, one of the other
two uses (1 Cor. 11:17) occurs in the context where Paul quotes traditions he
had received 'from the Lord' concerning the last supper (11:23–25). Another

---

28. On believers' sufferings, see Matt. 5:10–12, 43–44; 10:16–39; 24:4–25; John
    15:18–25. On sexual purity, Matt. 5:27–30; Mark 7:20–23. On the suddenness of
    the Day of the Lord, Matt. 24:36–44; Mark 13:32–37; Luke 12:35–40; 17:26–32;
    21:34–36.

29. So Fee, *Thessalonians*, p. 141; James Moffatt, 'The First and Second Epistles of Paul
    the Apostle to the Thessalonians', in W. Robertson Nicoll (ed.), *The Expositor's
    Greek Testament*, vol. 4 (1910; repr. Grand Rapids: Eerdmans, 1951, 1988), pp. 1–54,
    here p. 33; William Neil, *The Epistles of Paul to the Thessalonians*, MNTC (London:
    Hodder & Stoughton, 1950), p. 76.

30. BDAG, s.v. A.4.b; Albrecht Oepke, '*dia*', *TDNT* 2:67–68. Those who understand
    dia to be indicating the efficient cause or causal agent are inclined to read the
    expression as though Paul had said 'what instructions the Lord Jesus gave you
    through us'; see esp. Holtz, *Der Erste Brief*, p. 154; Légasse, *Thessaloniciens*, p. 206;
    A. T. Robertson, *A Grammar of the Greek New Testament in the Light of Historical Research*
    (Nashville: Broadman, 1934), p. 583; Otto Schmitz, '*parangellō*', *TDNT* 5:764.

31. On the general question of Paul's knowledge and use of Jesus' teachings, see esp.
    David Wenham, *Paul: Follower of Jesus or Founder of Christianity?* (Grand Rapids:
    Eerdmans, 1995), pp. 380–408.

pointer comes later in our present chapter, where Paul mentions a 'word of the Lord' (1 Thess. 4:15). Given the way he refers to what 'the Lord' has said,[32] this 'word' is more likely to refer to the teaching of Jesus than to the oracle of a Christian prophet.[33]

The exhortations Paul gave when he was with them urged the believers to live worthily of God (2:11–12). Now he tells them that they are to live in a way that is fitting for those whom God is calling into his kingdom and glory – their serving 'walk' is to reflect his saving work.

What relationship is there between the *euangelion*, the 'gospel', and the *parangeliai*, the 'instructions' – between the word of God and the will of God? The most obvious observation to make is that Paul brings the gospel to his hearers first (2:2–9), before he gives them instruction about the God-pleasing life. The latter is meant for those who have responded to the gospel in faith. Yet this does not mean that the gospel is no longer conveyed to those who have already heard and believed it. Paul continued to proclaim the gospel to those who had become dear to him as believers and for whose benefit he worked hard at supporting himself (2:8–9). The priority of the gospel over the instructions is thus more logical than chronological – both were a constant feature of the church's life; although the gospel was fundamental, the constant core of Paul's ministry of the word.

Secondly, presenting the gospel involves making an announcement and issuing an appeal – declaring what God has done and exhorting the hearers to respond appropriately (2:3, 12). As we have seen, the core response to the gospel is a twofold turning: the turning away from sin that is repentance and the turning to God-in-Christ that is faith. And this faith goes to work (1:3) – it expresses itself in godly living. So the instructions spell out the ways in which authentic faith works. If the gospel summons people to faith, the instructions show believers how their faith should express itself.

Thirdly, the gospel is in the indicative mood while the instructions are in the imperative. There is also an intermediate form of the indicative which is

---

32. In addition to 1 Cor. 7:10 and 11:23–25, see also 1 Cor. 9:14; cf. Acts 20:35. On this, see Werner Foerster, '*kyrios*', *TDNT* 3:1092.

33. See Frame, *Thessalonians*, pp. 171–172; Holtz, *Der Erste Brief*, pp. 183–184; Marshall, *Thessalonians*, pp. 125–126; Wanamaker, *Epistles to the Thessalonians*, pp. 170–171; Seyoon Kim, 'The Jesus Tradition in 1 Thess. 4.13–5.11', *NTS* 48.2 (2002), pp. 225–242 (at 235–237); Wenham, *Paul*, pp. 305–306. Confirmation of this view lies in the fact that Paul echoes a number of sayings of Jesus in 1 Thess. 4:13 – 5:11; see Kim, 'Jesus Tradition', pp. 231–235; Wenham, *Paul*, pp. 305–316.

not the gospel but which links the gospel and the instructions, both spelling out the implications of the gospel and forming the basis of the instructions. We see this in 5:4–10, where Paul is urging the Thessalonians to recognize what they are and so to be what they are, to let their practice reflect their status. Because God has made them his own, they are now all 'children of the light and children of the day'. This implication of the saving work declared in the gospel becomes the foundation for instructing them about living in the daylight, not as people who belong to the night.

Fourthly, the instructions teach a way of life that reflects on the horizontal plane what the gospel declares God has done on the vertical plane. The 'walk' taught by the instructions matches up with the work announced by the gospel. We see this at several points in the letter. God has set his love upon them – and so they are to live in love for one another and for all (1:4; 3:12; 4:9). God has given his Holy Spirit to each believer – and all are therefore called to live a holy life (4:3–4, 7–8). The call to a holy life is also embedded in the fact that God will establish their hearts in holiness at the coming of the Lord Jesus (3:13) – in addition to being what they are, they are also to become what they will be.

Fifthly, both the gospel and the instructions have a word-of-God character. The gospel is expressly said to be the 'word of God' (2:13), while the instructions are so by implication. To reject the instructions – Paul's teaching about God's will (4:3) and calling (4:7), and about his judgment (4:6) – is not to reject the human who speaks them; it is to reject God (4:8). Not only the apostolic gospel but also the apostolic teaching is thus to be received as the word of God.[34]

8. Authority and affection in ministry

This brings us to our eighth and final point. According to 1 Thessalonians, Paul's ministry of the word combined authority and affection. This emerges particularly clearly in the passage where he portrays himself in turn as a child, a mother and a father (2:7–12). As I have already suggested, Paul is defending himself against accusations from outsiders that he was interested in the Thessalonians only for what he could get out of them. He denies that his conduct cleverly masked such greed (2:5). It is true that, as an apostle, there

---

34. Holtz, *Der Erste Brief*, p. 166; Légasse, *Thessaloniciens*, p. 228; Marshall, *Thessalonians*, pp. 113–114; Wanamaker, *Epistles to the Thessalonians*, p. 158.

were rights he could have exercised, including the right to be supported while he carried out his ministry (2:6; cf. 1 Cor. 9:1–14). But instead of self-seeking, his conduct was self-giving, like that of a nursing mother with her children. So great was his love for the Thessalonians that, rather than burdening them in any way, he worked long and hard to support himself.

With the shift to the image of the father (2:11), the focus does not change from affection to authority, as though a father figure was seen only in terms of his authority. Rather, it combines the notion of authority with that of affection.[35] As the *paterfamilias* expressed his care for and authority over his children by taking responsibility for their education, their preparation for responsible adult life, so Paul took responsibility for ensuring that the Thessalonians knew how they should live their new life in Christ. He makes this clear in 2:12, where he speaks of himself as 'exhorting' (*parakalountes*) and 'charging' them (*martyromenoi*), as well as 'encouraging' or 'comforting' them (*paramythoumenoi*). With each of the Thessalonians he appealed for and insisted on a life worthy of God and his kingdom. The note of fatherly authority is also seen in 4:2, where Paul refers to the instructions – the *parangeliai*, the authoritative directives – he gave them.[36]

The blend of authority and affection is also to be seen in the fact that Paul puts himself in the position of both a father and a brother. Although he sees himself as having a father's responsibility for the Thessalonians (2:11–12), he also addresses them as his *adelphoi*.[37] He is both over them as a father and alongside them as a brother, with authority over them and also affection for them.[38]

It is the interplay of authority and affection that explains Paul's conduct in Thessalonica. As Christ's apostle, he has rights – but he does not take them up (2:6–7). This is because as the church's father, he has responsibilities – and he will not give them up. His affectionate commitment to their growth and progress in the faith is the reason why he chose to forego his right to be supported and chose instead to support himself. This choice to work hard is, in the context, at least part of what Paul has in mind when he refers to his exemplary conduct (2:10). The Thessalonians are to follow the old adage 'like father, like son'; as Paul worked to support himself, so they are to work in order not to give offence to outsiders by becoming dependent on them (4:11–12).

---

35. See Burke, *Family Matters*, pp. 58, 93–94, 137–138, 148–151.

36. This passage is connected with Paul's fatherly role in ibid., p. 137.

37. In 1:4; 2:1, 9, 14, 17; 3:7; 4:1, 10, 13; 5:1, 4, 12, 14, 25–27.

38. See Reidar Aasgaard, *'My Beloved Brothers and Sisters!' Christian Siblingship in Paul*, JSNTSup 265 (London: T. & T. Clark International, 2004), p. 289.

Conclusions

Our survey of Paul's ministry of the word enables us to draw some conclusions about our own ministries. Doing so rests on the assumption that authentic Christian ministry is to be grounded on and shaped by the apostolic message and models – in this case, what we see in 1 Thessalonians:

1. While face-to-face contact is preferable, it is not always possible. Yet it is still possible to have an effective faith-sustaining and faith-building ministry at a distance. In addition to prayer, this can be exercised by means of letters (as well as by other media made available by modern technology).
2. Our ministry of the word should be shared. Those who are leaders in this ministry should endeavour to involve suitably gifted people who (like Timothy) can develop into leaders themselves through their shared participation in the ministry of the word.
3. Prayer must go with proclamation, intercession with instruction. Our speaking to people about God and his saving work should always be accompanied by our speaking to God about his saving work in those people.
4. It is people's faith – faith in God; faith in the Lord Jesus; faith in the saving events – that is especially important and worth labouring and contending for.
5. A faithful ministry of God's word will involve suffering and is likely to provoke opposition. There is no possibility of a pain-free ministry of the word.[39]
6. It is not enough to declare the gospel; we must ensure that our lives match our words. Shepherds must be examples to the flock (1 Pet. 5:2–3).
7. The gospel must take priority: as the word of God par excellence it should be the basis and focus in all our ministry of the word.
8. When the gospel has priority, our ministry of the word will be Christ-centred, focusing on the person of Jesus as Son of God, Messiah and Lord, and eliciting deep and loyal devotion to him.
9. When the gospel has priority, our ministry of the word will centre on the salvation that comes to us through the death and resurrection of Jesus and with his final coming.

---

39. See 2 Tim. 1:8; 2:1, 3, 9–10; 3:10–12; 4:3–5, 10, 14–16.

10. It is not enough to declare the gospel, as we need to teach converts how to live a life that pleases God and is worthy of him. The apostolic letters consist of applied theology, and any ministry of the word that seeks to be true to the NT will maintain this 'applied' thrust, drawing the appropriate lessons for Christian living from the apostolic teaching.

11. Instruction about living a new life in Christ will, *inter alia*, teach people that they should expect to experience suffering, that they must be committed to sexual purity, that they must live responsibly without misusing the kindness of others, and that they should wait expectantly for the Lord's coming. These and other such teachings will stem to a significant extent from the Gospel accounts of Jesus' words.

12. An authentic ministry of the word will involve authority, because of the word, and affection, because it is a ministry.

© Allan Chapple, 2011

6. PREACHING AND THE CHURCH THAT IS FIT FOR PURPOSE: LESSONS FROM 1 TIMOTHY

William Taylor

The subject under consideration in this chapter is preaching that achieves an evangelistic end. It would not be accurate to describe the subject as 'evangelistic preaching'. Evangelistic preaching concerns individual sermons, the theology that lies behind an evangelistic sermon and the skill of crafting and delivering a sermon so that the message of the gospel is carried home to the heart of the unbeliever. That is not the issue under consideration here. Rather, this chapter has to do with biblical preaching and Bible teaching that achieves an evangelistic end. The contention is that preaching that achieves an evangelistic end is preaching that shapes and orders an entire congregation so that it is fit for purpose as an assembly of God, holding up and holding out the gospel to the local community.[1]

In order to explore the subject we will examine the author's purpose and method in the letter of 1 Timothy.[2] There will be two parts to the chapter:

---

1. We in the UK are deeply indebted to Peter Adam's regular visits to the Proclamation Trust and St Helen's, as God has used the breadth and depth of his ministry to shape a generation of preachers and to equip congregations to fulfil God's purpose for them.

2. The assumption of this chapter is that the letter of 1 Timothy is early, that Paul is the author and that he has one major pastoral aim in writing the letter that shapes

first, the congregation, the gospel and the purpose of God; secondly, the gospel, preaching and the congregation that is fit for purpose.

Put simply, the aim here is to demonstrate that the kind of preaching and teaching that achieves an evangelistic end is the kind of preaching and teaching through which an entire congregation is shaped to be active and credible in ministry.

It is, of course, the gospel alone that has all God's power for salvation, not the church. The gospel produces the local assembly of God's people. God calls, matures and presents his people perfect on the day of Christ through the gospel. It is the gospel by which God evangelizes, not the church. However, it is in the local church that the mystery of God's gospel is made manifest to the world as the gospel is proclaimed and lived. As others have observed, the church is the 'apologetic' for the gospel, or, put more strongly, the church is the 'plausibility structure' for the gospel. The pastor's chief goal is to preach and teach the gospel in such a way that God's people are called, matured and perfected in Christ. This is the kind of preaching that produces an entire assembly that is credible in ministry; thus achieving an evangelistic end. This goal is, I believe, Paul's objective in writing his first letter to Timothy.

Put negatively, for clarity, a pastor could preach evangelistically every Sunday and a congregation might declare that every Sunday is Evangelism Sunday. There might be sermons with all the power of a Billy Graham, all the passion of a John Wesley, and all the clarity and winsomeness of a John Chapman, but in so far as the pastor fails to preach in such a way that the entire congregation is grown, matured and perfected, so far will the impact of the evangelistic ministry of the congregation be impaired.

The congregation, the gospel and the purpose

At the heart of 1 Timothy we find a statement concerning Paul's purpose in writing, the identity of the church and its function in God's economy. Paul writes:

Footnote 2 (*cont.*)

 and directs every part of the letter as he writes. A useful summary of recent debate on the issue of authorship can be found in Donald Guthrie, 'The Pastoral Letters', in D. A. Carson et al. (eds.), *New Bible Commentary*, 4th ed. (Leicester: IVP, 1994), pp. 1292–1315.

I hope to come to you soon, but I am writing these things to you so that, if I delay, you may know how one ought to behave in the household of God, which is the church of the living God, a pillar and buttress of truth. Great indeed, we confess, is the mystery of godliness:

He was manifested in the flesh,
　　vindicated by the Spirit,
　　　　seen by angels,
proclaimed among the nations,
　　believed on in the world,
　　　　taken up in glory.
(1 Tim. 3:14–16)[3]

Paul's *purpose in writing* is that the local congregation in Ephesus be rightly ordered. As will be shown below, his concern is not with minor matters of liturgical correctness or administrative order. Rather, 'how one ought to behave' has to do with such vital matters as the evangelistic heart of the congregation, the selection and appointment of appropriate ministers so that the gospel is not brought into disrepute, and the godliness and growth both of Timothy and every group within the congregation in order that no slander be directed towards the gospel.

The *identity of the local church* is spelled out in the first half of verse 15. The church is both 'the household of God' and 'the church of the living God'. The phrase 'household of God' can refer either to the building or to the family that occupies the building. If Paul is using the phrase in the sense of a building, he must be referring to the local congregation as the dwelling place of God (cf. 1 Pet. 2:5; 1 Cor. 3:16). However, as Paul has already used the word to refer to families and family relationships in this chapter, it is more likely that he is speaking of the church as God's family. More widely, in 2 Samuel 7 God promises King David that he will establish his house and his kingdom for ever. The local church, then, is the family of God, brothers and sisters with one Father in heaven. The church is the royal family, the place in which and from which God's Kingdom is established and advanced across the world. The church is the dwelling place of God on earth.

The phrase 'church of the living God' is best translated 'assembly of the living God'. Just as God 'assembled' or 'churched' his people at the rock of Mount Sinai (Deut. 4:10), so the living God 'assembles' or 'churches' his

---

3. Bible quotations in this chapter are from the ESV.

people around the proclamation of the gospel, the rock of Peter's confession of Christ (Matt. 16:16–19). The universal church of all God's people through time gathered around the eternal throne of God (Heb. 12:18–24) has its local expressions in history as congregations of God's people assemble around his word.[4]

It is worth pausing at this point to consider who we are as we meet together week by week in our local assemblies. No matter that our assembly is small in number, weak in appearance, beset by any number of trials and difficulties; we are the royal family of God, we are the place in which and from which God extends his royal rule across the world, we are nothing less than the dwelling place of God. Elsewhere Paul writes, 'not many of you were wise according to worldly standards, not many were powerful, not many were of noble birth' (1 Cor. 1:26). We may be all too aware of our apparent insignificance, insecurity and impotence in the eyes of the world, but wherever we gather and whenever we gather we are the family of God.

God's *purpose for the local church* is spelled out at the end of 1 Timothy 3:15. The church is the 'pillar and buttress of truth'. This is a surprising description of the church. Elsewhere we read that the church is 'built on the foundation of the apostles and prophets, Christ Jesus himself being the cornerstone' (Eph. 2:20). The idea of the truth holding up the church is familiar. Here, however, it appears that the church holds up the truth. Paul seems to be suggesting that the local assembly of God's people is the place on earth in which God's truth is held up and held out to the watching world. Here, then, is God's purpose for his church. His intention is that the assembly of his people be the place from which the truth of the gospel radiates. Of course, as we have already noted, it is the gospel alone by which God calls, matures and presents his people perfect in Christ. But as the local congregation is called, matured and sustained, so God's truth is held up and held out verbally and visually to the world. The local assembly of the living God is the 'plausibility structure' for the gospel.

Again, we do well to pause and consider this claim. Ponder every news briefing, every broadsheet article and every website bulletin that has been broadcast over this last week. How often has the gospel of Jesus Christ been

---

4. Apart from these two expressions of church (church local and church universal) the Bible knows no other concept of church. There is no such thing as 'denomination' in the Bible. Article 19 of the Church of England has it right: 'The visible Church of Christ is *a* congregation of faithful men, in which the pure Word of God is preached' (emphasis added).

held up and held out? In my situation here in London the answer is: not once. Consider the local golf club, recreation centre, pub, town hall, or university common room. When and where is the gospel of Jesus Christ defended, proclaimed and held high? Again, more likely than not the answer is: not once. It is the local congregation of God's people that is God's strategy and programme for the defence and proclamation of his glorious gospel.

This then makes the life in the local congregation of God's people for which a pastor is responsible of vast, eternal and weighty significance in the purposes and designs of God. No matter how small or seemingly insignificant in the eyes of the world, the local church is the linchpin in God's purposes for the community in which it is set. To steal a phrase from the business community, if the local church is not 'fit for purpose', then the village, town, city suburb or inner-city centre in which it is set will not have access to God's truth.

This then makes the preaching and teaching of God's word in the local church of vital and eternal significance. Paul's point is that Timothy's teaching and preaching are designed to achieve the health and effectiveness of the local churches in Ephesus. I will demonstrate shortly that there are three key areas in the life of the local church for which Paul is particularly concerned. They are: an outward-facing gospel heartbeat, godly leadership and godliness in every area of life. Paul tells Timothy that he is to 'put these things before the brothers' (1 Tim. 4:6), 'command and teach these things' (4:11) and 'teach and urge these things' (6:2). Timothy is to defend the 'charge' with which he has been 'entrusted' as he fights 'the good fight of the faith' (cf. 1:18–19; 6:12). It is the task of the teaching elders of the churches to preach and teach in such a way that the disciples for whom they are responsible grow up and are shaped and equipped to fulfil God's purpose as they hold up and hold out the gospel. Failure to address these three areas in the regular preaching to believers will render the ministry of a church incredible to unbelievers. The teaching elders might preach 'evangelistically' every Sunday for ten years. They might address every seeker sensitively and personally from the pulpit in the most winsome ways imaginable. But if the local church as a whole is not shaped effectively through their preaching, then all the finest ministry plans and intentions will be rendered proportionately less effective.

This provides a timely corrective to many regular preachers and teachers of God's word. For many in a position of leadership, the godly desire for the 'unbeliever in our midst' to hear the gospel means that too often the direction of a preaching programme and the bulk of the application of sermons is addressed to the unbeliever or the immature. One friend tells me that he is a member of a church with fewer than forty members. Every week the senior pastor stands up and announces, 'You may be here as a visitor.' My friend tells me that with just forty adult members it is patently obvious that frequently there is no visitor there. He is not bothered by the announcement since he understands that the senior pastor is seeking to create an environment in which a visitor will feel welcome. However, too often the preacher's sermon follows a similar tack and has only the immature believer or unbeliever in its sights. The result is immaturity in the church. Ultimately, of course, the congregation fails to grow up and the preacher becomes the only evangelist in the congregation.

First Timothy 3:16 sums up the point that Paul has made in verses 14 and 15 with a six-line poem that encapsulates the heart of the letter. The poem divides into two. The first three lines address the earthly life and ministry of Jesus in the first century. The second three lines concern his ongoing work in the local church through the ages. Taken as a whole the poem concerns the 'mystery of godliness', which was clearly a major issue of contention amongst the false-teaching elders who had emerged so quickly in the churches in Ephesus. Though long before the highly developed Gnostic systems of the second century, these false teachers were promoting an early form of higher knowledge. Paul speaks of them as promoting 'what is falsely called "knowledge"' (6:20). Their religious practice and promotion of an 'inner ring' of the spiritual elite took the form of Jewish super-spirituality (1:3–7). Paul's point is that the 'mystery of godliness' is no secret available only to the inner circle. Rather, the 'mystery' is to be found in the person of Jesus and in the ongoing work of Jesus in the local church. The 'mystery' has been manifested in Jesus' incarnate life (line one), vindicated through his resurrection (line two), and confirmed through his enthronement in heaven (line three). Furthermore, the so-called 'mystery' is now being 'proclaimed amongst the nations' (line four) through the local church, which is the 'pillar and buttress of truth', is being 'believed on in the world' (line five) as men and women of every tribe and tongue hear the gospel and are joined to the local church, and will be consummated at the last day (line six) as Christ's people are 'taken up in glory'.

Thus this poem of verse 16 drives to the heart of the matter.

The local church is the place on earth in which God's truth is on display for the nations. There is no longer any special secret to be divined only by the inner circle of the super-spiritual elite (1:3–7). Rather, as the gospel is proclaimed, God assembles his people to be the 'household of God' and 'the assembly of the living God'. Paul's concern is that through the mature preaching and teaching of God's word by godly leaders, the local churches in Ephesus might grow up to maturity and thus function as God intended them to, namely as the 'pillar and buttress of truth'.

The gospel, preaching and the church that is fit for purpose

The way Paul addresses the key issues that need attention in the Ephesian context provides us with a perfect model of the kind of preaching and teaching we have been considering. The substance of the letter can be divided into three and is summed up in the three 'trustworthy sayings' found in 1:15, 3:1 and 4:8. Each trustworthy saying captures the essence of all that is under discussion in the section of the letter in which it is set. The first trustworthy saying has to do with the mission of Christ. 'Christ Jesus came into the world to save sinners.' This sums up everything written in chapters 1 and 2. The second trustworthy saying has to do with the leadership of the church. 'If anyone aspires to the office of overseer, he desires a noble task.' This governs chapter 3. The third trustworthy saying has to do with godliness in every area of the church's life. 'Godliness is of value in every way, as it holds promise for the present life and also for the life to come.' Godliness is the subject under discussion from chapter 4 through to the end of chapter 6.

The gospel heartbeat of the local church
The first trustworthy saying concerns the gospel heartbeat of the local church. 'The saying is trustworthy and deserving of full acceptance, that Christ Jesus came into the world to save sinners' (1:15). The saying is embedded in one of the most personal passages in the NT and follows Paul's analysis of the false-teaching elders in Ephesus. Eleven times in 1:12–17 Paul uses the first-person singular. Many of the technical commentaries appear to be at a loss to explain why Paul speaks so openly of himself. Gordon Fee sums up their error: 'This paragraph is so clearly a digression in the argument of the letter that it is easy to read it, or comment on it, apart from its immediate context. But to do so is to miss a large part of its significance.'[5] Once Paul's aim in this part of the letter is identified, it becomes apparent that, far from being a digression, Paul's testimony is perfectly deployed to achieve his purpose. His concern is with the false-teaching elders. He wants the churches in Ephesus to remain fit for the purpose God has given them as 'pillar and buttress of truth'. The false-teaching elders are promoting a form of godliness Jewish in tone and Gnostic in feel. Long before the second century the Christian 'inner ring' was already in evidence with its mysticism, asceticism and super-spiritual promotion of 'knowledge' available only to an elite inner circle (1:4–6; 4:1–4; 6:3–4, 20). This

5. Gordon D. Fee, *1 and 2 Timothy, Titus*, NIBC 13 (Peabody: Hendrickson, 1988), p. 50.

speculative, super-spiritual teaching was in danger of turning the churches in Ephesus in on themselves and limiting the reach of the gospel to the lost world. Once it is suggested that the 'mystery of godliness' is available only to a limited elite, the reach and scope of grace is lost. Such exclusive, restrictive tendencies can be found in forms of Christianity all over the world.

Paul's testimony (1:12–17), with its ruthless focus on his own sinfulness, completely contradicts the false teachers. Paul was 'a blasphemer, persecutor, and insolent opponent'. Paul was chief of all sinners. And Paul's conversion demonstrates the purpose of Christ who 'came into the world to save sinners'. Any attempt to restrict the grace of God and to limit it to a small inner circle of 'elect' who can be marked out by ethnic origin, exotic experience and ascetic practice flies in the face of the gospel charge with which Paul and Timothy have been entrusted. Indeed, in verse 16 Paul insists that he would have himself put on display as an example of precisely how far outside the inner circle God is prepared, in his grace, to reach with his glorious gospel.

Now, given that Paul's testimony is such a 'purple passage' full of evangelistic appeal, it would be almost impossible to preach it without the preacher addressing himself to the 'unbeliever in our midst'. What preacher and teacher of the gospel, when presented with a passage containing verse 15, could prevent himself from turning to the unconverted and preaching a full-blooded gospel sermon with an appeal at the end?

However, to preach this passage with the unbeliever as the key audience would be to miss its purpose and significance altogether. Paul's concern is for the churches in Ephesus. Paul's concern is for Timothy and the direction of his ministry. Paul's concern is that Timothy put before the believers in the churches the heartbeat of God so that the pulse of the church be redirected to the mission of Christ. Thus, in so far as the preacher fails to preach and apply 1:12–17 to the leaders of the church and the believers in the pew on Sunday, so far has he failed to teach the passage accurately and failed to reshape the direction of the church he is leading.

Paul's desire in chapters 1 and 2 is for congregations in Ephesus to have the same passion for the lost and a limitless desire to cross ethnic, cultural and social boundaries with the good news of the gospel. The preacher in the pulpit and the leader in the small group will need to teach and apply this *primarily* to the believer in order to achieve a church that is fit for purpose.

This same aim of redirecting the ministry of the church is to be found right the way across the first two chapters. In 1:18–20 Paul stresses that if Timothy is going to have churches in Ephesus that are outwardly focused and fit for purpose, he will have to fight for it. In chapter 2 Paul appeals to the character of God, 'who desires all people to be saved and to come to the knowledge of the truth' (2:3–4). He backs this appeal with a statement concerning the unity of God and the scope of his salvation: 'there is one God, and there is one mediator between God and men, the man Christ Jesus, who gave himself as a ransom for all' (2:5–6). This is preceded by a call to pray 'for all people, for kings and all who are in high positions' (2:1–2).

Even the section at the end of chapter 2 with its appeal to peace, modesty and male headship has the purpose of the local churches being ordered correctly for a ministry that reaches the lost.

Of course, none of this means that the preacher and teacher will need to ignore the unbeliever as he teaches this passage. There will be numerous opportunities in sermons on chapters 1 and 2 to address those in the congregation who are investigating the Christian faith and present to them the appeal of the gospel. However, Paul's pastoral purpose in writing these chapters is that the evangelistic heart of Timothy and the elders of the churches in Ephesus be reignited and thus the believers in the churches be reshaped in the passion and direction of their ministry. The preacher who fails to address this issue will have failed to preach in such a way that the church be rendered fit for purpose. If this is the hallmark of his ministry, he will, ultimately, become the only evangelist in the church.

Godly leadership of the local church

Paul's passion for the gospel heartbeat of the local church is matched by his concern for the godly leadership of the local church. The second trustworthy saying comes in 3:1, and this verse governs the whole of the chapter: 'The saying is trustworthy: If anyone aspires to the office of overseer, he desires a noble task.' Leadership in the church should be leadership that matches the privileged position of the local church. If the leadership of the church does not reflect the honour and privilege of this gathering of the living God, which embodies 'the mystery of godliness' that will one day be 'taken up in glory', then the impact of the church as 'pillar and buttress of truth' will be minimalized. We have seen this truth writ large in the failures within the Roman Catholic church over recent decades, but the failures of Roman Catholicism have been mirrored in numerous instances within Anglican churches in the United Kingdom. Indeed, one might say that the failure of public leadership in the church in England since the 1960s has done more damage to the proclamation of the gospel in our land than anything else.

The whole of 3:1–13 is devoted to leadership, and Timothy is expected to speak openly and publicly as part of his gospel charge, and to 'put these things before the brothers' and 'command and teach these things' (4:6, 11). 'If anyone aspires to the office of overseer, he desires a noble task' (3:1). The

world considers that leadership of the local church is for those who have
failed in worldly affairs. Images of church leaders presented on UK television
range from Dawn French as the *Vicar of Dibley* to Rowan Atkinson in *Four
Weddings and a Funeral.* One young friend of mine recently announced that he
was leaving a promising professional career to pursue ordained ministry. His
relatives declared, 'What a waste.'

God's opinion of those who would lead his household and assembly is
entirely different. It is a privileged position to lead the local church.

There is not time to run through the verses in detail. Suffice it to say that
the privileged position of church officers must be matched by consistent
lives. Paul's treatment of the qualities required of church leaders covers both
overseers and deacons. There is a plurality of leaders in the local church.
Paul insists that the personal life, family life and public reputation of leaders
be exemplary. This stands to reason, for if those in the privileged position
of leadership of God's household do not embody the truth of which the
assembly is pillar and buttress, then the evangelistic impact of the church
will be deadened. In the case of the lifestyle and family both of overseers and
of deacons, the reputation of the gospel is at stake. They are to be tried and
tested in godliness so that the gospel does not fall into disrepute. The overseers must be 'able to teach' and the deacons 'must hold the mystery of the
faith with a clear conscience'. There is no room given to the idea that a church
leader might publicly teach the official doctrine of the church whilst privately
holding a different view.

The false-teaching elders of the Ephesian church are variously described
as speculators, myth-makers, false handlers of God's law (1:3–7); ascetics
with seared consciences (4:1–3). They are quarrelsome, conceited, ignorant
men whose teaching leads to 'envy, dissension, slander, evil suspicions, and
constant friction' (6:3–5). Any so-called gathering of God's people marked
by these characteristics will never be effective in holding up and holding out
God's truth. Indeed, preaching evangelistic sermons against a backcloth of
such gospel-denying lives will be like firing bullets into a wall of rubber.

Given the impact of over 150 years of liberal theology in the churches of
our major denominations, much work in many local churches is going to be
painstakingly slow. Little attention has been given to the vital issue of leaders'
conduct in the local church. Much repair is needed. One leader of a major
denomination recently suggested he might be able to lead the denomination
whilst privately holding views that differ from the historic teaching of the
denomination to which he was appointed! Paul would not have had such a
man as the deacon in a local church. Another senior leader was recently discovered drunk and disorderly on the streets of London. Paul would not have

allowed such a man to lead a house group. Across the denominations and in local churches up and down our nation, men who fail to qualify on grounds both of morality and of doctrine are in positions of leadership. There is a vast work of repair and restoration needed in the local churches of our major denominations, and it will take men of steel empowered by God and armed with his gospel to accomplish it. They will have to address the issue of leadership in the local church in their preaching and teaching. Unless they do so, the context against which they preach the gospel will constantly be denying the truth they proclaim. Far from being the 'apologetic for the gospel', the local church will be a visual denial of it.

Of course, whilst speaking about leadership in the local church from the pulpit the church leader need not ignore the 'unbeliever in our midst'. There is nothing the unbeliever dislikes more in public leadership than hypocrisy. Sermons on leadership in the church will enable the preacher to hold up God's ideal of leadership for his church. Such preaching ought to be powerfully attractive to unbelievers weary of the compromised leadership on offer in the world and in worldly churches.

Godliness and the gospel life of the church

The final trustworthy saying of the letter is found in 1 Timothy 4:8, 'Godliness is of value in every way, as it holds promise for the present life and also for the life to come.' The issue here has to do with godliness and the gospel life of the church. The saying governs the rest of the letter. Paul is still addressing the issue of godliness in 6:6 and on into the final charges from 6:13. Paul appeals to Timothy to pursue godliness himself and to make progress in it (4:6–16). He insists that the welfare systems of the church be staffed by godly servants and limited to those whose godliness is proven (5:1–16). He urges that the reputation of the church be preserved both in the handling of accusations against elders and in the conduct of slaves towards their masters (5:17 – 6:2). Finally, even as he urges Timothy to persevere, he warns against the false teachers and those in the congregation who would support them (6:2–12). Throughout the section Paul's aim is unchanged. He would have Timothy 'keep the commandment unstained and free from reproach until the appearing of our Lord Jesus Christ' (6:14). It is Timothy's task to bring the gospel that produces godliness to bear both on himself and on every area of the church's life. It is as he preaches this gospel and lives it out in the midst of the congregation that the commandment will be kept unstained and the reputation of God's gospel will be intact as the 'mystery of godliness' is held up and held out to a lost world.

The subject under discussion in this chapter has been that of preaching that achieves an evangelistic end. Our concern has not been with evangelistic sermons per se; rather we have been considering biblical preaching and teaching that renders a congregation fit for the evangelistic purposes of God. The identity and purpose of the local church in God's economy is to be pillar and buttress of his truth, holding out the open secret of his gospel in a lost world. It is only as a congregation is itself impacted and shaped by the preaching and teaching of the gospel that it is enabled to fulfil its role. Bible teachers must preach to mature believers from their pulpits and seek to shape the whole life of the congregation under the gospel in order for the local church to be made fit for purpose. Preaching is not to be aimed solely at the 'unbeliever in our midst'.

Such preaching can be undertaken only by a man who has himself been deeply impacted by the truth he teaches.

7. THE MINISTER'S 'DEVOTIONAL' READING OF THE BIBLE

D. A. Carson

When I was told the general theme of this Festschrift for Peter Adam, I was asked to suggest the title of my own chapter. I must now confess that what I chose was a gentle exercise in misdirection: even though ministers and other Christians alike should read the Bible devotionally, I have long questioned whether there ought to be a separate category for 'devotional' reading of the Bible. It may be simplest to plunge ahead with six clarifying resolutions.

1. Resolutely abolish the distinction between devotional Bible reading and Bible study

One can see why the distinction is appealing and may even do some good. Where ministers devote all of their Bible-reading time to focused study on the passage or passages to be unpacked in the next sermon or house-group meeting, or where their Bible study is professionally competent, complete with rigorous exegesis and informed theological integration but devoid of joy and adoration, to talk about the importance of devotional reading of the Bible may be a good thing.

On the other hand, should any Christian ever read the Bible *non-*devotionally? Much depends on what is meant by 'devotionally'. (a) If 'devotional' Bible reading refers to Bible reading that declines to use lexica, commentaries and other helps, preferably done in a quiet context early in the morning or late at night, then however refreshing this may be, there must *also* be occasions when Christians, especially ministers, *should* engage in non-devotional Bible reading – that is, in close exegetical work using commentaries and theologies and other tools. (b) 'Devotional' Bible reading, however, often has a rather different flavour. Now the reading becomes 'devout' or even mystical, as opposed to the careful and 'objective' reading of the pastor-exegete. One simply listens to the text, prays over it, turns it over in one's mind and, frankly, expects to *feel* something of the Spirit's presence, to *hear* God speaking through his Word. By contrast, the exegete is so determined to get the interpretation right, to figure out what kind of use the genitive has in this line and decide whether this or that present-tense verb is in fact present-referring, that 'devotion' or a 'devout' attitude gets swamped by the need for diligence. Such 'devotional' Bible reading is distinguished from 'objective' or 'critical' Bible reading or from 'Bible study'.[1] And it is this latter polarity that should be for ever consigned to the abyss.

One understands the polarity, of course. Many a student entering seminary or Bible college begins formal study of the Bible only to discover that former delight in reading the Bible has dissipated into the hard work of memorizing Greek declensions. Not surprisingly, the most frequently offered advice to such students when they express their sense of loss and even of frustration is that they should preserve time and space for 'devotional' reading of the Bible. This is simultaneously moderately helpful advice (on the first understanding of 'devotional') and utterly atrocious and even dangerous advice (on the second understanding of 'devotional'). After all, God is committed to looking with favour on those who are humble and contrite and who tremble at his word (Isa. 66:2) – whether they are reading in the common language early in the morning or struggling with the exegesis of a passage in the middle of a second-year Hebrew class.

The polarity needs to be addressed from both ends. When we think we are reading the Bible 'devotionally' (in the second sense), we ought to take special pains to read carefully, to see what is there, to avoid merely sentimen-

---

1. Some readers may be uncertain about what I mean by 'critical', 'critically' and 'criticism' in this chapter. I do not mean that one becomes a critic, or somehow stands over Scripture to judge it. In literary endeavours, including Bible study, it is common to use these words to refer to exegesis that provides reasons and arguments in support of particular interpretations of the text, as opposed to readings that are little more than unfounded opinion.

tal notions that are not grounded in what Scripture *says* – in short, we need to read critically – whether or not we take time to fetch a reference work to help resolve some uncertainty in our minds. On the other hand, when we think we are engaged in serious Bible study, we ought to guard our hearts all the more intentionally and ask God to enable us to see wonderful things in his law (cf. Ps. 119:18). While struggling with the syntax of the Greek participle, we should be hungering no less to learn what God is saying through his Word, finding great comfort and joy in the work.

One remembers the somewhat analogous observation of C. S. Lewis:

> For my own part, I tend to find the doctrinal books often more helpful in devotion than the devotional books, and I rather suspect that the same experience may await others. I believe that many who find that 'nothing happens' when they sit down, or kneel down, to a book of devotion, would find that the heart sings unbidden while they are working their way through a tough bit of theology with a pipe in their teeth and a pencil in their hand.[2]

In a similar way, Christian ministers should preserve the goal of reading reverently, devoutly, 'devotionally' if you will, when they are at their most careful, dispassionate, studious and critical. Such study of Scripture should be accompanied by prayer and adoration, no less than the Bible reading undertaken under more casual or 'devotional' circumstances. Equally, as they read the Bible 'devotionally', ministers (and for that matter all Christians) should aim to bring watchfulness, precision and rigorous thinking to the task.

2. Resolutely set aside time for Bible reading beyond the Bible reading undertaken for the next sermon or Bible study

It is easy to overlook the importance of such pleasure and discipline in the urgency of ministry. It is easy to conclude that regular and systematic Bible reading is for *other* Christians – Christians who do not carry the responsibility of regular Bible teaching and preaching. There is of course some truth to such rationalization: if you are engaged in regular expository ministry, then *of course* you are constantly in the Scriptures in a way that many others are not.

---

2. C. S. Lewis, *God in the Dock: Essays on Theology and Ethics* (Grand Rapids: Eerdmans, 1970), p. 205. This is part of his essay 'On the Reading of Old Books' (pp. 200–211).

The negative result is twofold. First, if all of your Bible reading feeds directly into your public ministry, then your Bible reading becomes strictly utilitarian. However much you tell yourself it is not so, your Bible reading has become part of your job; you are paid to do it, and the primary reason you do it is to be prepared for the next public obligation. Suddenly there is little or no sense in which your public Bible teaching is the overflow of rich Bible reading; rather, whatever the quality of your teaching, it is the product of study undertaken for that particular ministry. Secondly, after a while you are no longer undertaking to read the *whole* Bible right through on a regular basis. You may enjoy expounding several biblical books over, say, a five-year period, while your knowledge of the rest of the Bible is allowed to become increasingly sketchy because it has not been refreshed by recent reading.

This is not to prescribe only one kind of Bible reading. Some pastors have committed themselves to following the M'Cheyne Bible reading scheme every year of their lives.[3] That scheme takes you through the NT and Psalms twice, and the rest of the OT once, every year (or one can halve the pace and cover the same material every two years). Others, myself included, follow that scheme for a time, and then undertake something else for a while before returning to M'Cheyne: to memorize a biblical book, to work through texts in the original language, to read repeatedly through the wisdom literature, to read repeatedly through one particular book, and so forth.

What one must nurture is one's sheer *delight* in reading God's Word. Several decades ago, while still a doctoral student, I went to the nearby laundromat, fairly late at night, to get my washing done. There I found a fellow-student, his head buried in his Bible, waiting for his clothes to stop spinning. If memory serves, he was reading Amos. Knowing that he was writing his doctoral dissertation on Paul, I asked him why he was reading Amos. His answer was not 'I'm trying to keep up on my Bible reading' or 'I'm having my quiet time' or anything of that sort. It was devastatingly to the point: 'Because I like it.'

The importance of thinking through Scripture is either taught or exemplified in many parts of Scripture. On assuming the mantle of leadership, Joshua is famously told, 'Keep this Book of the Law always on your lips; meditate on it day and night, so that you may be careful to do everything written in it. Then you will be prosperous and successful' (Josh. 1:8).[4] On his accession to

---

3. For an introduction to M'Cheyne's reading scheme, along with daily reflections on select Bible passages, see my *For the Love of God: A Daily Companion for Discovering the Riches of God's Word*, 2 vols. (Wheaton: Crossway, 1998–9).

4. Unless stated otherwise, Bible quotations in this chapter are from the TNIV.

the throne, the first task of the Davidic king was to write out for himself, by hand, a copy of 'this law' (the book of Deuteronomy? part of it [e.g. chs. 1 – 30]? the Pentateuch?) drawn from a copy held by the Levitical priests. He was then to read this copy 'all the days of his life so that he may learn to revere the LORD his God and follow carefully all the words of this law and these decrees and not consider himself better than his fellow Israelites' (Deut. 17:18–20). While unrighteous people take their cue from the wicked and sinners (Ps. 1:1), the righteous 'delight in the law of the LORD / and meditate on his law day and night' (Ps. 1:2). The lengthiest psalm in the canon is a meditation on the words, law, truth and revelation of God (Ps. 119). Why should it not be so? The Word of God cannot pass away (Matt. 5:18) any more than the words of Jesus (Matt. 24:35; Mark 13:31; Luke 21:33).

3. Resolutely set out to read the Bible in different ways

By 'different ways' I am not smuggling back into the discussion the merits of reading the Bible critically (that's *one* way) and then devotionally (that's *another* way) as alternative ways of reading. I have already insisted that we should never read the Bible without engaging critical faculties and without engaging our heart and devotion. By 'different ways' of reading the Bible I mean, rather, to draw attention to different tools and grids that we might deploy in our reading. For example, one might read the Bible grammatically. In that case one studies how words are used and what they mean (philology) and how words come together in grammatical units and what meaning those units convey (syntax). Alternatively, one might read the Bible with a heavy emphasis on the literary genre of each part: parable, proverb, genealogy, apocalyptic, history, chronicle, letter, discourse, lament, oracle, psalm, and much more. Merely grammatical study may leave the reader insensitive to issues of literary genre; a focus on genre must learn not to overlook careful exegesis of the grammar. What sorts of things may be said in a lament or a letter that one would never say in apocalyptic? Why do wisdom literature and apocalyptic share in common an absolute polarization – between Lady Wisdom and Dame folly, between the good guys who are suffering now but who will finally be vindicated and the bad guys who may triumph now but who will be thrown into the lake of fire – while narrative allows for human beings to be displayed in all their inglorious inconsistencies (think David or Peter)? Again, one might read the Bible theocentrically, or, more specifically, Christocentrically. One might read through the Bible with special focus on how the theme of covenant can be used to organize the material: one is reading the Bible covenantally. One can read many parts of the Bible historically – that is, either trying to understand, as accurately as possible, *what happened* according to those parts of the Bible that disclose such history, or trying to understand how any part of the Bible, even if that part is not history, fits into the broader stream of history conveyed in the Bible as a whole or in broader works that describe the same period of time. One then fastens rather more attention on exactly what happened, so far as our sources will warrant – for example, on the cross and on the tomb that was empty on that first Easter Sunday morning – than on the theology that flows from the cross and resurrection of Jesus. It is often helpful to read the Bible with one eye peeled on the literary structure of a passage. One can read the Bible holistically, seeking to unpack the message of the Bible as a whole; equally, one may read the Bible along the trajectories laid down by biblical theology, seeking to tease out the inner-canonical connections that hold the books of the Bible together. How do the themes of temple, priest, sacrifice, kingship, Passover, and many more, develop with time – in each book and corpus of the Bible, across the centuries when the Bible was written, until one clearly sees how God in his wisdom laid down these trajectories for our learning?

These are but a few suggestions of some of the ways one might profitably read the Bible. Many of the best readers will read the Bible in several of these ways at once without self-consciously picking and choosing among them.

4. Resolve to keep improving your Bible reading – that is, with increasing insight and integration

One of the things that this varied Bible reading should do is make us *better* Bible readers – that is, Bible readers who are more accurate, insightful, devout, and more greatly filled with the mind of God as God has disclosed himself to us through his Word. Provided we keep reading the Bible, this is likely to happen whether or not we are aiming for it to happen – yet we *should* be aiming for it to happen. After all, on at least five occasions Jesus rebukes his opponents for their *mis*reading of Scripture. Usually he begins his challenge with the formula 'Have you not read?' He knows, of course, that they *do* read the Scriptures and *have* read them; his question is not designed to provoke them into more reading but into better reading, into more insightful reading. In each instance Jesus corrects their improper conclusions by appealing to Scripture (Matt. 12:3, 5 [Mark 2:25; Luke 6:3]; 19:4; 21:16, 42 [Mark 12:10]; 22:31 [Mark 12:26]).

The issue is not merely how to read the Bible correctly, but how to read it insightfully. Several historical psalms report segments of Israel's history, the details of which were well known and not in dispute – yet they do so in such a way that fresh insight spins out of the account. This is true, for example, of Psalm 78. That is why the psalmist can say, on the one hand, 'I will open my mouth in parables, / I will utter hidden things, things from of old' – and, on the other, 'what we have heard and known, / what our fathers have told us' (78:2–3 NIV). In Acts 7 Stephen's speech covers a lot of historical turf that was not in dispute but, as he paints the pictures from the past, he shows how regularly the ancestors rejected the revelation that was given them, so it is scarcely surprising that their progeny, the people of Stephen's generation, reject the Messiah himself and in mob enthusiasm demand his crucifixion.

What this suggests is that our Bible reading should provide us with more than biblical data, the kinds of bitty information that show up in Bible trivia games. When I was a boy I learned choruses that taught me the names of the twelve sons of Jacob, the names of the twelve apostles, how to draw the main features of the land of Israel, and so forth. Doubtless all of this is good information to acquire. One might learn by heart the names of the monarchs of the united kingdom and then of Judah and Israel separately. Knowledge of such details, however, would not necessarily lead us to the *theological* conclusions teased out of these same texts by Asaph in Psalm 78 or by Stephen in Acts 7. Otherwise put, what we are looking for, in our systematic Bible reading, is what Paul commands Timothy to preserve, namely, 'the pattern of sound teaching' (2 Tim. 1:13) – more than unconnected data, but the *pattern* of sound teaching. A hint of what Paul means is on display in the words immediately following: 'with faith and love in Christ Jesus'.

The importance of faith and love flowing from this pattern of sound teaching I will pick up in the next point. That this pattern should issue in faith and love *in Christ Jesus*, however, demands a little more immediate reflection. The pattern of sound teaching is for Paul profoundly Christological: it focuses on Jesus Christ. Or, as he stipulates elsewhere when he outlines the gospel that he preaches with his emphasis on the matters 'of first importance' (1 Cor. 15:3), the content is not Jesus Christ as an empty cipher, but Christ crucified, dead, buried, risen again – according to the Scriptures (15:1–19). This leads to three further reflections.

First, many people do *not* learn to read the Bible this way. This was true in the first century (e.g. Acts 13:27). Many Jews read what we call the OT, the same Scriptures the early Christians read, and did not understand them the same way that Christians did. Doubtless they found many good things there, but they did not find the gospel of Christ crucified. Our situation is a bit different, of course. Today many Christians, while holding that Jesus died

on the cross for our sins and rose for our justification, read their Bibles with
scarcely any sensitivity to these integrating themes. They read them to find
private promises to lift their spirits, to seek guidance for choices they must
make, to address contemporary moral and ethical issues, to justify a responsible stance toward ecological challenges, to ramp up denunciation of social
trends of which they disapprove, and so on. Ministers of the gospel are not
exempt from these patterns of reading as they seek to gather material for their
next sermons. This is not to say, of course, that the Bible does *not* provide
wonderful promises, relief from discouragement, moral guidance, and insight
into contemporary challenges. Rather, it is to say that if we 'discover' such a
plethora of useful themes while leaving them unintegrated into what the Bible
itself designates as the matters of first importance, it is highly doubtful that we
are improving in our Bible reading.

Secondly, the Bible-reading skill that integrates the Bible around Jesus and
his cross and resurrection is not something acquired by mere discipline and
resolution. Two other factors should be introduced here.

(a) There is no unambiguous evidence that Jewish readers of the Bible in
Jesus' day anticipated a messianic king who would also be a suffering servant,
a triumphant king in David's line who would die in ignominy and torture by
Roman execution – still less that he would rise on the third day. Even when
the apostles confess Jesus' messiahship in Caesarea Philippi (Matt. 16), they
still have no category for a messiah who suffers and dies. If Peter and the
others do not get it, how much does anyone else? Even when Jesus was
buried, they did not get it. It was only the resurrection that brought with it the
first flicker of real understanding – a theme powerfully presented in John's
Gospel (e.g. John 2:19–22). In other words, for Jesus' first disciples, *one of the
things necessary for discerning how antecedent Scripture works was time – time until the
resurrection of Jesus, from which vantage point everything looked different.* They had to
wait until that next great turning point in redemptive history had taken place,
Jesus' resurrection, or they were not going to understand. Doubtless there
was some culpability associated with such ignorance (cf. Luke 24:25–27), but
it was also part of God's wise plan: the gospel itself, and many individual parts
of it, are simultaneously presented in the Bible as what has been prophesied
in the past and fulfilled in the present, and as has been hidden in the past and
only now revealed (see esp. Rom. 16:25–27).[5] Before Jesus' resurrection, Peter

---

5. For more detailed articulation of this point, see my 'Mystery and Fulfillment:
   Toward a More Comprehensive Paradigm of Paul's Understanding of the Old and
   the New,' in D. A. Carson, Peter T. O'Brien and Mark A. Seifrid (eds.), *Justification*

and the other apostles – not to mention everyone else – failed to understand how the OT pictorially and typologically anticipates the Messiah's death (e.g. in the sacrifices of Yom Kippur and Passover, in the priestly system, in the temple structure). But this is not exactly the sort of misunderstanding that anyone alive in the twenty-first century could experience the same way. For their misunderstanding could be removed only by the dawning, in time, of the next great redemptive-historical event, Jesus' resurrection, while our contemporaries, even if they cannot accept that the Messiah must suffer, do not need to wait for a great redemptive-historical event to open their eyes. The great event has already happened; millions understand it and can talk about it. Paul regularly speaks of his ministry in terms of unpacking this mystery, unfolding what has been hidden in time past and is now publicly disclosed (e.g. Eph. 3:4). So this first factor is what led to the understanding and integration of thought of the first Christians as they read their Bibles, but we cannot exactly reproduce how the first Christians came to integrate their Bibles. That brings us to the second factor.

(b) Even *after* Jesus' cross and resurrection, many Jews did *not* believe: they did not read the Scriptures in a way that mandated or even permitted the Messiah's death and resurrection. Saul, the arch-persecutor of the church, was one of them. He could not have failed to understand what the Christians whom he was persecuting were saying; he simply did not believe them because he thought that the way they integrated Scripture was monstrous. After his conversion on the Damascus road, Saul could no longer think that Jesus was dead and damned. Jesus was alive and vindicated – so Saul was forced to rethink how he put what we call the OT together. But the interesting thing is that, as far as the evidence goes, Paul does not try to convince unconverted Jews that they too will come to read the Bible in the way Christian Jews do, if only they have a Damascus road experience equivalent to his own. There is no hint of that sort of reasoning anywhere in his writing. Rather, (i) *he reasons with them from the Scripture* to prove that the anticipated Messiah really is Jesus (which presupposes that his conversion has transformed his own ways of integrating Scripture), and (ii) *he insists that however much people ought to believe on the basis of his exegesis of Scripture, they will not do so apart from the illumination of the Holy Spirit* (cf. esp. 1 Cor. 2:9–16), the Spirit poured out in the wake of Jesus' triumphant resurrection, ascension and session on the right hand of the Majesty.

---

and Variegated Nomism, vol. 2: *The Paradoxes of Paul* (Tübingen: Mohr, 2004), pp. 393–436.

The point, then, is that first-century Christians came to read the Bible a certain way; namely, they came to grasp the pattern of sound teaching, not only because certain great and unrepeatable redemptive-historical events came to pass (notably the cross and resurrection of Jesus), but also by the illumination of their minds by the Holy Spirit. There was both a public revelatory event and inner revelatory disclosure.

Thirdly, the early church never gave up on the importance of teaching, not least teaching believers how to read the OT. That was part of how the reading of the Scriptures by Christians and among Christians (where the reading was aloud so that those who could not themselves read might listen) was improved: by teaching how those Scriptures were to be understood, by uncovering the pattern of sound teaching. The NT writers not only wanted their readers to understand what *they themselves* wrote (e.g. Rev. 1:3), but most of them took pains to teach their readers how to understand what they read in the OT.[6] In other words, the need for illumination from the Holy Spirit did not vitiate the need for apostolic teaching, and the presence of apostolic teaching did not reduce the need for the Spirit's inner disclosure. The Word–Spirit link is what he appeals to, rather than a particular personal experience.

What this means for our own Bible reading is that we too can benefit from teachers. It makes no sense so to appeal to the inner work of the Spirit when we are having our 'devotions' that we refuse, because of the Spirit's work, to read commentaries, sermons, theologies, reference works and other helps, when the NT writers devote as much space as they do to unpacking the earlier Scriptures. Equally, it makes no sense to suppose we will improve our reading of the Bible out of nothing more than disciplined study, absent the illumining work of the Holy Spirit.

One of the practical outcomes of these reflections is that it is a mistake to think that the only thing one is permitted to do in one's 'devotional' reading of the Bible is – to read the Bible! Of course, reading the Bible comes first and last. Reading devotional or doctrinal books is no substitute. One might even decide, while reading an extended passage, not to interrupt the reading by looking up reference works to better understand difficult bits – and in that case it may be a good idea to keep a pencil or an iPad handy to jot down what you want to look up later. But there is nothing intrinsically wrong with reading through, say, Amos, and reading an excellent commentary on the side. If the commentary is a good one, you are simply listening to teachers explain to

---

6. Cf. G. K. Beale and D. A. Carson (eds.), *Commentary on the New Testament Use of the Old Testament* (Grand Rapids: Baker; Nottingham: Apollos, 2007).

you the pattern of sound teaching. Of course, one must not permit the commentary to take over and become the focus of one's reading. The aim must be to become a better reader of the Bible, more faithful, more insightful, more integrative.

5. As you read, resolutely pursue faith and obedience, individually and corporately, situating yourself and your church in the cosmic contest between good and evil, God and the devil, the temporary and the eternal

This counsel could be extended indefinitely. For our purposes it will suffice to offer two reflections.

First, it is wise and good to cultivate spontaneous doxology. In the midst of expounding justification, Paul's mention of the Son of God prompts him to erupt with the modifier 'who loved me and gave himself for me' (Gal. 2:20). While writing his closing charge in his first letter to Timothy, the apostle anticipates 'the appearing of our Lord Jesus Christ, which God will bring about in his own time' – and then immediately adds, 'God, the blessed and only Ruler, the King of kings and Lord of lords, who alone is immortal and who lives in unapproachable light, whom no one has seen or can see. To him be honour and might for ever. Amen' (1 Tim. 6:14–16). What might almost be called a pattern of irrepressible praise surfaces repeatedly in Paul's writings. It is as if thinking through who God is and what God has done in Jesus is enough to prompt spontaneous adoration.

So also our reading of Scripture, our meditation on what it discloses of God – his character, attributes and activities, not least his redemptive purposes in Christ – *ought* to prompt spontaneous doxology. Whether expressed in prayer, song, holy joy, a heart bursting with gratitude, contrition or renewed faith and courage, this spontaneous doxology should not be long suppressed. It seems somewhat paradoxical to speak of working hard to develop and maintain spontaneous doxology, but that is what we must do. For a start, it will transform our Bible reading into worship and reduce the moments when the exercise seems arid.

Secondly, the improving integration of Scripture with our lives, values, churches, outlook and practice presupposes not only that we have an improving understanding of Scripture but also that we have an increasingly penetrating grasp of our culture in the light of Scripture. This is true in a general sense. John Frame is right when he insists not only that 'the law is necessary to understand the world' but also that 'the world is necessary to understand the law': to grasp what 'you shall not steal' means, I must know something of what property is and what it means to say that certain property belongs to me or to my neighbour.[7] More specifically, however, if the Bible is to have a bearing in our own minds, on a vast array of cultural artefacts, choices, realities and trends, we must think through the culture in which we find ourselves, and how our knowledge of God mediated through Scripture changes, or ought to change, all of our perceptions regarding that culture.[8]

So you are standing in an interminable queue at an airline counter, waiting to get your ticket changed now that a flight has been cancelled because of a faulty fuel gauge that cannot be repaired until a new part is flown in at least ten hours from now. You can feel the stress and exasperation in the people all around you, and you yourself can hardly wait to get home. Along with everyone else, including the young woman in front of you with two children under the age of five, you are hoping to get transferred to another flight. What does faithful reading of the Bible have to do with this situation? If you are integrating what you are reading with how you look on life as a Christian, then surely you will instinctively gravitate to thoughts such as the following:

- It is surely true that the habits of a clock-watching culture exacerbate tensions in this sort of experience into frustration. What does it mean, in this particular situation, to put people, God's image bearers, ahead of most kinds of deadlines?
- God is sovereign, Romans 8:28 has not been snipped out of the Bible, and I can trust him, I must trust him, when I am tired. He knows best.
- As people mutter in the line around me, am I furthering the rebellious reaction with my own muttering, or making a gentle joke out of it to provoke grins and friendly conversation?
- I wonder if there is a way I can help the young mother in front of me without being too intrusive?
- When it is my turn at the counter, how can I encourage the airline representative who has been taking quite a lot of sullen abuse from frustrated passengers? After all, it's not her fault that a part of the plane malfunctioned.

---

7. Cf. John Frame, *The Doctrine of the Knowledge of God* (Phillipsburg: Presbyterian & Reformed, 1987), pp. 66–67. I am indebted to Dan Doriani for the reference.
8. For an excellent stimulus to this sort of thinking, cf. Kevin J. Vanhoozer, Charles A. Anderson and Michael J. Sleasman (eds.), *Everyday Theology: How to Read Cultural Texts and Interpret Trends* (Grand Rapids: Baker, 2007).

- I wonder if God wants me to use this delay and hiatus as something that will provide a 'heavenly appointment' with some stranger or other whose heart God has prepared to hear the gospel?
- How can I best relieve the worries of those waiting for me at home?
- *Dear heavenly Father, thank you for your sovereign providence. I'd like to get on an early alternative flight, and I'll try my best to arrange it, but help me to respond to this very minor setback in such a way that somehow your Son will be glorified and I will be faithful (for I remember that your Word tells me that in everything I do, even eating and drinking, I am to do all for your glory [1 Cor. 10:31]).*

Of course, one can multiply life situations: strife within a congregation, visiting an art gallery or a rock concert, sorting out relationships in a growing family, driving a car or riding a bike, reading a book or going to a movie, helping out some needy folk in your area, working with others on a project with deadlines, preparing for an exam, nursing a baby, telling a joke, building a friendship, and on and on. In absolutely every situation in life, a little imagination nurtured by Scripture reading will disclose how we are pleasing Satan, who regularly masquerades as an angel of light (2 Cor. 11:14), deceiving, if it were possible, the very elect (Matt. 24:24), or pleasing Jesus Christ, who came to destroy the devil's work (1 John 3:8). You will begin to see whether you are living for yourself in this transient age or investing in the new heaven and the new earth that stand for ever. The gospel will become more precious to you, and you will all the more eagerly hunger to learn better how to share it, articulate it and live it out.

6. While you read your Bible, resolutely fasten on the grace of God in the gospel

In some ways, this is merely a development of my fourth resolution: resolve to keep improving your Bible reading – that is, with increasing insight and integration. Nevertheless it is worth making a separate point of this one.

The reason is perhaps shocking. The very discipline of regular Bible reading, or for that matter of any of the 'spiritual disciplines' widely encouraged today (some of them useful, others with precious little biblical sanction), easily becomes the basis on which we establish a new moralism almost untouched by grace. Whatever we read in the Bible, many of us instantly gravitate toward what we should *do* or how we should *act* on the basis of what we have just read. Many is the preacher who follows the same course: regardless of the text, every sermon ends up with an *ought* or a *must do*, along with a threat, implicit or explicit, that failure at this point marks us out as at best inferior Christians.

God knows there are many demands, commands, requirements and standards in the Bible. They are so high that at the end of the day God demands that we be perfect, as he is perfect (Matt. 5:48). Certainly, we are to love God with heart, soul, mind and strength, and our neighbours as ourselves. The demands are there and inescapable. But are they transforming and life-giving?

If all those who have failed to meet these two most important commandments were in every age removed from the face of the earth, this earth would have only ever witnessed one human being. In the light of the Bible's teaching, why should we think that moralism ever transformed anyone in such a fundamental way that he or she is ready to meet God, ready for the new heaven and the new earth? Why do both our preaching and our Bible reading frequently have the effect of either turning us into self-righteous prigs (thank God we are not as other people are!) or driving us into bleak despair?

What is missing is the integrating vision that shows us how much of the Bible's storyline is an effective display of the grace of God. It is the account of the holy God pursuing and saving countless numbers of this rebel brood of his image-bearers. And what encourages us, transforms us and lifts our hearts in joy, confidence, faith and hope toward our Maker, Redeemer and Judge is a steadfast reliance on the grace of God in the gospel. So while you read your Bible, resolutely fasten on the grace of God in the gospel.

Tolle, lege (take up, read).

© D. A. Carson, 2011

8. PREACHING GOD'S WORDS AND WALKING IN GOD'S WAYS: SCRIPTURE, PREACHING AND THE ETHICAL LIFE

Graham A. Cole

Introduction

Scandal in the churches raises many questions about their ethical integrity, and many Christians are disheartened by such scandal. Paedophilia in the Roman Catholic Church is a striking example. The secular media rightly draws attention to our hypocrisies and misuses of power and status. Evangelical churches too are not exempt from charges of hypocrisy and abuse. When prominent evangelical preachers and pastors fall into spectacular sin – sexual, abuse of power, embezzlement of church funds – the question emerges as to whether the evangelical has somehow been disconnected from the ethical.[1] Indeed, an emphasis on the ethical seems to be missing from much evangelical preaching, at least in the USA. There are plenty of inspirational and counselling-oriented sermons dressed up with some biblical proof texts, but not much exposition of Scripture – let alone the ethical application of such exposition.[2]

---

1. The Christian should always be disappointed by sin in the church, but never surprised. For example, of the seven churches referred to in Rev. 2 – 3, five come under divine criticism for wrong doctrine and/or behaviour.
2. I recall an American Christian magazine cover with an intriguing question: 'Will

My aim in this chapter is to explore the interface of preaching the words of God and walking in God's ways. Preaching the words of God presupposes that God has spoken. In other words, that there is a special revelation from God. Walking in God's ways assumes that the divine desire is for us to image his character in the world. In the ancient Near East the king as image of God was a designated representative of the gods, ruling on their behalf. As Terrence Fretheim comments on Genesis 1:24, 'The image functions to mirror God to the world, to be God as God would be to the non-human, to be an extension of God's own dominion.'[3] For the evangelical committed to a high view of biblical theology there can be no divorce of the Great Commission (Matt. 28:18–20) from the Great Commandments (22:34–40).[4] The Great Commission mandates the discipling of the nations through teaching. The Great Commandments mandate the love of God and the love of one's neighbour. The evangel (gospel) and the ethical are not to be confused but neither are they to be separated.

We begin with the need for special revelation from God. We need to hear God's words.[5] Next we explore what God has revealed in general terms before considering in particular the biblical idea of walking in God's ways. Then we examine a NT example of the balance between the evangelical and the ethical in Paul's letter to the Thessalonians, one of the earliest documents in the NT. Lastly, we reflect on the significance of the discussion for today's preacher before drawing a conclusion.

Footnote 2 *(cont.)*

the therapist replace the preacher?' In the background was a pulpit. In the foreground were couches not pews.

3. Terence E. Fretheim, 'The Book of Genesis: Introduction, Commentary, and Reflections', in *The New Interpreter's Bible*, vol. 1 (Nashville: Abingdon, 1994), pp. 317–674, quote p. 345. Gen. 1 presents humanity in royal terms and Gen. 2 in priestly. It is no accident then that in the eschaton redeemed humanity functions as kings and priests (Rev. 1:6; 22:3, 5). The image has been recovered and renewed.

4. There is a specious argument that runs like this: The most loving act I can do for my neighbours is to preach the gospel to them. Anything less is a distraction. If that were true, it is hard to know why the letter of James was ever included in the NT.

5. I have used 'preaching God's words' in the title of this chapter with two of Peter Adam's books in mind: *Speaking God's Words: A Practical Theology of Preaching* (Leicester: IVP, 1996) and *Hearing God's Words: Exploring Biblical Spirituality*, NSBT 16 (Leicester: Apollos; Downers Grove: IVP, 2004).

The need for special revelation

If we are to walk in God's ways, then we need to know what they are. Hence there is a need for special revelation.[6] The need for special revelation is further underlined by the facts of human finitude and fallenness. As finite creatures we cannot obtain the knowledge of God without divine aid. The living God needs to be pleased to make himself known. Otherwise we grope in the dark. This is unsurprising if God is personal, because persons can only be really known if they self-reveal. If they don't, we are left only with our best guesses concerning them. In addition, as fallen creatures we have a bias against God and a resistance to believing his words. The Christian doctrine of original sin explores this bias, its origin and nature. Indeed, a case can be made that the primordial sin in the garden story was not pride, not sensuality, but unbelief.[7]

The good news is that God has addressed both needs. With regard to our finitude, there is a special revelation from God. Finite though we are we can know the living God both by description and acquaintance. 'Description' refers to knowing true propositions about God. 'Acquaintance' refers to knowing God through personal dealings. With regard to knowledge by description, the writer to the Hebrews puts it:

> In the past God spoke to our forefathers through the prophets at many times and
> in various ways, but in these last days he has spoken to us by his Son, whom he
> appointed heir of all things, and through whom he made the universe. (Heb. 1:1–2)[8]

This special revelation is now to be found crystallized as Holy Scripture, which is the words of God in the words of humankind (2 Pet. 1:21). In relation to knowledge by acquaintance, Peter writes:

> Though you have not seen him, you love him; and even though you do not see
> him now, you believe in him and are filled with an inexpressible and glorious

---

6. Theologians draw a distinction between special revelation (what God makes
   known about his character, will and ways to only some in the course of history)
   and general revelation (what may be known by anyone, anywhere and at any time
   through the created order).
7. As I argue in 'Reinhold Niebuhr on Pride', in Andrew Cameron and Brian
   Rosner (eds.), *Still Deadly: Ancient Cures for the 7 Sins* (Sydney South: Aquila, 2007),
   pp. 103–120, esp. pp. 108–109.
8. Unless stated otherwise, Bible quotations in this chapter are from the NIV.

joy, for you are receiving the goal of your faith, the salvation of your souls.
(1 Pet. 1:8–9)

Paul could put it in autobiographical terms: 'Yet I am not ashamed, because I know whom I have believed, and am convinced that he is able to guard what I have entrusted to him for that day' (2 Tim. 1:12).

With regard to our fallenness, there is also the illuminating work of the Spirit who gives the regenerate affection for the revealed words of God:

> The Spirit searches all things, even the deep things of God. For who among men knows the thoughts of a man except the man's spirit within him? In the same way no one knows the thoughts of God except the Spirit of God. We have not received the spirit of the world but the Spirit who is from God, that we may understand what God has freely given us. (1 Cor. 2:10–12)

Our fallenness does not consist of a cognitive disability but an affective disinclination that the Spirit overcomes through regeneration.

Furthermore, it is the Spirit who makes the written words a contemporary word. For example, for Jesus, Paul and the writer to the Hebrews, Scripture is God's contemporary word and not merely his past word.[9] Jesus says to the Sadducees in a debate about the resurrection, 'have you not read what God said *to you*?' (Matt. 22:31, emphasis added). Jesus then quotes from the *tôrâ* to make his point (Matt. 22:32, citing Exod. 3:6). The *tôrâ* was that part of the OT that the Sadducees took as authoritative. Paul makes a similar point in addressing the behavioural problems in the Corinthian congregation. The apostle draws their attention to the example of the grumbling Israelites in the wilderness and argues, 'Now these things happened to them as an example, but they were written down *for our instruction*, on whom the end of the ages has come' (1 Cor. 10:11 ESV, emphasis added). For both Jesus and Paul, Scripture has more than the original one readership in view. Scripture is a contemporary word. Neither Jesus' words nor Paul's refer to the Spirit per se. However, the letter to the Hebrews makes explicit the work of the Spirit with regard to the contemporaneity of Scripture. In Hebrews 3 – 4 the writer quotes Psalm 95 and applies the text to the life situation of his readers. He warns them of the dangers of unbelief and of not heeding the warning of God. Clearly, for the writer Psalm 95 is not simply what God said once in the past. Rather, the

---

9. It was my theology teacher, D. B. Knox, who first drew my attention to this phenomenon in the text.

psalm is the Spirit's present word to the Hebrews. Indeed, the writer describes Psalm 95 as the 'living' word of God (*zōn . . . ho logos tou theou*), which is like a sword in its effectiveness (4:12). Psalm 95 is no dead letter. The preacher who faithfully expounds the words of God is not without divine help in doing so.

The divine comedy

A useful way to consider Scripture as a whole is to adopt a literary approach. As Christian novelist Frederick Buechner puts it, 'The Good Book [is] a good book.'[10] In literary categories the good book presents a divine comedy. According to literary scholar Leland Ryken, a comedy is 'a work of literature in which the plot structure is U-shaped, with the action beginning in prosperity, descending into potentially tragic events, and ending happily'.[11] The *Dictionary of Biblical Imagery* develops this point:

> The overall plot of the Bible is a U-shaped comic plot. The action begins with a perfect world inhabited by perfect people. It descends into the misery of fallen history and ends with a new world of total happiness and the conquest of evil. The book of Revelation is the story of the happy ending par excellence, as a conquering hero defeats evil, marries a bride and lives happily ever after in a palace glittering with jewels.[12]

We see this U-shaped structure working itself out from Genesis to Revelation. The canon moves from the harmony of Genesis 1 – 2, through the disharmony of Genesis 3 to Revelation 20, to harmony again (indeed of a higher kind) in Revelation 21 – 22.

In this comedy the triune God comes before us as the chief actor in the story, and in fact its architect. The conflict between good and evil drives the plot. According to the *Dictionary of Biblical Imagery*:

> Almost every story, poem and proverb in the Bible fits into this ongoing plot conflict between good and evil. Every human act or attitude shows people engaged in some

---

10. Frederick Buechner, 'The Good Book as a Good Book', in *The Clown in the Belfry: Writings on Faith and Fiction* (San Francisco: Harper, 1992), p. 44.

11. Leland Ryken, *The Literature of the Bible* (Grand Rapids: Zondervan, 1980), p. 359.

12. Leland Ryken, James C. Wilhoit and Tremper Longman III (eds.), *Dictionary of Biblical Imagery* (Downers Grove: IVP, 1998), 'Comedy as Plot Motif', pp. 160–161, quote p. 161.

movement, whether slight or momentous, toward or away from God in this story of the soul's choice.[13]

Again the *Dictionary of Biblical Imagery* is helpful with regard to the core of the story:

> This history focuses on God's great plan to save people from their sin and its eternal consequences. Human history in the Bible unfolds within the providential framework of God's acts of redemption and judgment, as God deals with evil in the universe.[14]

God is reclaiming a people for himself. We can sum up the goal of the divine project in these terms: To secure God's people in God's place under God's rule living God's way enjoying shalom in God's holy and loving presence to God's glory.[15] W. J. Dumbrell finely sums up God's project in these terms as he reflects on the theological significance of Revelation 22:6–11:

> The history of salvation has ended, and the journey has been long. We have moved from creation and Adam to Israel and redemption, to Jesus as suffering Israel, to the creation of a new people of God through the cross and resurrection of Jesus . . . The biblical search for order is now at an end. Though the divine intention for humankind and the world had been signaled by Genesis 1–2, God patiently bore with sinful humankind until imposing order at the end of the canon. The movement in the Bible from creation to the new creation was made possible only by the fact that God was in Christ, in the historical factor of the cross outside the city of Jerusalem in the midpoint of salvation history, reconciling the world unto himself.[16]

A key feature of the project is the divine desire that God's people are to live God's way. To this important biblical idea we now give our attention.

---

13. Ibid., 'Bible', pp. 90–92, quote p. 91. I am much indebted to the discussion in this section.

14. Ibid., p. 92.

15. Graeme Goldsworthy, *Gospel and Kingdom: A Christian Interpretation of the Old Testament* (Exeter: Paternoster, 1981), p. 47. I have expanded Goldsworthy's summation of the biblical story, which he takes to be a kingdom-of-God story. His formulation runs, 'God's people in God's place under God's rule.'

16. William J. Dumbrell, *The Search for Order: Biblical Eschatology in Focus* (Grand Rapids: Baker, 1994), p. 346.

Walking in God's ways

Genesis presents human beings as creatures in God's image (Gen. 1:27): 'So God created man in his own image, in the image of God he created him; male and female he created them.' J. I. Packer unpacks the biblical phrase 'in God's image' in the following helpful way:

> The statement at the start of the Bible (Gen. 1:26–27, echoed in 5:1; 9:6; 1 Cor. 11:7; James 3:9) that God made man in his own image, so that humans are like God as no other earthly creatures are, tells us that the special dignity of being human is *that, as humans, we may reflect and reproduce at our own creaturely level the holy ways of God*, and thus act as his direct representatives on earth. This is what humans are made to do, and in one sense we are human only to the extent that we are doing it.[17]

Packer rightly sees that walking in God's ways is a persistent biblical theme.

Sadly, the story of God's image takes a tragic turn in Genesis 3. Adam and Eve are exiled from the garden where they walked with God. But God has not abandoned his project. The Creator is determined to have a creature that images his character in the world. Abram/Abraham's call is integral to the plan. God covenants with Abraham and thus begins the divine plan to restore the creation order (Gen. 12:1–3; 15:1–21). Later in the *tôrâ* we find that Abraham's children – God's corporate son Israel – is delivered from Egyptian bondage to become 'a display-people, a showcase to the world of how being in covenant with Yahweh changes a people'.[18] Displaying God in his world involves walking in God's ways:

> The LORD will establish you as his holy people, as he promised you on oath, if you keep the commands of the LORD your God and *walk in his ways*. Then all the peoples on earth will see that you are called by the name of the LORD, and they will fear you. (Deut. 28:9–10, emphasis added)[19]

Ideally, this means that Israel is to be morally different from other nations such as Egypt (Lev. 18:1–5) and Canaan (20:22–23). Israel is

---

17. J. I. Packer, *Concise Theology: A Guide to Historic Christian Beliefs* (Wheaton: Tyndale House, 1993), p. 71, emphasis added.
18. John I. Durham, *Exodus*, WBC 3 (Waco: Word, 1987), p. 263 on Exod. 19:6.
19. The theme of walking in God's revealed ways is found especially in Deuteronomy; e.g. 5:33; 8:6; 10:12; 11:22; 19:9; 26:17; 30:16.

to be a nation set apart (20:24). Israel is to be holy as God is holy (19:2).

The theme of walking in God's ways continues in the NT. Corporately speaking, 1 Peter 2:9 reaffirms the 'display-people' motif of Exodus 19:5–6: 'a chosen people, a royal priesthood, a holy nation, a people belonging to God'. Individually speaking, the OT *imitatio Dei* becomes the NT *imitatio Christi*: 'Whoever claims to live in him must walk as Jesus did' (1 John 2:6).[20] The classic gospel story embodying *imitatio Christi* is found in John 13. Walking in Christ's ways is to be the servant who takes the humble place. Here is other-person-centeredness on display. Jesus makes the intent of his actions clear:

> You call me 'Teacher' and 'Lord', and rightly so, for that is what I am. Now that I, your Lord and Teacher, have washed your feet, you also should wash one another's feet. I have set you an example that you should do as I have done for you. I tell you the truth, no servant is greater than his master, nor is a messenger greater than the one who sent him. Now that you know these things, you will be blessed if you do them. (John 13:13–17)

It is important to note, however, that not all of Jesus' actions are to be imitated by us. The wise preacher discerns the difference between the imitable and the unique. John 13 presents the imitable as we have seen. However, Jesus as the mediator between God and ourselves is a unique vocation: 'For there is one God and one mediator between God and men, the man Christ Jesus, who gave himself as a ransom for all men – the testimony given in its proper time' (1 Tim. 2:5–6).

1 Thessalonians: a case study in balance

Paul spent only three sabbaths preaching in the synagogue in Thessalonica, the capital of the Roman province of Macedonia, before opposition forced him out and ultimately hastened him on to Berea (Acts 17:1–10). Although rejected by the synagogue folk, Paul was far more successful among the Gentiles in Thessalonica. Indeed, these Gentile converts became Exhibit A of the power of the gospel. Paul writes:

----

20. The NIV translation here is more a faithful paraphrase than a translation (lit.
    'The one claiming to abide in him [Jesus] ought to walk as that one walked').

And so you became a model to all the believers in Macedonia and Achaia. The
Lord's message rang out from you not only in Macedonia and Achaia – your
faith in God has become known everywhere. Therefore we do not need to say
anything about it, for they themselves report what kind of reception you gave
us. They tell how you turned to God from idols to serve the living and true God
[clearly he is not referring to Jews], and to wait for his Son from heaven, whom
he raised from the dead – Jesus, who rescues us from the coming wrath. (1 Thess.
1:7–10)

This is a priceless summary of the Pauline gospel to the Gentile world: faith
in God, the break with idolatry, the service of the real God, expectation of
Christ's return, the risen Christ who as saviour delivers his people from the
coming righteous judgment of God, his wrath. Patently, the embrace of the
Pauline gospel was so life transforming that the news of the Thessalonians'
experience had travelled widely.

Importantly for our purposes, we observe that Paul not only left these
Thessalonians with an evangel (gospel) but also with an ethic. He reminds
them, 'For you know what instructions we gave you by the authority of the
Lord Jesus' (4:2). The apostle then elaborates:

It is God's will that you should be sanctified: that you should avoid sexual immorality;
that each of you should learn to control his own body in a way that is holy and
honourable, not in passionate lust like the heathen, who do not know God; and that
in this matter no one should wrong his brother or take advantage of him. The Lord
will punish men for all such sins, as we have already told you and warned you. For
God did not call us to be impure, but to live a holy life. Therefore, he who rejects
this instruction does not reject man but God, who gives you his Holy Spirit.
(1 Thess. 4:3–8)

A holy God desires a holy people. Sexual propriety is part of that desideratum.
Living an other-person-centred lifestyle does no harm to another Christian's
interests. These Thessalonian Christians, then, are no longer to live like they
did as heathens 'in passionate lust'.

It is worth noting that Paul couches his ethical instruction in relational
terms. This is no mere duty ethic. The point he makes is that they must
please God: 'Finally, brothers, we instructed you *how to live in order to please
God*, as in fact you are living. Now we ask you and urge you in the Lord
Jesus to do this more and more' (4:1, emphasis added). In fact, unless this
relational dimension is frequently highlighted in preaching God's words and
walking in God's ways, the Christian ethic could all too easily degenerate into

mere moralism. Christian duty must not lose its connection with devotion.[21]

On a historical note, the Reformers (Luther, Calvin and Cranmer) preserved this Pauline balance in their understanding of catechizing (instructing) church members. The Christian was to be taught a creed to confess (the Apostles' Creed), a way to relate to God devotionally (the Lord's Prayer) and a code of conduct (the Ten Commandments). Teaching these three was the Reformers' strategy for bringing new life to the sixteenth-century church at a grass-roots level.[22] This strategy remains relevant in my view.

Today's preacher

Paul instructs his younger associate Timothy concerning Timothy's preaching ministry in these terms: 'Do your best to present yourself to God as one approved, a workman who does not need to be ashamed and who correctly handles the word of truth' (2 Tim. 2:15). 'The word of truth' in this context is the gospel. It is no great leap, however, to argue that the principle has wider application; namely, that it applies also to the handling of God's Word written. 'Word of God' in the NT is applied most often to the oral presentation of the gospel, but also in places to the Scriptures (cf. 1 Thess. 2:13; Heb. 4:12–13).

What is involved in the right handling of the word of truth today? To start with, the faithful preacher needs to make wise discriminations in expounding the words of God and making ethical applications. Four categories of biblical material need to be distinguished: the *described*, the *prescribed*, the *proscribed* and the *permitted*. For example, although 1 Kings 11 describes Solomon's polygamy, it does not prescribe polygamy as a God-pleasing lifestyle. In fact, the unfolding narrative shows the reverse. We read:

> As Solomon grew old, his wives turned his heart after other gods, and his heart was not fully devoted to the LORD his God, as the heart of David his father had been.

---

21. The great Jewish thinker Abraham Joshua Heschel recognized a similar danger in Judaism when *halakhah* (the moral walk) eclipses *haggadah* (the story of Israel's redemption): it could lead to the loss of God at the centre. See David Hartman's foreword to Fritz A. Rothschild (ed.), *Between God and Man: An Interpretation of Judaism from the Writings of Abraham Joshua Heschel* (New York: Free Press Paperbacks, 1997), p. 2.

22. For the substance of this paragraph, see J. I. Packer, *I Want to Be a Christian* (Wheaton: Tyndale House, 1977), pp. 13–16.

He followed Ashtoreth the goddess of the Sidonians, and Molech the detestable god of the Ammonites. So Solomon did evil in the eyes of the LORD; he did not follow the LORD completely, as David his father had done . . . The LORD became angry with Solomon because his heart had turned away from the LORD, the God of Israel, who had appeared to him twice. Although he had forbidden Solomon to follow other gods, Solomon did not keep the LORD's command. (1 Kgs 11:4–6, 9–10)

These marriages made Solomon into a king like those of the nations around about and declension set in, as can be seen above. Recently I read an argument for gay marriage along the lines that the Bible has polygamy in it and is therefore no guide for a twenty-first-century marital ethic. The *Newsweek* writer Lisa Miller writes:

> Let's try for a minute to take the religious conservatives at their word and *define* marriage as the Bible does . . . Abraham, Jacob, David, Solomon and the kings of Judah and Israel – all these fathers and heroes were polygamists.[23]

This journalist has clearly confused what is simply described in Scripture and what is prescribed with divine approval. Her citing of Solomon's story is a case in point.

The Bible not only contains descriptions of human behaviour: some good, some bad. Scripture also prescribes behaviours, usually by way of divine commands. For example, Scripture does *prescribe* the love of God and neighbour and does not simply describe it (Matt. 22:34–40). Scripture can be negative too. For instance, Scripture does *proscribe* idolatry and does not merely describe it, and does so in both the OT and the NT (e.g. Exod. 20:1–6; 1 John 5:21). Lastly, in places Scripture *permits* a practice and does not simply describe it, prescribe it or proscribe it. Marriage may be embraced but the Christian is not obligated to be married according to Paul (1 Cor. 7:8–9).[24]

The wise preacher also knows that the Bible must be conceived as a whole and not atomized. A text to be preached on needs to be placed in its context in its literary unit in its book in the canon, and considered in the light of the

---

23. Lisa Miller, 'Our Mutual Joy: Opponents of Gay Marriage Often Cite Scripture. But What the Bible Teaches About Love Argues for the Other Side', *Newsweek* (6 Dec. 2008), <http://www.newsweek.com/id/172653/output/print> (accessed 20 Sept. 2010), emphasis added.

24. Personifying Scripture in this way ('Scripture permits') has good apostolic precedent (e.g. Gal. 3:8: 'The Scripture foresaw').

flow of the redemptive history delineated in the Scriptures. Suppose the text is Matthew 13:44–47 with its two brief stories about what ought to be valued.[25] The text runs:

> The kingdom of heaven is like treasure hidden in a field. When a man found it, he hid it again, and then in his joy went and sold all he had and bought that field.
>
> Again, the kingdom of heaven is like a merchant looking for fine pearls. When he found one of great value, he went away and sold everything he had and bought it.

The second block of teaching material that occurs in Matthew's account (13:1–53) provides the context of these two parables about God's kingdom values.

Our two parables are found in the Gospel of Matthew with its explicit links to the OT. It is no accident that early Christianity placed Matthew first in the NT canon. It opens with a genealogy that links Jesus to Abraham, King David and the messianic expectations of Israel (1:1–17). Indeed, the context of our two parables explicitly links Jesus' parabolic teaching with Isaiah 6:9–10 and Psalm 78:2. In terms of the flow of redemptive history, Jesus our parable teacher is speaking of a kingdom that is the hope of Israel. The era of fulfilment has come (13:35). Thus the moral question raised by the parables remains relevant: What ought we to prize?[26] Are we what we eat, as Feuerbach famously argued? Are we what we wear, as the character Meryl Streep plays in the movie *The Devil Wears Prada* might argue? Or are we what we prize, as Jesus taught? 'For where your treasure is, there your heart will be also' (6:21).

Preaching Scripture in a way that draws out its ethical applications needs care. The preacher needs to be sensitive to this need. On the one hand, such preaching must not confuse law and grace. Preaching can easily become moralistic when biblical imperatives lose their connection with the great indicatives of grace. A ladder ethic may replace a response one, as

---

25. Each story is a parable. A parable may be a short comparison, as in the two examples here, or an implied analogy as in Luke 15:3–7, or a longer narrative as in Matt. 13:1–9. See Stephen I. Wright, 'Parables', in Kevin J. Vanhoozer (ed.), *Dictionary for Theological Interpretation of the Bible* (London: SPCK; Grand Rapids: Baker Academic, 2005), pp. 559–562.

26. This is a moral question because it is couched in terms of 'ought'. This is the language of moral obligation.

though by doing the right I climb my way into God's favour. The genius of divine revelation in both OT and New is the way that the nexus between what God has done and how we are consequently to live is shown. Thus in Exodus 20 we find that the Ten Commandments (Exod. 20:3–17) are predicated on God's gracious rescue of Israel: 'I am the LORD your God, who brought you out of Egypt, out of the land of slavery' (20:2). The Ten Commandments are not obligations dropped out of heaven into a relational vacuum. Similarly, in the NT we see Paul argue that we are to '[forgive] each other, just as in Christ God forgave [us]' (Eph. 4:32). Likewise, John maintains that 'we . . . ought to love one another' because God 'loved us and sent his Son as an atoning sacrifice for our sins' (1 John 4:10–11). On the other hand, the preaching of grace and the freedom it brings ought not to lead to licence. Paul develops such an argument in Galatians 5:13–15. He begins with this very point: 'You, my brothers, were called to be free. But do not use your freedom to indulge the sinful nature; rather, serve one another in love.' He elaborates on the notion of love: 'The entire law is summed up in a single command: "Love your neighbour as yourself."' Then he applies his point to the Galatians themselves: 'If you keep on biting and devouring each other, watch out or you will be destroyed by each other.'

One of the challenges facing the preacher of God's words with regard to walking in God's ways is to discern whether there is a key *presupposition* informing a given text, or whether the text enshrines a pertinent moral *principle* or presents a *prescription* to obey. Ephesians 6:1–3 exhibits all three. The passage runs, 'Children, obey your parents in the Lord, for this is right. "Honour your father and mother" – which is the first commandment with a promise – "that it may go well with you and that you may enjoy long life on the earth."' The presupposition relevant to understanding this text and preaching on it pervades both the OT and NT. Relationship brings responsibility is that presupposition. Children are in a relationship that brings obligations.[27] Those obligations are encapsulated in one of the Ten Commandments; namely, honour your father and your mother. That is the principle. But what does the embrace of that principle look like in life? It shows itself in obeying one's parents. 'Obey your parents in the Lord' is the specific prescription. Helpfully, this text shows the character of Paul's moral reasoning because he cites both

---

27. Likewise, fathers are relationally responsible to their children: 'Fathers, do not exasperate your children; instead, bring them up in the training and instruction of the Lord' (Eph. 6:4).

his principle as well as makes a specific application of it to a section of his readership (children).[28]

One way to distinguish between a moral presupposition, moral principle and moral prescription is to recognize that a moral presupposition is more general in nature than a moral principle, which in turn is more general that a moral prescription. Or put another way, the movement is from general to specific.

Finally, the preacher needs to distinguish between what is local in a passage and what is translocal in its import.[29] Paul commends the Philippians for so many aspects of their congregational life (e.g. their partnership in the gospel, Phil. 1:4–5). However, there was a problem with two women who had worked with the apostle in gospel ministry. They could not agree, so Paul appeals to them in 4:2: 'I plead with Euodia and I plead with Syntyche to agree with each other in the Lord.' The local is clearly to the fore. However, when Paul writes to the Romans, he has a prescription by way of a command that is equally clear but translocal in force: 'Hate what is evil; cling to what is good' (Rom. 12:9).

Aristotle, the ancient Greek philosopher, realized that good communication involves more than words. The speaker's life has its own eloquence or shows the lack of it. Ethos, or character, matters.[30] The apostle Paul knew that truth too. He reminded the Thessalonians of the sort of person they found him to be: 'You know how we lived among you for your sake' (1 Thess. 1:5). Later in the letter he elaborates:

> As apostles of Christ we could have been a burden to you, but we were gentle among you, like a mother caring for her little children. We loved you so much that we were delighted to share with you not only the gospel of God but our lives as well, because you had become so dear to us. Surely you remember,

---

28. It is worth noting that for Paul children were fully members of the congregation and therefore worth addressing in their own right.

29. I prefer as more useful and less question begging the distinction between the local and the translocal as opposed to the distinction between the cultural and transcultural.

30. Words did matter to Aristotle. Good communication (rhetoric) involves *logos* (argument) addressed to the mind and *pathos* (moving stories) addressed to the emotions. However, good communication cannot be reduced to *logos* and *pathos*; *ethos* is needed too. See the summaries at <http://courses.durhamtech.edu/perkins/aris.html> (accessed 20 Sept. 2010).

brothers, our toil and hardship; we worked night and day in order not to be a burden to anyone while we preached the gospel of God to you. You are witnesses, and so is God, of how holy, righteous and blameless we were among you who believed. For you know that we dealt with each of you as a father deals with his own children, encouraging, comforting and urging you to live lives worthy of God, who calls you into his kingdom and glory. (1 Thess. 2:6–12)

I have learned from many years of ministry and observing those in ministry that a person's skill-set may make that person a better preacher from a technical point of view (well-organized ideas, carefully chosen illustrations, and so on), but ethos can give the preacher a better hearing. Thus a less skilful preacher may be more effective in impacting a congregation than a more technically able one. Character matters.

Conclusion

God has spoken. God's people need to hear these words of God. The preacher expounds the words of God. Expository preaching is a corollary of special revelation. But the exposition of God's Word written needs to be applied to the conscience. Exposition without application is abortion. We need to know what we ought to believe. We need to know what we ought to value. We need to know how we ought to live. How we ought to live involves at the very least walking in God's ways as we image God's character in the world. Indeed, whether the OT is on view or the New, God's people are to walk in God's ways. On this point there is continuity between the Testaments. Even so, by the NT period the general imitation-of-God theme becomes the more specific imitation of Christ, the image of God. In that light, the preacher wrestles with the ethical implications of the text. Is the text merely descriptive or is it prescriptive or proscriptive or permissive? The preacher also needs to discern whether on view in the biblical text is a moral presupposition or a moral principle or a moral prescription. In addition, the preacher of God's words needs to work out whether the text has only local significance or has translocal relevance. Above all, the evangelical and ethical need each other. There is the gospel (the evangel). An evangelical strength is to recognize, prize and preach the gospel. But there is also 'walking worthy of the gospel' (an ethic). That accent too is in the NT. Over recent years an evangelical weakness I have observed in some churches is to be so fixed on the Great Commission – and with it church planting – that the great Commandments are neglected.[31] Both matter. Faithful preaching of all the words of God can help restore the balance.

© Graham A. Cole, 2011

---

9. REVELATION AND THE JUDGMENTS OF GOD

Peter Jensen

The date 7 February 2009 has been designated 'Black Saturday' in Australia because that was the day of horrendous bushfires in the state of Victoria causing widespread loss of life and property. Three days later, Catch The Fire Ministries (an unfortunate name in the circumstances) released a media statement headed, 'Abortion laws to blame for bush fires?'[1] The release expressed grief for the victims of the tragedy and an appeal for practical action by way of support for victims. But it went further:

> CTFM leader, Pastor Danny Nalliah said he would spearhead an effort to provide every assistance to the devastated communities, although he was not surprised by the bush fires due to a dream he had last October relating to the consequences of the abortion laws passed in Victoria.
>
> He said these bushfires have come as a result of the incendiary abortion laws which decimate life in the womb . . .

The release then proceeded to quote some of the detail of his earlier personal revelation:

---

1. 'Media Release – Abortion Laws to Blame for Bush Fires?' (10 Feb. 2009), <http://catchthefire.com.au/blog/2009/02/10/media-release> (accessed 20 Sept. 2010).

'In my dream I saw fire everywhere with flames burning very high and uncontrollably. With this I woke from my dream with the interpretation as the following words came to me in a flash from the Spirit of God.

'That His conditional protection has been removed from the nation of Australia, in particular Victoria, for approving the slaughter of innocent children in the womb.'

The media release added more of the pastor's response, now that the fires were indeed raging:

'Australia is based on Judeo-Christian values. How far have we as a nation moved from these principles instilled in our nation's inception? How much does it take for a nation to return to God? The Bible is very clear, if you walk out of God's protection and turn your back on Him, you are an open target for the devil to destroy.

'Can we stop the fires? Yes we can! But it will take God's children to rally together and repent and cry unto Him as in 2 Chronicles 7:14.'

Pastor Nalliah had first reported his dream to his national network three months earlier and asked for prayer, although his earlier account contained some differences:

'I saw a man firing randomly with a weapon at people on the streets and many were falling dead. I was very disturbed and was crying. Then the scene changed and I saw fire everywhere with flames burning very high and uncontrollably. With this I awoke from my dream with the interpretation as the following words came to me in a flash from the Spirit of God, "My wrath is about to be released upon Australia, in particular Victoria, for approving the slaughter of the innocent children in the womb. Now, call on My people to repent and pray!" '[2]

The outcry following the publication of the later release was highly critical. Many other Christians were dismayed. Leading newspapers quoted prominent Christian and former Treasurer of Australia Peter Costello as saying:

To link the death and suffering of bushfire victims to other political events is appalling, heartless and wrong. Those who have suffered deserve every support

---

2. 'STOP PRESS – URGENT PRAYER NEEDED REGARDING AUSTRALIA, ESPECIALLY THE STATE OF VICTORIA!!!' (7 Nov. 2008), <http://catchthefire.com.au/blog/2008/11/07/stop-press> (accessed 20 Sept. 2010).

and sympathy. It is beyond the bounds of decency to try to make moral or political points out of such a tragedy.[3]

It was pointed out that amongst the victims there were doubtless those who opposed abortion and there were certainly Christian believers. How could they have been the victims of the wrath of God?

This was no trivial matter. It is worthy of theological reflection for a number of reasons, of which the pastoral is only the most obvious. Indeed, it was not only the reputation of Pastor Nalliah that was at stake, but the reputation of God himself. Two issues confront us at once. First, is it the case that God uses human disasters to express his wrath on the world? Secondly, is it the case that God gives personal revelations of his purposes so that we may understand and explain prophetically what he is doing? To bring the two sharply together, can we say, in the name of God and on the basis of the dream of Pastor Nalliah, that the fires in Victoria were an outcome of the decision by the state of Victoria to loosen the laws concerning abortion?

At one level, the outcry against Pastor Nalliah makes him simply a victim of the age in which we live. His view that we may see God's judgment at work through catastrophes or deliverances was the commonplace of an earlier era. Nor was this merely at a popular level. Theologians certainly endorsed the view that God is active in history and nature and that we may see the outworking of his purposes in the events around us. But they did this without making a claim for a personal revelation about the meaning of the events.

For a comparison, I turn to another Australian example, this time a nineteenth-century sermon. Its short title was, 'The Counsel and Pleasure of God in the Vicissitudes of States and Communities', and its explanatory subtitle ran, 'A sermon, preached in the church of St James, Sydney, on Thursday, November 12, 1829, being the day appointed for a General Thanksgiving to Almighty God, in acknowledgement of his mercy in putting an end to the late severe drought, and in averting his threatened judgments from this colony.' The preacher was the leading local Church of England clergyman of the time,

---

3. Rick Feneley, 'Pastor's Abortion Dream Inflames Bushfire Tragedy', *Sydney Morning Herald* (10 Feb. 2009; rev. 11 Feb. 2009), <http://www.smh.com.au/national/pastors-abortion-dream-inflames-bushfire-tragedy-20090210-832f.html> (accessed 20 Sept. 2010); Christian Kerr, 'Peter Costello Slams Cult's Victorian Bushfire Retribution Claims', *The Australian* (11 Feb. 2009), <http://www.theaustralian.com.au/news/costello-slams-cults-retribution-claims/story-e6frg6of-1111118814587> (accessed 10 Feb. 2011).

Archdeacon (later Bishop) William Grant Broughton, and the sermon was, we are told, 'Published by Direction of His Excellency the Governor.'[4]

Broughton, an English high churchman, had no doubt whatsoever that we may see in the operations of nature the providential hand of God:

> If we can look upon passing events, even those which are apparently the least
> important, and persuade ourselves that they so happen by the impulse of chance
> or fate, or whatever other name we may bestow upon the controlling power,
> instead of acknowledging that all proceed under the wise direction and continual
> superintendence of Him who is the Creator and Governor of all things, then is
> our system no better than one of direct Atheism.[5]

His text was Isaiah 46:10, 'My counsel shall stand, and I will do all my pleasure' (AV), which he readily admitted belongs to Israel in the first instance. But the historical affairs of Israel give a window into God's rule over all the nations. He did not regard the parallel as a simple one. As the context in Isaiah demonstrates, Israel is a special case both in her relationship to God and in the way in which the blessings and judgments of God came upon her miraculously: 'the marks of divine interposition, in their temporal success and failure, were more direct and more visible than are now witnessed, or can be expected with regard to other nations'.[6] Nonetheless, such is the sovereignty of God over his world that communities of men should expect the interposition of 'the finger of God' in their affairs and in accordance with his moral and redemptive purposes.

Broughton claimed that this work of God can be read off the pages of history. According to him, 'every people, in whatever country, has had some appointed purpose to execute in the great scheme of earthly Providence'.[7] But he made special mention of the way in which nations and empires have a role to play in the dissemination of the gospel. He saw the case of Great Britain as the outstanding contemporary example of how God works though human affairs at a national and international level. In the rise of the influence of England throughout the world he perceived a special providence by God, and so called on his hearers to read the signs of the times. He admitted that

---

4. William Grant Broughton, 'The Counsel and Pleasure of God in the Vicissitudes
   of States and Communities' (Sydney: Mansfield, 1829), p. 1.

5. Ibid., p. 5.

6. Ibid., p. 8.

7. Ibid.

many may see the exaltation of the English as merely the result of commerce or curiosity or competition, but when he consulted 'that Sacred Book in which the will and purposes of the great Governor of the world are recorded', he saw that the diffusion of the English, with the accompanying civilization, was a consequence of the will of God to plant the gospel throughout the world. He contrasted the desolation of Australia without the gospel to the 'evident design of Almighty God that this vast tract of country should be, in his own season, replenished with a race of men to whom it is granted to "sanctify the Lord God in their hearts"'.[8] That design his hearers were called upon to play their part in fulfilling.

This was the context in which he addressed the subject of the great drought and the recent blessing of rain. Clearly, God was offering the nation his discipline. The drought could be spoken of as a manifestation of his wrath on their iniquities, a judgment 'we most justly deserved'.[9] In vivid terms, Broughton described what could have happened to their community had God allowed the drought to continue – anarchy, destruction and 'the groans of despair'. Broughton called on his hearers to give thanks to God, and to recognize their utter dependence upon him, for no human aid would have saved them in the drought and famine. But he went further.

Broughton believed that he could see in what had occurred, 'with the plainness of demonstrative evidence', the deepest intention of God:

> It is the counsel and pleasure of God, I repeat, to raise up here a Christian nation; and if by our distresses we are so turned from our former vain conversation as to become indeed doers of the word and not hearers only, then he will bless us in turning away from us the punishment due to our iniquities. National mercies demand national thankfulness; and national thankfulness is best shewn by national reformation.[10]

I have chosen Broughton's sermon because of the similarity of teaching, of provenance and of occasion to the words of Pastor Nalliah, and yet as coming from an utterly different Christian tradition and a different time. Without doubt the point could be illustrated a thousand times over, that it is a commonplace of Christian teaching that God blesses and judges us in this life through historical and natural means and that this may be applied personally as well as communally, to non-Christians as well as to believers. And yet

---

8. Ibid., p. 11.
9. Ibid., p. 13.
10. Ibid., p. 17.

Broughton's sermon was printed and disseminated at the behest of Governor Darling, while Pastor Nalliah's effort was excoriated even by Christians. Why? There are a number of reasons, but one is that the position adopted by Broughton and Nalliah has simply become culturally implausible.

There are two main reasons for implausibility in this connection.

First, as a society, we now have a different conception of God's relationship to the world. To take one illustration only, the state of human knowledge about the weather in Broughton's day was infinitesimally smaller than it is now. It was still possible to experience weather conditions as capricious and unknowable, basically far more like the work of a personal being than the result of the movements of far-off weather events and patterns. Forecasting was close to mere guesswork. Causation could only be a matter of speculation at best. The absence of knowledge could be filled in with prayer and hope for something better. Today, although surprising events may still occur, a prayer for different weather conditions works against the grain of the sheer success of forecasting. Why pray about what will occur in any case?

In his study of secularization, Duncan MacLaren puts the point like this:

> Why ask God to do something that he may or may not do (such as heal a sick person) when the technology has been developed that will do it for certain? In the face of expanding technology, Christian claims about God became increasingly limited to the sphere of unseen, moral transactions (repentance, faith, forgiveness) and withdrew from making instrumental claims about say, healing, crop production, or the weather. The world ceased to be 'charged with the grandeur of God' (as the poet Gerard Manley Hopkins wrote) and instead suffered 'disenchantment'.[11]

When, in our minds, God occupies the sphere of the uncontrollable and the arbitrary, his power seems as vast as our ignorance. The suddenness of the earthquake is easily related to God until we have a history of the earth and a knowledge of tectonic plates. Then we see that earthquakes are not eruptions of God's will wreaking his fury on sinful human beings, but rather the inevitable consequence of the natural history of the world. They are virtually predictable. The animistic-like personalization of world events can hardly survive the advance of science.

But there is a second and even more telling reason why talk of God's providential ordering of the world has become implausible in modern culture. We have changed not just in our attitude to God and the world, but in our attitude

---

11. Duncan MacLaren, *Mission Implausible* (Milton Keynes: Paternoster, 2004), p. 35.

to the character of God. Indeed, this alteration could be said to pre-date the scientific attitude to the world. Take Voltaire's response to the huge disaster of the Lisbon earthquake of 1755 in which over thirty thousand people perished. Famously, he wrote:

Say ye, o'er that yet quivering mass of flesh:
'God is avenged: the wage of sin is death'?
What crime, what sin, had those young hearts conceived
That lie, bleeding and torn, on mother's breast?
Did fallen Lisbon deeper drink of vice
Than London, Paris, or sunlit Madrid?
In these men dance; at Lisbon yawns the abyss.[12]

The problem is in the moral character of God. By what reasoning can we attribute such a mindless disaster, such an indiscriminate slaughter, to the God of justice? In particular, what of infant mortality in such a catastrophe? But not just infant mortality is on view, for the sense that the victims of earthquake or famine or disease are especially cursed and that they have sinned so deeply that God is right to exact vengeance upon them in this manner is difficult to square with any version of modern sensibility. Nor is this to do only with historical events; the 'decline of hell', that is, decline in the belief in judgment and eternal punishment, is also a well-documented phenomenon.[13] If men and women of the western world are inclined to believe in God, it is a God who does not judge adversely and certainly not a God who sends sinners to hell and eternal destruction.

Implausibility is of course not a synonym for falsehood. Our first theological task is to compare modern thought with the truth of God's self-revelation. If in fact that investigation yields a position very close to the traditional one, it remains our task to speak that truth, however uncomfortable. It is equally an obligation that we seek to speak it in a way that will communicate the truth and not distort it or provoke needless opposition. And yet we must acknowledge that in a world which has embraced the gospel of a God without wrath, any reference to his judgment in this life or in the world to come is likely to create furious reaction, and we cannot judge theological rightness or even

---

12. Voltaire, 'Poem on the Lisbon Disaster', *Selected Works of Voltaire*, tr. Joseph McCabe (London: Watts, 1911), p. 1.

13. The phrase comes from Daniel P. Walker, *The Decline of Hell: Seventeenth-Century Discussions of Eternal Torment* (London: Routledge & Kegan Paul, 1964).

missional correctness merely by the strength of negative response. We must therefore turn to the Scriptures. As we do, some preliminary observations may be of help.

First, we ought to note the presence of a strong liberal theological view, which would agree that the older tradition is both implausible and theologically defective. Concerning our view of God's relationship with the world, it would be argued that we cannot now read an inerrant Scripture as though it is making deliverances better left to science to establish. Whether it is best to think of God as somewhat detached from the daily operations of the world (as in deism) or whether we think of him as not being in full control of the world but, so to speak, interacting with it in a generally beneficent way (as in open theism), these are serious attempts to make sense of what most people now believe about the world in which we live while retaining the essence of the Christian message, which is Jesus Christ.

Furthermore, those who refresh the Christian message in this way are also very conscious of the moral difficulty of relating God too closely to catastrophic events in the world by way of judgment. John Macquarrie writes:

> Needless to say, we reject the view that natural evil is to be understood as an instrument of God's justice, whereby he punishes the wicked. This ancient and tenacious belief is already shown to be inadequate in the Old Testament drama of Job, and it is explicitly rejected by Jesus, as when he states that the eighteen people killed by the falling of a tower were not struck down because they were worse than other people.[14]

Proponents wish to stress the biblical message of the love of God and his inclusiveness to all human beings, not his wrath and judgment. Once again, we have a biblical hermeneutic in which the very heart of the biblical story – the presence and activity of Jesus Christ understood as a perfect expression of the love of God – is the controlling element for reading the Bible as a whole. The Scriptures are, so to speak, read out from that centre, and statements or stories or promises in Scripture that seem inconsistent with the love of God are relativized.

Such responses are not to be dismissed out of hand. They constitute an attempt to remain faithful to God's revelation in Christ while making sense of the modern world. Nonetheless, they must be tested against the whole of

---

14. John Macquarrie, *Principles of Christian Theology*, 2nd ed. (London: SCM, 1977), p. 258. The reference is to Luke 13:4–5.

Scripture for faithfulness to the Christian message as it has been delivered to us by those inspired by the Holy Spirit. There comes a moment when our restatement loses touch with the original and becomes inauthentic. Then a new way forward must be found, since even the most plausible restatement must still be true to the revealed gospel.

While we might come to the view that Pastor Nalliah's utterances are more faithful to Scripture than those of many other Christians, there may well still be a weakness in his biblical interpretation. By referring to Australia as being under the 'conditional protection' of God, he seems to equate this nation with Israel. If so, he needs to observe the context of biblical theology as a whole. Broughton made use of the OT, notably Isaiah 46:10. But, as we have already observed, he did so with caution, recognizing its context as part of an address to Israel.

What, however, of the main point? Is it the case that God uses human disasters to express his wrath on the world? Surveying the biblical evidence, we must say the following.

First, God is the righteous Judge and Lord of all. The biblical evidence for this is so abundant that we may take one case chosen almost at random:

> For you are not a God who delights in wickedness;
>   evil may not dwell with you.
> The boastful shall not stand before your eyes;
>   you hate all evildoers.
> You destroy those who speak lies;
>   the LORD abhors the bloodthirsty and deceitful man.
> (Ps. 5:4–6)[15]

God's righteousness is fundamental to his holiness and glory. It necessarily expresses itself in his government of the world, first in the declaration of his moral will for all humanity and then in the condign justice with which he treats those who keep and those who breach his law. Consequently, whether the evidence points to a judgment within history or not, it is perfectly clear that there is to be a Day of Judgment when the deeds, words and even the thoughts of the heart will be tested and rewarded. Hence the words of Paul 'But because of your hard and impenitent heart you are storing up wrath for yourself on the day of wrath when God's righteous judgment will be revealed' (Rom. 2:5).

We have noted already that modern culture regards such a view of God

---

15. Bible quotations in this chapter are from the ESV.

as implausible and that there is an overwhelming temptation for modern Christianity, whether popular or learned, to accept this verdict. There are, however, two major difficulties with this cultural mood and its reflection amongst Christian people. In the first place, it is so thoroughly inconsistent with the teaching of the Bible from first to last that what remains when it is removed is another gospel altogether. It is not merely an adjustment to the Christian religion, a course-correction, so to speak; it is the emasculation of the whole message. Christians may continue to speak of Christ and atonement and of the Holy Spirit, but they are unable to give proper context to these topics, and they have to read the Bible with a constant self-denying ordinance about its obvious sense. More than this – if God is not righteous, then he is not love either; for the God who is love must be righteous and must act righteously as part of the love he bears toward us. Naturally, this is but a small problem for those who have abandoned the Christian faith. It is a major problem, recognized or not, for those who still wish to profess Christ.

The other difficulty with this suppression of the wrath of God is its inconsistency with our aspirations for and experience of the world. The portrait of God admitted by our culture, with his glory and holiness suppressed, is the typical idol. He is less than those who have created him. For even the least morally sensitive of our people seek righteousness in the community and hope that unrighteousness will be punished. When placed in positions of authority as parents or at work or in a voluntary association, they will exercise the prerogatives of the judge and pass sentence on behaviour of which they approve or disapprove. They are quick to condemn others; sometimes they will praise; sometimes they will praise or even condemn themselves. They will seek to put right that which is wrong. So much is the expectation and practice of righteousness a part of human experience that it passes as unremarked as the law of gravity. The unwillingness to attribute it to God is not the superior vantage of the modern person, but the perennial exercise in idolatry that is sinful.

Secondly, God is the creator and sovereign ruler of the world. Once again, this is a statement of the biblical view so easily verified that it is hardly necessary to supply evidence. God is the one who 'created all things, and by your will they existed and were created' (Rev. 4:11); he 'works all things according to the counsel of his will' (Eph. 1:11); he feeds 'the birds of the air' and 'clothes the grass of the field' (Matt. 6:26, 30). Whether it is the plant, or the worm that eats the plant (Jon. 4:6), or the mighty behemoth itself (Job 40:15–24), God made, and God rules. His rule includes his control over the nations of the earth (Isa. 10:5) and his capacity to turn evil to good (Gen. 50:20; Rom. 8:28). The effortless sovereignty of God is signalled in the opening chapter of the Bible in the description of his act of creation through speech alone. This is a theme taken up and deepened by the revelation that God's Word is personal and that he himself 'upholds the universe by the word of his power' (Heb. 1:3).

It is, of course, this view of God and his world that is now judged so implausible that even theologians seek for ways to recalibrate the faith. Once again the result is a small god, so far less than the biblical claims for the true God as to make him a reflection of the human race rather than the sovereign Lord. We cannot underestimate the power of the competing world view, which has created a crisis for the classical view of the sovereignty of God, but nor can we satisfactorily meet it by conceding the very ground on which we need to be standing. Perhaps instead there are two things worth exploring further: the real status of human existence and the nature of divine causation.

Concerning human existence, we need to analyse far more closely the nature of our frailty and dependence. The resources of the modern Western city have contributed to the sense we have of being invulnerable. We have food, shelter, power, communications, mobility, work, medicine, and we have such things in abundance. There is every reason to think we have mastered the world and done so without God. But this, too, is a delusion. It is true that we have enlarged the circle of our power considerably; yet in the totality of the universe that circle of power remains tiny and liable to collapse inward. An ancient city may only have been a week from famine; a modern city may be three months. But, as is demonstrated when a catastrophe occurs, the city we rely on can be turned to rubble and anarchy can be let loose in the world. The chaotic abyss is closer than we think.

Furthermore, our systematic examination of the world and the wondrous results it has brought forth via the scientific revolution have beguiled us into worshipping ourselves as though we alone are the masters of all this knowledge, and it leaves no room for God. But two great biblical principles have been forgotten. The first is that we do not merely look for God in the sphere of the uncontrollable and arbitrary, making his power only as large as our ignorance. The biblical account of God sees him in everything: the tiny as well as the huge, the ordered as well as the disordered, the visible as well as the invisible, that which we understand as well as that which we do not understand. To use the language of a previous generation, God is not 'the God of the gaps', the explanation beyond our explaining, the cause merely of the spectacular, the unexplained, the spooky and the unknown.

The second matter to explore is the mode of God's first-order 'causation' – the biblical description of Christ the Word upholding all things by the word of his power. Here is the personal, all-powerful, all-encompassing undergirding principle beyond our investigation and yet one that is the presupposition of all others. We may not investigate this principle directly, but we may acknowledge its presence indirectly, for it is the source of the perceived order of the universe that enables scientific work to proceed, and it is the source of the sense of meaning and purpose that animates research and continues life itself. This is not to declare wrong the animistic sense that there is in the universe a necessary answer to the questions of why events occur and who is responsible for them. The sense is accurate although the answers are inadequate. They find their proper conclusion in the Lord who upholds all things, who is before all things and in whom all things hold together (Col. 1:17).

Indeed, the fact that all things co-inhere in Christ is a reminder of another key biblical principle: that in him 'are hidden all the treasures of wisdom and knowledge' (Col. 2:3). The extraordinary increase in human understanding of the world has both deceived and emboldened us. Even compared with what may be known, let alone compared with what we do not and will never know, our present knowledge is trifling. We have become arrogant, bloated with our achievements and it has blinded us to the nature of reality. But if Christ is the Word, the organizing principle of the whole universe, then to be ignorant of him is to be ignorant of the very nature of all that is, except at the most superficial level. Conversely, to know him, even though uneducated otherwise, is to know what matters. A scientific knowledge of the world, with its brilliant explanations and accurate predictions, still fails to yield information about the fundamental questions of meaning and purpose.

Thirdly, the world is portrayed in the Bible as an arena of suffering because it is fit for humans alienated from God. The moment of expulsion from Eden is highly significant for the nature of human life in the world. It is an expulsion from joy, from fulfilment, from fellowship with God, from harmony amongst humans, from fruitful labour, from life itself. Deliberately God curses the typical spheres of life with a new bitterness: for the woman, childbirth and family; for the man, his labours in the field. Man and woman are expelled and the way back is barred. They now suffer the heart of death in alienation from God and are propelled towards the pain of death, seeing it first in the murder of one son by another. The murder indicates what becomes clear in the days of Noah: that a large part of the suffering of humanity is self-induced; the sin now carried forward in each person and in every generation creates much of the pain and suffering experienced as the human lot in this world. 'What causes quarrels and what causes fights among you? Is it not this, that your passions are at war within you? You desire and do not have, so you murder. You covet and cannot obtain, so you fight and quarrel' (Jas 4:1–2).

There is a paradox at work here that must be accepted if we are to make sense of what we hear from Scripture and what we may say as a result. On one side, it is true to say that suffering and sin are linked. If we are to think of God's intervening with judgments such as drought and fire, we need first to recognize that the world in itself is a place where judgment is the common experience. It is that sort of world because we are that sort of people. We actually worsen the pain by our exploitation of the world and careless disregard for its operating principles, moral and physical. Our sin contributes mightily to our suffering and to the pain of others. The great, occasional catastrophes – the earthquakes, eruptions, tsunamis, famines and droughts (predictable and explicable or not) – all remind us that we have been expelled from Eden, that we are a wandering tribe, far from our proper home, living with sin in a world antagonistic to sinners. Of all these things, death itself is the symbol and reality of the curse under which we labour as the enemies of God, 'for the wages of sin is death' as Romans 6:23 says succinctly. Indeed, the occasional great catastrophes constitute only the speeding up of the grim harvest death is gathering. Because we are so used to death, we do not see how his work represents the huge and ultimate catastrophe of the human race. Whether in the few hours of Lisbon or in an ordinary day, death afflicts the newborn child and the mature, the wicked and the righteous together. Lisbon only concentrates the mind on the truth all around us.

But there is the other side to this paradox. If in general terms we suffer because we have become alienated from God, this is not necessarily and specifically the case. Even in the general case God deals with us individually. Classically we have the tale of Job, which stands athwart the simplistic equivalence of suffering and sin; indeed, it stands as a testimony to the limits of human wisdom and knowledge and as a perennial reminder that we do not know all there is to know about God's ways. There is a need for caution about too glib an appeal to mystery when the problem is not so much mystery as our unwillingness to hear what God is saying to us. But in this case we rightly come to the limits of human understanding, and the word 'mystery' is not only appropriate, but is reverently necessary:

Who is this that darkens counsel by words without knowledge?
Dress for action like a man;
    I will question you, and you make it known to me.
Where were you when I laid the foundation of the earth?
(Job 38:2–4)

How wise the wisdom of Elihu, 'Behold, God is great, and we know him not' (36:26), and even of Job:

Behold, these are but the outskirts of his ways,
    and how small a whisper do we hear of him!
(26:14)

Hence, too, Jesus testifies to the same truth when he is in the presence of a blind man and is asked a simplistic question, 'Rabbi, who sinned, this man or his parents, that he was born blind?' His response dispelled any notion that all suffering is the direct result of the sin of the sufferer. 'It was not that this man sinned, or his parents, but that the works of God might be displayed in him' (John 9:2–3). So, too, Joseph suffered the punishment of prison for a crime he did not commit and yet experienced this as part of the purpose of God in his plan to bless his people (e.g. Gen. 50:20).

And yet the direct intervention of God in bringing justice to bear within history is also the clear testimony of Scripture. Ananias and Sapphira suffered in this way (Acts 5:1–11). So did Herod, who was struck down by an angel of the Lord, 'because he did not give God the glory, and he was eaten by worms and breathed his last' (12:23). Nor is this merely individuals, nor is it only Israel who suffers the vengeful hand of God within history; the first and second chapters of Amos demonstrate that God's wrath is experienced within the historical process by nations and communities who breach his commandments. Jonah is dispatched to preach judgment to the people of Nineveh. Memorably, Assyria and its king are both the rod of God's fury against his people and the object of his wrath (Isa. 10:5–19). In the opening chapter of Romans the wrath of God is being experienced even now both for and by the behaviour of those who refuse to have the knowledge of God before their eyes. Instances can be multiplied many times over.

In short, there is abundant biblical warrant for those who warn about the present judgment of God on those who break his laws and commandments. Indeed, it may be that one of the reasons for vapid preaching is that we are unwilling to do what our ancestors did in full measure and apply the teaching of Scripture, with the full demands and standards of God, to the social and personal sins of our own day with warnings about the potential consequences of offending God. There is no gospel without the call to repentance, and our repentance involves more than merely the minor faults that are often the worst our feeble consciences make us aware of.

And yet, it is well to remember the further threefold paradox of God's 'strange work' (Isa. 28:21 AV), his work of judgment.

First, although God punishes sin within the present fields of nature and history, there is mystery here, a limit to our knowledge. We ourselves should hesitate before saying directly and simply that we are dealing with God's specific judgment on specific sin. We remember that the man born blind was not thus because either he or his parents sinned. In any case it is almost always good to pause in memory of our own sins and the way in which they also merit the severity of God. This in fact is the word of Jesus. Contrary to the inexact exegesis of John Macquarrie, Jesus did not explicitly reject the view that natural evil is to be understood as an instrument of God's justice. On the contrary, both the moral evil of Pontius Pilate in killing people and the natural evil of the falling tower could be ascribed to a judgment on sin. But he gave no warrant for commenting on the fate of others or speculating on the connection between their fate and their sin. Rather his message was directed to those who invited such speculation: 'unless you repent, you will all likewise perish' (Luke 13:1–5).

There is a further element of paradox. It has to do with the nature of our sin and the nature of the divine response. The original Genesis account is a witness to a certain blessed tension – it tells us that the sin of Adam and Eve was worthy of instant death ('in the day that you eat of it you shall surely die', Gen. 2:17); but in fact they did not die on that day, nor for long afterwards. Instead, the Lord graciously made for Adam and his wife, Eve, garments of skin and clothed them (3:21). Thus, too, although our sin is worthy of instant condemnation, God both waits patiently for repentance and also constantly blesses us through that same natural world which is the arena of our pain (see Acts 15:15–17). Our warnings of his present judgment should be modest enough to acknowledge that God constantly 'makes skins' for us, overlooking the times of ignorance and showering upon us all the riches of his kindness and forbearance and patience (see Acts 17:30; Rom. 2:4). Of course, such modesty must not obscure the fact that there is a final and complete judgment of God and that his intention in showing mercy is to summon us to repentance (Rom. 2:5; 2 Pet. 3:8–9). In short, the preaching of judgment and wrath needs to be eschatological – it must in any case point to the Day to come when God will bring all things to reckoning.

The third aspect of the paradox belongs to the cross. We have noted the temptation of liberal theology to read the Scriptures from a centre that overcomes all references to the wrath and judgment of God, where Jesus Christ is understood as the perfect expression of the love of God. But the death of Jesus Christ, in which we see both utter innocence and the propitiation of the wrath of God by God himself, is the supreme moment when mercy and judgment meet. God's righteous judgment, and so his love, is vindicated in a vicarious and penal death. Hence Paul's great words 'For our sake he made him to be sin who knew no sin, so that in him we might become the righteousness of God' (2 Cor. 5:21). It is not much use preaching either the present love or the present judgments of God unless we do so from the perspective of the cross, for that is where repentance must take us and only there is wrath turned away. Then, too, our present experience can be seen only in the light of God's final purposes, 'through him to reconcile to himself all things, whether on earth or in heaven, making peace by the blood of his cross' (Col. 1:20).

I am addressing two questions. First, is it the case that God uses human disasters to express his wrath on the world? To that I have given a positive reply in that the daily groaning of the world is caught up in the sin of humanity and constantly reminds us that we are under the judgment of God, and also we have evidence that God sends his judgments within the natural and historical order to afflict us from time to time. Thus we may rightly affirm that abortion is an evil, and that it both brings its own painful reward to a society which practises it, and also that it may be that God deals with us in his specific judgment on it here and now.

But there are limits to what we know about specific cases, and always the possibility of misinterpretation. Hence the second question: Is it the case that God gives revelations of his purposes beyond the Scriptures so that we may understand and explain prophetically what he is doing?

In Pastor Nalliah and Archdeacon Broughton we see two different answers to the question. One relies on prophetic inspiration connected to a dream. The second relies on a reading of providence. Although different answers, they have in common what we may perhaps call a reliance on extra-biblical revelation (one special and one general) in order to give particular poignancy to their message. Is this wise?

What should we make of claims to special revelations? One obvious difficulty is the uncontrolled nature of such testimonies. Experience shows that such claims are not confined to Protestant Christianity but are made in Roman Catholicism in connection with alleged appearances of Mary the mother of Jesus, and likewise with religious experiences in non-Christian religions. Likewise, some appear to be vindicated by subsequent events, while many others fail this test. In the case of failures it is frequently said that the lapse was one of interpretation rather than truth.

On the theological front, however, we may express our hesitations differently. The supreme revelation of God is that of his Son, Jesus Christ, as he comes to us in the Scriptures. So great is this revelation that it bears two key characteristics. First, its finality, its sufficiency, its supremacy. Here is the voice and deed of God when faced with the great catastrophe of human sin and the prospect of judgment. The prophecies of the rest of Scripture point to him. The danger with elevating contemporary human experience to the status of special revelation is that it draws attention from Jesus and the reason for his coming into the world. Secondly, there is the public nature of God's revelation of himself. The Scriptures are a public document, addressed to us all. The promises are to all; the commands are to all. The shape of Christian faith and the obedience that flows from it do not come from private revelation of uncertain provenance, but from this great Christ-centred revelation, which all may hear and which all should believe. A catastrophe such as the Victorian bushfires should provoke us to compassionate help in the first instance. But like all disasters, and indeed death itself, it should make us also ponder our personal and corporate relationship with God in the light of his word and lead to repentance for our many failings. In one sense we do not need to know what may be the specific sin for which we are being chastised – our response will be to turn to the Lord with all our heart and to live under the sure guidance of his Word.

None of this is to doubt the sincerity of Pastor Nalliah or others who report similar experiences. But we recognize that we have only his account of God's warning. Further, God's threat was not actually as specific as the later press release intimates; it was not until the advent of the fires that Nalliah could interpret his earlier dream such that the imagery of fire was literal and dominant, while that of a rampaging gunman was only symbolic and secondary. Finally, Nalliah's whole message is set in a framework in which reference is made to the removal of part protection from the nation – a reference that seems to be based on a misreading of Scripture. In my opinion, it would be both going far beyond the evidence and theologically insecure to endorse the view that the bushfires were a direct result of the abortion legislation of the Parliament of Victoria.

Broughton did not claim a direct personal revelation. But he did 'read' providence and applied his sermon in accordance with his reading. In his case there is a far more careful nuancing of what is said; fewer claims are made for it, and the call for thanksgiving and repentance is not actually based on his reading of providence as such. Furthermore, his 'providentialist' account is set within the grand sweep of Scripture as a whole – it is to do with God's stated intention that the gospel is to be planted in all the world. And yet even here there is room for hesitation. By placing the expansion of the British Empire so centrally in the contemporary working out of God's plans – a not impossible thought as we look back in history – he nonetheless overstresses the darkness of the human landscape before the arrival of the British in Australia. Part of the tragedy being enacted on Australian soil even as Broughton was preaching arose from too sanguine a view of the benefits of European civilization and too dismissive a view of the 'primitive' nature of the existing human settlements.

And yet that said, Broughton was on firm biblical grounds in his sermon and challenges us not to concede too much to secular notions of plausibility. We may draw back from claims to personal revelations and sure words about God's mind on contemporary events. But we may draw back too far. There is what we may call a general revelation of God in nature and history, which we may read (with caution) in the light of the special revelation of Scripture, and there should be moments when we call our church, our denomination and our society to account. In so doing, in the right way and the right time we may also indicate that sin has its wages, part of which we experience in the sufferings of this world. Indeed, our unwillingness to apply the Scriptures thus creates a vapid and ineffectual preaching focused on personal piety but not on the working of God's will in the affairs of humanity. But, as we do so, it must always be with the word of Jesus in mind: 'Do you think that they were worse offenders than all the others who lived in Jerusalem? No, I tell you; but unless you repent, you will all likewise perish' (Luke 13:4–5).

10. THE 'HOLY HUSH': BIBLICAL AND THEOLOGICAL REFLECTIONS ON PREACHING WITH UNCTION

Michael Raiter

Introduction: the day the hush descended

Over a long weekend back in January 1989 I spoke at the Katoomba Youth Convention. Beautiful Katoomba, in the Blue Mountains outside Sydney, Australia, hosts a series of Bible-teaching conferences each year, and thousands attend these conventions to hear God's Word expounded and applied. Back then the conventions were held in a large tent that could seat up to four thousand people. This was the first convention I had been invited to participate in and was understandably very nervous. The theme for that weekend was 'Sin in the Life of the Believer'. Traditionally, on the Sunday night one of the speakers has been asked to deliver an explicitly evangelistic address, calling on people to confess their sins and commit their lives to the Lord Jesus Christ. I chose Hebrews 10 for my text, and spoke on sin, the cross and forgiveness. Like every talk delivered by the speakers that weekend, this one was bathed in prayer. Preaching, for the first time, to a crowd of thousands (well in excess of the fifty to a hundred, which had been my normal congregation) is a great motivator for unceasing prayer. As the talk drew to a close, I came to the point where, having explained Christ's atoning work, I began to call on people to turn to the Lord Jesus. At that point in that large tent something remarkable, and utterly unforgettable, happened: an almost tangible stillness fell on the whole crowd. People stopped shuffling. Chairs stopped scraping. The perpetual, gentle hum that accompanies such large gatherings was silenced. It seemed as if everyone stopped moving and listened with a hushed intensity. As I gazed upon that large crowd I knew that, for those few moments, *every one* was listening to every word. And, just as remarkably, at that point I, the speaker, felt myself at one with the crowd. While I was speaking the words, it was as if I was more one of the audience than the one addressing them. For those few moments I knew that the gospel was coming to the crowd with special convicting power. Indeed, later, when the meeting was finished and people had been invited to come to the front to meet and pray with counsellors, I wasn't surprised to see many come forward. The number who responded that night bore testimony to the fact that, indeed, the Spirit had accompanied the preaching of the gospel with unusual blessing.

Not surprisingly, I have often thought of that night. I had experienced the same thing some years earlier as a young preacher, in a small Uniting Church on a Sunday evening, but nothing like it since then. I have proclaimed the Word of God and preached the gospel countless times and, like every preacher, have seen God working through his Word, convicting, rebuking, challenging and transforming people. But I have never known another night like that one. Never again have I experienced that kind of holy stillness, which accompanied my preaching, and have never again seen such a response to my call to turn to Christ.

But others have in their preaching. As I read books on preaching, and the stories of great preachers through history, again and again I have read testimonies of preaching events similar to the one I have just described in my own life. Such moments are sometimes referred to as 'the holy hush', or, more simply, 'the anointing'. Most commonly, though, this kind of special endowment of spiritual power and blessing on preaching is referred to as 'preaching with unction'.

Of course, preachers and theologians from the Reformed wing of evangelicalism have traditionally viewed with great scepticism, if not scorn, any attempt to build a theology of faith or practice, including the practice of preaching, upon the shaky sands of subjective experience. But here is the interesting thing: many of those who testify to, and argue most passionately for, unction in preaching do so out of the Reformed tradition. Indeed, I wonder if it is at this point that two of the church's most uncomfortable bedfellows, the Pentecostal and the Reformed Christian, actually share some common ground: many from both camps testify to, and promote, a theology of unction in preaching.

In this brief chapter in honour of a friend and co-worker in the gospel of the Lord Jesus Christ, Peter Adam, whose preaching I both admire and have been blessed by, I want to explore what is meant by 'preaching with unction' and, in particular, critically examine the biblical justification often presented to support and endorse the experience.

What is preaching with unction?

In the article 'What's Wrong with Contemporary Preaching?' Johnson Lim investigates some of the oft-repeated failings of contemporary preachers. For example, he reprimands them for being professionals before they are preachers. Further, they are passionless; they spend more time preaching *about* God than leading people into *an encounter with* God. And the list goes on. But what, if anything, is at the heart of the modern malaise in preaching? Lim's diagnosis is that 'much of modern preaching is *powerless* because it is *unctionless*'.[1] Therefore, if we want preaching that is genuinely powerful and life-transforming (and that is certainly what our people also want), then we need to rediscover unction in our preaching.

So what is this 'unction'? Of course, 'unction' (Latin *unctus*) has been a well-known theological term referring to any rite of anointing. I suspect that in the contemporary church it is heard more commonly in Pentecostal circles. Sacramentally, the anointing has usually referred to the practice of anointing with oil those who are sick or near death. More widely, it can refer to any endowment of the Holy Spirit that enables or empowers someone for ministry. Consequently, when applied to preaching it is that special endowment of the Holy Spirit that transforms a preacher's words such that they come to the congregation with special awakening and transforming power. In the words of Lee Eclov, 'Unction means the anointing of the Holy Spirit upon a sermon so that something holy and powerful is added to the message that no preacher can generate, no matter how great his skills.'[2]

Defining the indefinable
But can we be more specific? What are the identifiable features of this anointing such that a preacher can recognize whether or not he or she is preaching with unction? While preachers can catalogue the requirements for obtaining

---

1. Johnson T. K. Lim, 'What's Wrong with Contemporary Preaching?', *Church & Society* 4.3 (2001), pp. 115–124, quote p. 120.
2. Lee Eclov, 'How Does Unction Function?', in Haddon Robinson and Craig Larsen (eds.), *The Art and Craft of Biblical Preaching* (Grand Rapids: Zondervan, 2005), p. 81.

the anointing (a holy life, preaching from the Word, preaching soaked in prayer), the experience itself seems shrouded in mystery. Eclov testifies to 'those *inexplicable* moments when I find myself soaring'.[3] The nineteenth- and early twentieth-century pastor, preacher and writer of a classic work on prayer E. M. Bounds describes it as 'this *mysterious* power'. 'Unction', he observes, 'is that indefinable, indescribable something . . . in preaching that cannot be ascribed either to matter or expression, and cannot be described what it is, or from whence it cometh.'[4] Bounds agrees with those who are much more conscious of the presence of unction than its absence. Waxing lyrical he says:

> Every one knows what the freshness of the morning is when orient pearls abound on every blade of grass, but who can describe it, much less produce it of itself? Such is the mystery of spiritual anointing. We know, but we cannot tell to others what it is.[5]

Occasional or continuous?

Is this mysterious unction a continuous, ever-present experience of the preacher or, as in the case of my own personal testimony, is it more of an isolated, unpredictable working of the sovereign God? At this point those who promote the necessity of unction do not agree. Ben Awbrey, Assistant Professor of Preaching at Midwestern Baptist Seminary, observes:

> Though unction is not automatic so that it will be present every time a preacher preaches, it is true that a preacher can preach with unction consistently. There are preachers whose preaching is characterized by unction from sermon to sermon throughout the years.[6]

If at this point I may be permitted a cheeky observation, I would suggest that

---

3. Ibid., p. 84.

4. E. M. Bounds offers two chapters, titled 'Unction, a Necessity' and 'Unction, the Mark of True Gospel Preaching', as chs. 14–15 of his *Preacher and Prayer* (1907) = *Power Through Prayer* (1912). Citations are taken from *The Complete Works of E. M. Bounds on Prayer* (Grand Rapids: Baker, 1990), here p. 478, emphasis added.

5. Bounds, *Complete Works*, p. 477, citing C. H. Spurgeon, 'The Preacher's Private Prayer', *Lectures to My Students* (London: Passmore & Alabaster, 1897), p. 49.

6. Ben Awbrey, 'Preaching with Power: The Need for Unction in Proclaiming God's Word', *Preaching* 24.4 (2009), pp. 6–10, quote p. 9. The article is condensed from Awbrey's *How Effective Sermons Begin* (Fearn: Mentor, 2008), pp. 150–168, where the quote appears at p. 159.

the claim that an individual's preaching is regularly marked by unction is one made more often by the speaker than the listeners!

On the other hand, many of the testimonies of those anointed in their preaching point to an activity that is special, unpredictable and very occasional. For example, in his book *Power in the Pulpit* Jerry Vines testifies to a time in 1976 when he spoke with special power at a conference on evangelism:

> When I began to preach, however, something happened. When I was barely five minutes into the message, the Spirit of God seemed to take complete possession of me. The congregation of mostly preachers was caught up as well. I felt as if I were actually in another world looking on the event. The conference of preachers seemed to be swept along in a flood tide of joy and spiritual excitement. When I was finished, we were all aware that God had visited us. *Never before nor since have I been so stirred and moved by the Holy Spirit.*[7]

I confess that his testimony resonates very closely with my own. However, while recognizing the uniqueness of this particular event, Vines asserts that some preachers (like Spurgeon) did experience such occurrences on an almost weekly basis, and that all preachers should continually seek the Lord for this kind of blessing on their ministry in the expectation that, to varying degrees, they might experience it.

The Doctor and unction

The year 2011 marks the fortieth anniversary of the publication of one of the contemporary Christian classics on preaching, *Preaching and Preachers* by Doctor D. Martyn Lloyd-Jones. The book, which is a transcript of a series of lectures on preaching delivered at Westminster Seminary two years earlier is, according to his biographer Iain Murray, 'in some respects, his most important book'.[8]

The book deals with topics that have become the staple of many books on preaching: the primacy of preaching, the preparation of the preacher, the shape of the sermons, illustrations, pitfalls in preaching, and so forth. The

---

7. Jerry Vines, 'Laying the Foundation', in Jerry Vines and Jim Shaddix (eds.), *Power in the Pulpit* (Chicago: Moody, 1999), p. 67, emphasis added.
8. Iain Murray, *D. Martyn Lloyd-Jones: The Fight of Faith, 1939–1981* (Edinburgh: Banner of Truth, 1990), p. 620.

book's final and climactic chapter is entitled 'Demonstration of the Spirit and of the Power'. In short, it is an apology for the necessity of unction in preaching.

So influential has been Lloyd-Jones as a preacher, and so important this book, that it is worth rehearsing for a moment Lloyd-Jones's argument in this chapter. Lloyd-Jones begins this chapter with the words 'I have kept and reserved to this last lecture what is after all the greatest essential in connection with preaching, and that is the unction and the anointing of the Holy Spirit.'[9]

How does Lloyd-Jones understand unction? He goes on to say:

> It is the Holy Spirit falling upon a preacher in a special manner. It is an access of power. It is God giving power, and enabling, through the Spirit, to the preacher in order that he may do his work in a manner that lifts it up beyond the efforts and endeavours of man to a position in which the preacher is being used by the Spirit and becomes the channel through whom the Spirit works.[10]

To support the contention that unction is 'the greatest essential' in preaching, Lloyd-Jones offers two arguments. First, he seeks to demonstrate that unction in preaching is securely founded upon the witness and teaching of Scripture. Secondly, he then shows how this biblical expectation of anointed preaching can be demonstrated from countless examples in history. The chapter is evenly divided between these two arguments.

First, what biblical evidence does Lloyd-Jones offer to demonstrate that preachers should seek, and expect, to find their preaching blessed with Holy Spirit anointing? To begin with, he points to John the Baptist and the Lord Jesus, both of whom are described by Luke as being anointed with the Holy Spirit, and the expression of this anointing was in their preaching ministry (citing Luke 1:15–17; 3:15–17; 4:18–22). Not surprisingly, the experience of the apostles at Pentecost and throughout the book of Acts is critical for Lloyd-Jones's argument. The 'baptism of the Spirit' which they received, and displayed publicly at Pentecost, 'is not regeneration or sanctification; this is power, power to witness'.[11] Importantly, Lloyd-Jones affirms that 'this 'effusion of power' is not something 'once for all'; it can be repeated, and repeated many times. Along with the preaching of the apostles as described in Acts,

---

9. D. Martyn Lloyd-Jones, *Preaching and Preachers* (London: Hodder & Stoughton, 1971), p. 304.

10. Ibid., p. 305.

11. Ibid., p. 308.

Lloyd-Jones examines the preaching of Stephen and Paul, noting in each instance the relationship between their powerful and effective preaching, and the recognition of the presence of the Spirit. Significantly, he also observes that in every instance this anointing is not announced beforehand, planned or orchestrated; rather, 'they never knew when it was going to happen'.[12] It was a spontaneous dispensation of the Sovereign God.

Turning from the descriptive narrative of the book of Acts to the more prescriptive letters of Paul, Lloyd-Jones finds in Paul's references to his own preaching ministry a number of allusions to, what Lloyd-Jones interprets to be, the apostle's own experience of unction. Importantly, in 1 Corinthians 2 Paul reminds the church how his ministry amongst them of preaching and church planting, while embodied in weakness, fear and faltering human speech was, nevertheless, 'a demonstration of the Spirit's power' (1 Cor. 2:4).[13] For Lloyd-Jones, 'this is the vital and controlling statement with respect to the entire matter'.[14] In short, Paul recognized that his effectiveness as a preacher was not founded upon either the presence or absence of rhetorical or oratorical skills, but the presence or absence of the powerful working of the Spirit. Lloyd-Jones sees this as lying behind Paul's words just two chapters later, that 'the kingdom of God is not a matter of talk but of power' (4:20). Lloyd-Jones also finds allusions to the anointing behind Paul's repeated statements in 2 Corinthians 4 that his effectiveness amongst them was not due to crafty methods, but 'by setting forth the truth plainly' (2 Cor. 4:2), and that 'this all-surpassing power is from God' (4:7). Paul does not deny human effort in preaching but recognized that, while he laboured and struggled, he did so 'with all the energy Christ so powerfully works in me' (Col. 1:29). For Lloyd-Jones, 'that is what is meant by unction': it is divine power achieving what human effort, by itself, is impotent to achieve. In a similar vein, Lloyd-Jones notes Paul's words in 1 Thessalonians 1, which he calls, 'the definitive and controlling statement concerning preaching and evangelism':[15] 'For we know, brothers and sisters, loved by God, that he has chosen you, because our gospel came to you not simply with words but also with power, with the Holy Spirit and deep conviction' (1 Thess. 1:4–5).

Finally, and interestingly, Lloyd-Jones suggests that John's experience of being 'in the Spirit' on the island of Patmos on the Lord's Day, as recorded

---

12. Ibid., p. 311.

13. Bible quotations in this chapter are from the TNIV.

14. Ibid.

15. Ibid., p. 313 (both quotes).

in Revelation 1, is also a reference to his anointing to proclaim the visions he saw.

For Lloyd-Jones this 'clear and unmistakable' weight of biblical evidence confirms his assertion that unction is the central and necessary ingredient for effective preaching. Then, against the cessationists, who would suggest that such unction passed with the death of the last apostle, he presents a sweeping overview of the history of preaching, starting with the Reformers, identifying numerous incidents of men who preached with the same kind of spiritual power as John, Jesus and the apostles. This survey not only supports his contention that unction remains the determinative factor in powerful, transformative preaching, but also demonstrates what form this anointing takes. In other words, by looking at the testimonies and experiences of preachers over the past five hundred years we can read back into the NT and identify what shape the apostolic 'demonstration of the Spirit and of power' took.

There is no need to rehearse Lloyd-Jones's catalogue of anointed preachers, which reads like the *Who's Who* of homileticians (Luther, Calvin, Latimer, Cotton Mather, Wesley, Whitefield, Howell Harris, Daniel Rowlands and D. L. Moody). Of note is an account Lloyd-Jones relates of John Livingstone, a seventeenth-century Scottish preacher. He was a humble, godly man, and a gifted preacher. But on one occasion, after a night of continual prayer, he preached the next morning with great power, 'and as a result of that sermon 500 people were added to the churches in the locality'. Significantly, 'Livingstone lived many years after that but he never had such an experience again.'[16] The experiences Lloyd-Jones recounts vary. For some, like Livingstone, the unction is a one-time, unrepeatable, event; for others, like David Morgan, it marked two years of his preaching ministry.

How, then, does Lloyd-Jones describe this experience? In terms with which we are already familiar he writes:

> How does one know it? It gives clarity of thought, clarity of speech, ease of utterance, a great sense of authority and confidence as you are preaching, an awareness of a power not your own thrilling through the whole of your being, and an indescribable sense of joy . . . when this happens you have a feeling that you are not actually doing the preaching, you are looking on. It is not your effort; you are just the instrument, the channel, the vehicle: and the Spirit is using you, and you are looking on in great enjoyment and astonishment. There is nothing that is in any way comparable to this.[17]

---

16. Ibid., p. 317.
17. Ibid., p. 324.

In summary, Lloyd-Jones asserts that Scripture testifies to this kind of unction in preaching. Church history bears ample testimony to its repeated presence. And even I, who am the least of all the witnesses, can bear testimony to its presence in my own life. But does that settle the argument? Is 'unction in preaching' something we ought to expect ('Seek it' is Lloyd-Jones's final, passionate plea) because our exegesis of the NT has led us to expect it, or have we read back into the writings and testimonies of the apostles our own contemporary experiences? Does the Scripture help us to understand and interpret this experience? Is unction in preaching biblical and, if so, should we be joining the respected Doctor in exhorting all preachers who desire to see their preaching empowered to seek this special anointing regularly? The rest of this chapter will seek to address these questions.

The Bible and the anointing

Anointed apostles

A number of the assertions of those who testify to, and promote, preaching with unction are incontestable. First, the preaching of the Word of God must be accompanied by the ministry of the Holy Spirit for the word to have any lasting effect on the lives of the hearers. Secondly, while the gospel is still preached to saving effect through men and women with false motives (Phil. 1:17), generally speaking the character of the life of the preacher either adorns or belies the truth of the message (1 Thess. 2:3–12). Thirdly, no one would deny the inextricable unity of the Word of God and prayer. The apostles announce to the church in Acts 6, as it faces its first internal crisis, that they must give their attention to prayer and the ministry of the Word. Almost certainly, the prayer referred to here is prayer offered for the effectiveness of the preaching of the gospel. David Peterson comments:

> Even though the word of God is represented in Acts as the powerful means of winning converts and growing churches . . . *prayer* was a necessary accompaniment because it expresses dependence on the Lord, to give boldness in speaking the word, to protect its agents, and to provide opportunities for the word to be heard and believed.[18]

---

18. David G. Peterson, *The Acts of the Apostles*, PNTC (Grand Rapids: Eerdmans; Nottingham: Apollos, 2009), p. 234.

Lloyd-Jones notices the repeated references in the book of Acts to the apostles receiving a special anointing to preach the gospel. At Pentecost, having been filled with the Spirit, Peter stands up and preaches Christ. Later, in the presence of the hostile Sanhedrin, he is again filled with the Spirit and proclaims Christ (Acts 4:8). Following the release of Peter and John, when a large number of believers are gathered together they pray that God might 'enable your servants to speak your word with great boldness', attesting this word with miraculous signs (4:29–30). Luke then records the remarkable answer to this prayer: 'After they prayed, the place where they were meeting was shaken. And they were all filled with the Holy Spirit and spoke the word of God boldly' (4:31).

Repeatedly, then, the apostles receive spiritual power to preach the Word boldly. Mind you, not every reference to being filled with the Spirit in Acts refers to preaching so directly. Stephen is said to be 'full of the Holy Spirit' (7:55) *after* his sermon. Facing the fury of the Sanhedrin, he is given, presumably, a Spirit-filled calmness and a vision of the ascended Christ. In Acts 13 Paul is filled with the Spirit, enabling him to expose the deceit of the false prophet Elymas prophetically. The other significant example of the pairing of the Spirit and bold preaching is the ministry of Apollos. He is described by Luke as 'burning in the Spirit' (a better translation than 'great fervour' [e.g. NIV] or 'burning enthusiasm' [e.g. NRSV]), teaching accurately about Jesus and speaking boldly in the synagogue (18:25–26).

What conclusions are we to draw from this? Lloyd-Jones argues that all preachers should expect this same kind of anointing, which is a special access of power falling upon the preacher. Of course, we would want to exhort every preacher of the gospel to ask the Lord that he or she be filled with the Spirit to preach the Word of God accurately and boldly. This filling is an ongoing experience for the preacher, as much as the individual Christian. But what is the manifestation or expression of this boldness? Luke does not describe any physical manifestations, except for the occasion when the 'place in which they were gathered was shaken'. This seems to be a unique occurrence and, while the Lord may undoubtedly perform a similar work again, no one is suggesting that shaking rooms should consistently accompany anointed preaching. If one feature stands out about the Spirit-empowered preaching of the apostles, it is boldness. Indeed, they are recorded as explicitly praying for this, and this is what is powerfully given to them. It is also worth noting that the apostles pray for, and are granted, boldness in preaching in the context of a hostile environment. In the face of persecution and the threat of death, a prayer for boldness is particularly appropriate. This is not to say that we, too, who preach in quite a different context in our Western churches, do not also need to preach boldly, but the stakes are much higher when your audience is antagonistic and confronts you with murderous intent. So, while agreeing that our preaching should always be accompanied by prayer, and prayer for the word to work powerfully in the lives of the hearers, any suggestion that such anointing is marked by the kinds of physical accompaniments Lloyd-Jones and others describe, and are said to manifest when the preacher experiences unction, is in the end an argument from silence.

1 Corinthians 2:4

> My message (*logos*) and my preaching (*kērygma*) were not with wise and persuasive words, but with a demonstration of the Spirit's power (*en apodeixei pneumatos kai dynameōs*).

Lloyd-Jones and others buttress their arguments for the importance of unction both from the testimony of the book of Acts, but also on some key allusions to it in the letters of Paul. Space does not permit us to examine every reference that has been marshalled to provide biblical warrant for preaching with unction, so we will examine just the two verses regularly seen to speak most directly to the issue.

For those teachers who advocate the necessity of preaching with unction, 1 Corinthians 2:4 is the cardinal verse. Paul explicitly disavows human methods of persuasion, relying solely on the power of the Spirit. It is then assumed that this 'demonstration of the Spirit's power' is referring to the same experience of unction that many preachers have testified to subsequently.

Surprisingly, given the importance of this verse, I am not aware of any attempt by homileticians to engage seriously with what the apostle is actually saying here. For example, Robert V. Rakeshaw in a robust defence of unction begins his section 'Is the Concept Biblical?' with this verse.[19] However, apart from mentioning it, there is no attempt to unpack its meaning. It seems that the very mention of the Holy Spirit in the context of preaching is sufficient to establish the case that 'unction' should accompany every proclamation of the Word.

But is Paul speaking here of unction? Did the 'holy hush' descend upon the people of Corinth when Paul brought the gospel to them? The account

---

19. Robert V. Rakestraw, 'The Power of the Holy Spirit in Your Preaching' (24 Feb. 1992), <http://people.bethel.edu/~rakrob/files/Power_HS_Preaching3.htm> (accessed 20 Sept. 2010).

in Acts of Paul's ministry in Corinth does not provide us with any help. Luke simply notes that 'many of the Corinthians who heard Paul believed and were baptized' (Acts 18:8). However, in the opening chapters of his first letter to the Corinthians Paul reflects on his preaching ministry. Most commentators agree that Paul is reminding the church he founded that he deliberately rejected any style of preaching that smacked of self-promotion or the display of his own cleverness. This is of a piece with the entire section (1:18 – 2:5). Paul repeatedly contrasts God's work amongst them with the seductive methods and worldly wisdom of the wandering sophists. The power God displayed amongst them was, paradoxically, a power displayed in weakness and foolishness. God's foolishness is evidenced threefold in the message of a crucified Saviour (1:18–25), the calling of 'the foolish things of the world' into his church (1:26–31), and the weak and, by the worldly standards of the Corinthians, ineloquent preaching of the apostle (2:1–5).

Renouncing such worldly techniques, Paul encourages the Corinthians to reflect upon his ministry amongst them, which was a demonstration of the Spirit and power. 'Spirit' and 'power' here are probably used as a hendiadys and so the TNIV rightly captures Paul's intention by rendering the phrase 'the Spirit's power'. But what does Paul mean by this? The expression is very brief and, really, our interpretation must be governed by the wider context. Gordon Fee is surely right in suggesting that the *dynamis* here is not a reference to signs and wonders.[20] Given that Paul has just castigated the Jews for their desire for signs and wonders, he would hardly then turn around and seek to authenticate his own ministry by this very thing.

What, then, is Paul referring to? The apostle has not left us completely in the dark, however, as he goes on in the next section (2:6–13) to elaborate on the ministry of the Spirit in the proclamation of the Word. In short, the gospel, which is the power of God to salvation, is appropriated by people as the Spirit of God reveals its mystery to those who, by his grace, have become spiritual (v. 10). It is the Spirit who enables us to know (in the sense of to comprehend or understand) 'what God has freely given us' (v. 12). So what is the evidence that the believers in Corinth are 'spiritual'? It is that, by the power of the Holy Spirit, they have understood the gospel, the mystery of God, having been persuaded by the preaching of the apostle. The person without the Spirit cannot receive such things, but the person with the Spirit rightly judges the truth of the gospel as made known in the preaching of the apostle.

---

20. Gordon D. Fee, *The First Epistle to the Corinthians*, NICNT (Grand Rapids: Eerdmans, 1987), p. 95.

In the light of this, what is 'the demonstration of the Spirit and power'? The demonstration is evidenced in the response of the Corinthians. Their own believing response to the gospel and the subsequent establishment of a church demonstrates that God worked powerfully in their midst.

So is 1 Corinthians 2:4 a reference to Paul's experience of unction in his preaching? I am suggesting that the demonstration of spiritual power Paul refers to here is a reference to the work of the Spirit, through the preaching of the Word, seen in the lives of the hearers. Paul is not speaking of a subjective awareness he might have had of the Spirit speaking through him.

Of course, this is not to say that Paul was not, in some sense, anointed when he spoke. It all depends on what we mean by that. If we mean that, as Paul proclaimed the gospel of the crucified Christ, the Spirit worked and brought understanding, leading to repentance and faith, to the minds and hearts of the hearers, then yes, he was anointed. However, if we are suggesting that some 'holy hush' descended upon the hearers, or there was 'a sense or awareness of God's presence and guidance during (his) preparation and delivery', then there is no evidence that Paul was thinking in those terms.

1 Thessalonians 1:4–5

> For we know, brothers and sisters loved by God, that he has chosen you, because our gospel came to you not simply with words (*en logō*), but also with power (*en dynamei*), with the Holy Spirit and deep conviction (*plērophoria*).

In what is probably Paul's first reference to the Holy Spirit in his letters, the apostle gives to the Thessalonians the grounds for his confidence that God has chosen them (v. 4). It is this immediate context that illuminates the meaning of Paul's words in verse 5. Two significant questions of interpretation bear on Paul's meaning here, and therefore the extent to which this verse can be used to establish either the presence or the necessity of unction in preaching.

First, what was Paul referring to when he spoke of the gospel's coming to the Thessalonians in both 'word' and 'power'? The expression is virtually the same as the one we have just examined in 1 Corinthians 2 and, while a number of commentators prefer to see 'power' here as a reference to Paul's miracles (or, at least, not excluding these in the apostle's mind), it seems preferable to see the meaning here as consistent with the one in 1 Corinthians. In other words, he is speaking of the impact of the gospel on the lives of the hearers. This is consistent with the evidence Paul has already, implicitly, given of their election; namely, the exhibition in their lives of faith, love and hope (1 Thess.

1:3). Further, he then goes on to share with them the reputation they have gained amongst the other churches, both for their open-hearted reception of Paul and his co-workers (v. 9), but also the dramatic life change they underwent as a result of the preaching of the gospel (v. 10). To turn from idols to the living and true God is, indeed, the work of the powerful Spirit.

Secondly, we need to address the question of what Paul meant when he wrote that the gospel came to the Thessalonians with 'deep conviction'. The Greek expression (*plērophoria pollē*) is variously rendered 'full assurance' or 'fullest conviction'. Scholars debate whether this 'full conviction' refers to 'the assurance and confidence with which the missionaries presented the message' or 'the Thessalonians' deep inward persuasion of the truth of the gospel, a token of the Holy Spirit's work in their hearts'.[21] Paul uses the same word in Colossians 2, where he longs for the believers to grasp a deeper understanding (*plērophoria*) of the mystery of Christ. Here in 1 Thessalonians Paul is speaking of this same certainty, and perhaps the assurance that comes with it, that the Spirit engendered in the minds of those who heard the apostles' gospel. What else could have provoked these believers to commit the seditious act of rejecting the gods of their city and empire and turn to One who claimed universal lordship?

In summary, then, the reference here to the power of the Spirit at work through the preaching of the apostles is not a reference to their signs and wonders (although, indisputably, they were a feature of their ministry), nor is it a reference to any observable unction that came upon them and their hearers. It is, again, a reference to the powerful convicting, life-changing impact of the Word of God on the minds and hearts of the hearers.

Hindering the hush

All I have attempted in this brief chapter to this point is to suggest that the attempt to justify biblically, and demand of preachers, preaching with unction understood as a kind of 'holy hush' is questionable. The NT simply does not describe the kind of experience that I, and many others, bear witness to. This does not invalidate the experience but it does, at least, suggest we should be more temperate in our remarks about unction.

---

21. Respectively, I. Howard Marshall, *1 and 2 Thessalonians*, NCB (Grand Rapids: Eerdmans, 1983), p. 54; F. F. Bruce, *1 & 2 Thessalonians*, WBC 45 (Waco: Word, 1982), p. 14.

So, to repeat, this chapter is not intended to be a debunking of 'preaching with unction'. But I am unpersuaded by the rather thoughtless proof-texting that seeks to undergird it, and I am concerned by the way it is presented in some contemporary literature on homiletics. Let me just mention four areas of concern.

First, in order to experience 'unction' the preacher is called to a level of spiritual intensity that, quite simply, I do not find in the NT, and is certainly not true to the experience of most preachers I know. Listen to this writer's description of the kind of attitude necessary for preaching with unction:

> Every preacher should step to the pulpit with a heart that has been God-tested and blood-bleached. But there are times when preachers have an experience akin to Isaiah's, when it seems as though a burning coal from an angel's hand has cauterized our tongue . . . He is the man whose heart has been broken till 'all the vain things that charm me most' have been emptied out, and he waits to speak from a holy hollowness, having for the first time a great capacity for God . . . He has somehow seen the Lord, high and lifted up, till his knees went weak and his tongue tied. Yet when he preaches – gasps, really – the sermon burns with holy oil . . . And we begin to smoulder with some inward poetry, some lyric that fairly jumps from our lips on Sunday . . . [T]here are times, too, when the sole sufficiency of Christ very nearly takes our breath away.[22]

In the year that Uzziah died, Isaiah experienced a vision that, indeed, was profound and unique. It was also his calling to his special ministry. It is not presented to us, though, as a paradigm for the experience of a preacher who desires to proclaim the Word of God faithfully and boldly. Of course, I do not deny that there will probably be times in preachers' lives when certain gospel truths are impressed upon their minds and souls with special, even breathtaking, force; but to imply that such experiences are necessary for effective, Spirit-anointed preaching goes beyond the teaching of the Bible. While acknowledging that such events may not mark every sermon, the clear implication is that this kind of spiritual intensity should be pursued on a regular basis. Paul's advice to Timothy, by contrast, is much plainer: 'Preach the word; be prepared in season and out of season; correct, rebuke and encourage – with great patience and careful instruction' (2 Tim. 4:2). More helpful is George Marsden's description of the preaching style of the obviously anointed Jonathan Edwards:

---

22. Eclov, 'How Does Unction Function?', p. 83.

Although Edwards had none of the dramatic gestures of a Whitefield or a Tennent and was said to preach as though he were staring at the bell-rope in the back of the meetinghouse, he could be remarkably compelling. An admirer described his delivery as 'easy, natural and very solemn. He had not a strong, loud voice; but appeared with such gravity and solemnity, and spake with such distinctness, clearness and precision; his words were so full of ideas, set in such a plain and striking light, that few speakers have been so able to demand the attention of an audience as he.' Through sheer intensity he generated emotion. 'His words often discovered a great degree of inward fervor, without much noise or external emotion, and fell with great weight on the minds of his hearers. He made but little motion of his head or hands in his desk, but spake so as to discover the motion of his own heart, which tended in the most natural and effectual manner to move and affect others.' The combination of controlled but transparent emotion, heartfelt sincerity both in admonition and compassion, inexorable logic, and biblical themes could draw people into sensing the reality of ideas long familiar.[23]

Secondly, there is a demand for a degree of human effort that can be unhelpfully guilt-inducing. One writer urges every preacher, before each sermon, that 'we need to feel our deep need'. Further, if we want the anointing in our preparation, 'We need to knock . . . Do it with confidence, and expect the power to flow.'[24] Bryan Wilkerson observes:

> I have discovered a real and predictable correlation between the condition of my soul and my sense of the Spirit's empowering activity in my preaching. For that reason, I cannot afford to let my devotional connection with God become routine or inconsistent.[25]

I wish I could confess that my devotional life is consistently passionate and vibrant, that I rarely miss a daily quiet time, and that they are seldom perfunctory or pedestrian. Sadly, that is not my experience, nor that of most honest Christians with whom I speak. Does that breed in me complacency? Not at all. I continue to work hard at this important Christian discipline. But at the same time, I do not flail myself because my congregations are robbed of anointed preaching because I haven't met the necessary daily devotional requirements.

---

23. George M. Marsden, *Jonathan Edwards: A Life* (Yale: Yale University Press, 2004), p. 220.

24. Rakestraw, 'Power of the Holy Spirit'.

25. Bryan Wilkerson, 'Unction Junction', *Leadership* 30.1 (2009), p. 57.

Again, let me emphasize that I am not minimizing the importance of the Christian character of the preacher. The preacher's words carry authority when they spring from a life consistent with the message. My concern is that this kind of talk, which peppers most writings on unction, can put the faithful proclaimer of God's Word under considerable guilt. When we read that 'Preaching that will and can transform lives is only possible by "the Holy Spirit and with strong conviction" . . . only a sermon empowered by the Spirit is life transforming', we certainly agree, but the obverse is not the case.[26] Many preachers will testify to delivering sermons that appear to have had little impact on the hearers or, indeed, to having preached for long periods with little evident fruit. Are we to conclude that they lack unction? When I read the long list of conditions for obtaining unction, and there seems little evidence of my sermon having profoundly connected with the congregation, am I to conclude I have not been prayerful enough? Or that I have not sufficiently felt my deep need? Or that I have not knocked enough? Or believed enough? There may be a whole range of reasons why there is little evident response to the gospel, as the apostle Paul and countless missionaries and evangelists have testified.

Thirdly, I am uneasy that inherent in some contemporary expressions of unction is a two-tier approach to preachers; there are the 'haves' and the 'have nots'. E. M. Bounds maintains there is 'a wide spiritual chasm between the preacher who has it and the one who has not'.[27] Certainly, I share the concern of the critics that too many sermons today are not biblically based. Yes, we need to rebuke those preaching entertainers who tickle people's ears with what they want to hear, and do not confront them with the demands and delights of living under Christ's lordship. At the same time, many (perhaps most?) faithful teachers and preachers of God's Word would testify to knowing nothing of the unction Lloyd-Jones and others speak about. And this is *not* an indictment on their preaching or character. Others, like myself, would testify to the very occasional nature of such an experience. Yet, such faithful, godly and, I would say, Spirit-filled preachers can be made to feel disempowered by some of the comments made. While we have rightly rejected orthodox Pentecostal theology, which advocated two types of Christian, the regenerate but powerless 'ordinary' Christian and the empowered 'Spirit-baptized' believer, unfortunately, what we have rejected in our pneumatology we are advocating in our homiletics.

---

26. The citation is from Lim, 'What's Wrong with Contemporary Preaching?', pp. 122–123.
27. Bounds, *Complete Works*, p. 478.

Fourthly, I have noticed in my own preaching, and from the testimonies of others, that there have been numerous times when it has become clear, usually subsequent to the preaching event, that God has worked powerfully through the preached Word and yet at the time I was far from conscious of any special anointing or enabling. To the contrary, I felt at my most powerless. I well recall speaking at a church camp on a Sunday morning, having spent the whole sleepless night before vomiting and feeling absolutely wretched. On top of all that I had lost my voice and could barely be heard. The very last thing I was conscious of was, in Lloyd-Jones's words, an 'awareness of a power not your own thrilling through the whole of your being'; yet, to my surprise and joy, I was informed some weeks later that the message had a remarkable impact on the gathered community. I only mention this because, I suggest, for most preachers this is a far more common experience than the holy hush. Moments when one feels one's great inadequacy as a communicator are the moments the Lord chooses to demonstrate his power. Of course, 'holy hushers' would not disavow this testimony but, again, it warns us against giving undue weight to such experiences of power.

Have we silenced the hush?

In his book *Five Evangelical Leaders*, Christopher Catherwood quotes John Stott, who observes:

> The most privileged and moving experience a preacher can have is when, in the middle of a sermon, a strange hush descends upon the whole congregation. The sleepers have woken up, the coughers have stopped coughing, and the fidgeters are sitting still. No eyes or minds are wandering. Everybody is attending, though not to the preacher. For the preacher is forgotten, and the people are face to face with the living God, listening to his still, small voice.[28]

I know exactly what John Stott is describing, and so do many other preachers. I do not doubt that there are some preachers who experience this unction regularly, although I have never sat under the ministry of such a person. Not only has the 'holy hush' been an isolated experience in my own ministry as a preacher, but I also confess that I am hard pressed, as one who has heard

---

28. Christopher Catherwood, *Five Evangelical Leaders* (London: Hodder & Stoughton, 1984), p. 37.

thousands of sermons, to recall a similar experience as a listener. Again, none of this invalidates the experience. Just as God in his sovereign wisdom sends times of revival to his church, he will similarly, in an extraordinary way, send special blessings on the ministries of those who proclaim the gospel. I, for one, continue to pray that the Lord, for his own glory and the salvation and sanctification of his people, may be pleased to work through this jar of clay in a similar way in the future.

In the meantime, I am suspicious of those who wish to take the special and extraordinary and seek to mandate it as the normal and ongoing. I am sceptical of any regimen of conditions for receiving what God alone, freely, sovereignly and graciously bestows. So, as a preacher of the gospel and a teacher of the Word of God, I keep on exercising this ministry as faithfully, accurately and passionately as I can, God being my helper. I take heed to my life and my doctrine. I recognize that apart from the work of the Spirit, the words I utter are empty gasps of breath. And I know that, under this Spirit, God's Word is powerful and will achieve its purpose in the lives of his people.

11. THE *HOMILIES* AND THEIR USE TODAY

Gerald Bray

Introduction

On 27 January 1542 the convocation of the province of Canterbury voted to produce a series of sermons designed to explain basic Christian doctrine to lay people who were disorientated by changes that had followed the break with Rome eight years earlier. Twelve topics, divided equally into doctrine and discipline, were assigned to members of the convocation, who then went home and wrote up their sermons. They were brought back to the convocation on 16 February 1543, but what happened to them after that is not clear. The king was in a reactionary mood and probably blocked their publication, because they did not appear until soon after the accession of Edward VI in 1547. They must have been popular though, because the idea caught on. After England was reconciled to Rome in 1553, Edmund Bonner, the restored bishop of London and a contributor to the earlier volume, issued his own book of sermons, even recycling two of those that had appeared in 1547. Bonner's book never got very far, but after the restoration of Protestantism, in 1559, yet another book of homilies was issued. Along with those of 1547, they were made part of the church's official teaching in Article 35 of the Thirty-Nine Articles of Religion. After Queen Elizabeth I was excommunicated by the pope in 1570, a further sermon was added to the 1559 book, warning people of the dire consequences that would follow from rebellion against the civil government. No further additions were made, and since 1623 the two Protestant collections have been published together as the *First and Second Books of Homilies* and have enjoyed a semi-official status in the Anglican Church as an important source of its official teaching.[1]

As a technique for instilling Christian principles, the *Homilies* were influential enough to inspire John Wesley to write forty-four sermons of his own, which soon became (and have remained) central to Methodism. In 1859 John Griffiths produced a critical edition of them which has never been superseded and remains the standard source for the text used today, though it was reset and published in a modern format as recently as 2006. Reprints of other nineteenth-century editions have also appeared in recent years, which may indicate that there is a growing interest in the *Homilies*, but for the most part they remain among the least known and least studied texts of the sixteenth-century Reformation.

This is unfortunate, because the *Homilies* are unique, both in their structure and in the role they played in the formative years of the reformed Church of England. No other Christian church, apart from the understandable exception of Methodism, has such a collection of sermons as part of its foundational documents, and nowhere else did anyone try to promote the Reformation by such means, although preaching was clearly central to the ministry of the Reformers. For at least two generations after 1570 the *Homilies* were widely read in churches, especially by those ministers who were not licensed to preach their own sermons. The longer ones were broken up into manageable chunks, so that they could all be read in the course of a year, and for many people they became the chief means by which they absorbed Christian teaching. Even when the *Homilies* were not read on a regular basis they were well known, because their teachings were absorbed by ministerial candidates, who then integrated them into the mind and soul of the church. It was not until the nineteenth century that they passed out of general use, and only in modern times have they become almost completely unknown.

The *First Book of Homilies* is clearly divided into six doctrinal sermons and six disciplinary ones, following the form (though not the content) of the Ten Articles of 1536. The doctrinal section is not comprehensive, but concentrates on those points most in need of elucidation after the Reformation. Pride of place is given to the interpretation of Scripture, because the Bible was henceforth to be the church's sole authority in matters of faith. As Article 6 clearly states, what could not be shown to derive from it was not to be imposed on

---

1. *The Homilies to Be Read in Churches*, Bishopstone, Herts.: Brynmill, 2006.

the church. The reader is then taken in quick and logical succession through the fall of mankind, salvation, faith, works and love. The disciplinary section is very different, with the emphasis falling on practical matters of personal belief and behaviour. A homily on the dangers of swearing is followed by one on backsliding and another on the fear of death. From there it moves on to obedience (enjoined), fornication and contentiousness (both forbidden). The choice of topics gives us a good idea of what the leaders of the church feared most at the time, but as all but one of them (the one on fornication) is anonymous, we do not know how representative the individual authors were. This is in sharp contrast to the doctrinal half, where no fewer than four of the sermons were written by Thomas Cranmer, although the other two were penned by conservative opponents of the Reformation (Edmund Bonner and John Harpsfield).

Topical preaching

As a collection of topical sermons, the *Homilies* are somewhat unusual in the history of Christian preaching. For many centuries before the Reformation it had been understood that sermons should be expository, the preacher taking a text of Scripture and expounding it to make it relevant to the hearers. Whole collections of such sermons survive from ancient times and men like John Chrysostom and Augustine of Hippo were acknowledged masters of the genre. In fact, Chrysostom was enjoying a revival of interest at the time of the Reformation, having been virtually unknown in Western Europe for most of the medieval period. The leading Reformers clearly preferred to preach expository sermons, and Calvin (in particular) approached the challenge in a systematic way, aiming eventually to cover the entire Bible. Modern readers of these sermons sometimes wonder what they have to do with the passage supposedly being expounded, and it must be admitted that digression is often at least as prominent as commentary, but however many lapses there may have been, the expository principle was normally preserved. If a preacher wanted to tackle a particular subject, he would find a text dealing with it and develop it from there. A good example of this procedure can be found in the convocation sermons of the province of Canterbury, many of which survive from the fourteenth century to the present day. They invariably start from a biblical text, but as they deal mainly with the burning issues of the day, they cannot be regarded as expositions in any normal sense. In this respect, the Anglican *Homilies* are something of a novelty, because although they could easily have followed this traditional pattern, they did not. It is true that biblical texts were introduced in the course of the homily in order to support its argument, although modern readers may find some of the verses quoted in this way less than convincing. That does not necessarily invalidate what the homilies are saying, which may be justified on other grounds, but it must make us cautious about claiming that they were 'biblically based' in the way we would understand that term today. For example, the long homily against civil rebellion is egregious in its quoting of the Bible, but this is open to question because it is clear that the main motive behind it was political and that the Word of God was being used to support established government in ways that even then seemed dubious to many.

It would have been possible for the English Reformers to have composed sermons dealing with what we would now call 'the great themes of the Bible', but they did not do so. Their aim was to address the issues that lay at the heart of the Reformation and to apply them to the lives of their hearers. A strong case can be made for saying that those issues occupy a prominent place in the Bible and that choosing to expound them was not 'unbiblical', but even so, it must be acknowledged that it was the circumstances of the time and not the general drift of the Scriptural text that set the agenda for the *Homilies*. Because of that, their usefulness and applicability today depends not so much on their exposition of the Bible, but on the continuing importance of the doctrines and disciplines they deal with. In other words, the *Homilies* are significant for the life of the modern church to the extent that the issues raised at the time of the Reformation remain vital for its spiritual health and godly witness. They are not really models of exposition, even if good exposition can be found in them, but sources of applied doctrine. It is in this respect that they retain their value as a model and challenge for preachers today.

The first difficulty in preaching a series of topical sermons is choosing what to cover, and here the *Homilies* are highly selective. No one would dispute that the doctrinal subjects in the first book are of prime importance, but a great deal has been left out and the choice reflects an age in which basic Christian principles were more widely understood and accepted than they would be now. If we were to create a new book of homilies for the use of the modern church, we would need to include a wider range of fundamental theological topics, including subjects like creation and Christology, that were taken for granted in the sixteenth century but are misunderstood or even unknown today. This does not invalidate the *Homilies* of course, but it reminds us that modern people are beginners in the Christian faith to an extent that was not generally true in the sixteenth century. Most of what they say assumes a degree of Christian knowledge that is increasingly rare, and it is sobering to reflect that, in spite of our greatly improved access to information and technology, in spiritual terms we have fallen far behind most of the people for whom the *Homilies* were originally written. They are no longer an Alpha course, as they were meant to be, but somewhere further down the road – an Omicron perhaps, in relation to the complete Omega! This needs to be said because a modern enthusiast for the *Homilies* might try to use them without taking account of the change of context and draw the wrong conclusions from his failure to communicate their message. The nature of this problem can perhaps best be measured by looking at the first homily, which in many ways is the one closest to our modern concerns. This is the homily on Scripture itself, which we now recognize as the work of Thomas Cranmer.

A modern preacher would probably give his sermon on this subject a title like 'Can the Bible Be Trusted?' or 'Is the Bible True?' It is no longer taken for granted that the Bible is the Word of God and most modern discussions of the subject, even among believing Christians, concentrate on such matters as its infallibility and inerrancy. Cranmer, by contrast, says nothing about any of those things. In his day nobody questioned the trustworthiness of Scripture, and virtually everyone assumed it was both infallible and inerrant, even if they did not use those words. This meant that he could safely ignore such issues and move on to something of greater practical importance: how the text should function in the life of the believer and of the church. His approach is clear from the opening lines:

> Unto a Christian man, there can be nothing either more necessary, or profitable, than the knowledge of Holy Scripture; forasmuch as in it, is contained God's true Word, setting forth his glory, and also man's duty. And there is no truth nor doctrine, necessary for our justification, and everlasting salvation, but that is, or may be, drawn out of that fountain, or well of truth. Therefore, as many as be desirous to enter into the right, and perfect way unto God, must apply their minds, to know holy Scripture; without the which, they can neither sufficiently know God, and his will, neither their office and duty. (*First Book*, first homily)

The profundity of these words is evident to anyone who reads them carefully, but a modern preacher might have to devote several sermons to them, whereas Cranmer evidently felt that his hearers would be convicted by them without further explanation. Perhaps the most interesting thing about this passage is the way in which he explains what the Bible is about: God's glory and man's duty. For him, the Bible was not a collection of spiritual insights from ancient times designed to help us along our spiritual journey, but a word from the Lord which makes it perfectly clear who God is and where we stand in relation to him. The issue of its divine inspiration Cranmer tackles like this:

The words of holy Scripture be called, *words of everlasting life*, for they be God's instrument, ordained for the same purpose. They have power to convert, through God's promise, and they be effectual, through God's assistance; and being received in a faithful heart, they have ever, an heavenly spiritual working in them. (*First Book*, first homily)

Here we have epitomized the doctrine of divine inspiration, explained not from any theory of how it might have occurred but from the results it effects in the lives of people who hear and believe. Those who might question the doctrine need only try it out and see for themselves whether it works or not. Cranmer was in no doubt that such an experiment would prove him right. His quotations from the Bible are of the kind we see here (John 6:68) rather than those we might expect from a modern apologist (e.g. 2 Tim. 3:16; 2 Pet. 1:21). Of course, we live in the twenty-first century, not in the sixteenth, and we cannot make the same assumptions he did, but the danger for the modern expositor is that he will err on the side of 'objectivity' in trying to prove what the Bible is and ignore what for Cranmer was ultimately more important: what it *does* in the hearts and lives of Christians, a concern that remains valid for us today. We may have to package it differently and explain it more fully, but we must not lose sight of the reality that the ultimate proof of the pudding is in the eating. The modern church is often tempted to become too cerebral and academic, but the *Homilies* never fall into that trap. The theological principles are there, to be sure, but they are applied, and it is the challenge to do that which strikes us most forcefully now.

What should we do then with this first and most fundamental of the homilies? To preach it as it stands is possible – it would take about forty minutes to read, but as it is divided into two parts it could be stretched over two Sundays without undue strain on the hearers – but it would probably not be very effective, if only because it is too rich in content. Every word needs to be pondered and every thought absorbed, which is impossible in the setting of most modern worship. Almost certainly therefore, the best use of the homily today is as a text for use in the classroom. It might be taken up by an adult Sunday school class, but it would probably make more sense to use it as a textbook for the training of preachers. After all, they are the ones who most need to think through the principles it contains and find ways of applying them in their own biblical exposition today. This homily might never be mentioned in a modern sermon, but it could serve as a hermeneutical guide to the way in which the preacher treats his text. Preaching that remains purely theoretical is useless, but preaching that applies the text in ways that do not glorify God and show us our duty in the light of that can be downright harmful. Getting the balance right is what preaching is all about, and it is in preaching that the power of Scripture as the Word of God is most clearly seen. Those basic truths have not altered since Cranmer's time, and it is at that level that we must absorb his message and recycle it for use in the church today.

Another problem with preaching topical sermons is knowing what to include in them and when to stop. A subject like Christology could easily occupy an entire lecture series and it is difficult to condense all that needs to be said about it into a single sermon. Nowadays however, people seldom follow a series all the way through (though they may listen to a recording) and that restricts the preacher's scope. For example, the third homily, on justification or salvation, is a masterpiece of condensation, but it would still take at least an hour to deliver and is so full of important points that few people could grasp it in such a short space of time. As always, Cranmer's gift for brevity shines through, and we are left in no doubt of what salvation is about:

> Because all men be sinners, and offenders against God, and breakers of his law and commandments, therefore can no man by his own acts, works, and deeds, seem they never so good, be justified and made righteous before God; but every man of necessity, is constrained to seek for another righteousness or justification, to be received at God's own hands, that is to say, the remission, pardon and forgiveness of his sins and trespasses, in such things as he hath offended. And this justification or righteousness, which we so receive by God's mercy and Christ's merits, embraced by faith, is taken, accepted and allowed of God, for our perfect and full justification. (*First Book*, third homily)

It would be hard to come up with a more succinct definition of the gospel, but to begin a modern sermon in this way would probably lead to mental overload and be counterproductive. Worse still, those few who have heard it all before would be tempted to nod their heads in agreement and fail to contemplate the deeper significance of what is being said here, much in the same way that we recite the creeds without actually thinking about their content. As with the homily on Scripture, we are dealing with a course of theological study that the preacher needs to unpack if he is going to communicate it to a modern congregation. At the same time, the homily reminds us that we are touching on a concept that cannot simply be analysed and dealt with one piece at a time, without constant reference to the whole picture. To preach that we are miserable sinners, but not get to the gospel until week six of the series, would be irresponsible and (in spiritual terms) impossible. Conviction of sin must be accompanied by a word of deliverance, since otherwise its purpose is misdirected. As Jesus himself said, he did not come into the world to condemn it, but to save it (John 3:17), and for us to give any other impression would be to deny both him and his message.

But there is only so much that can be said in twenty minutes, and given such time constraints, the temptation to gloss over the nasty bits can be overwhelming. This is what we all too often find in the modern church. Jesus is presented to us as the answer, which he is, but the exact nature of the problem is never explained! What is he the answer to? Why do I need him, if there is nothing very obviously wrong with me? An alcoholic or a drug addict may need to be delivered from his troubles – we can all understand that – but why should an ordinary, clean-living citizen bother with Jesus? Modern people do not really believe they are sinners in any fundamental sense, and getting that message across is one of the hardest tasks a preacher faces. It takes time, and may have to be gone into in great detail, as Cranmer actually does in his first sentence. We may need to have the message brought home to us in all its different aspects before we actually accept it, and the deficit of 'hellfire and brimstone' preaching today is one of the main causes of the modern church's spiritual weakness. But preaching of this kind, necessary as it is, can never be separated from the promise of redemption. That too has many aspects that need to be expounded, which can be understood properly only as we grow in awareness of our needs as sinners. What the homily helps us to see is that it all has to be kept within a framework, the 'big picture' as people say nowadays. To analyse it to the point of fragmentation is to miss the wood for the trees and lose the message, but to talk about the wood without examining the trees would be just as bad. What Cranmer has done has been to provide us with a way we can do both, and if we understand that, then his homily on salvation can come alive for us as it did for those who first heard it.

The use of the Bible

A third difficulty with topical preaching is the need for the preacher to justify his argument from the Bible. Here he can find himself in a real dilemma. If he restricts himself to a minimum number of proof texts, he may be accused of basing his argument on too narrow a selection of passages; but if he refers to everything he can find on the subject, he may be taking his hearers on a text-hunt through the Bible that causes them to lose his train of thought. Either way, the subject is likely to be lost in distraction and the point he is trying to make be obscured. The problem is that although the Bible handles a wide range of subjects, including all of those found in the *Homilies*, it does not treat them thematically. Instead, the biblical writers introduce them as they go along, weaving them into a wider narrative or assuming that readers will be able to work out how what they are saying is related to fundamental principles. The apostle Paul frequently exhorted churches to remember what they had been taught without specifying what that was, leaving us to piece it together from the way in which he dealt with errors or misunderstandings. On justification by faith, for example, he disposed of a number of obstacles that hindered the Galatians from accepting it, and in doing so appealed to the OT in ways that sometimes seem strange to us, as in his references to Hagar and Sarah. For us to reconstruct his doctrine of justification, we have to understand how Paul read the whole Bible, in order to explain what he was talking about in Galatians. For a systematic expositor this can cause problems if he digresses from the text before him and his hearers get lost en route. In the sixteenth century it was common for expositors to do just that. Martin Bucer's lectures on Ephesians, given at Cambridge in 1551, are full of doctrinal digressions that provide the context needed to explain the epistle, but some of them are so long that by the time Bucer gets back to the text the reader has forgotten what it was all about. John Calvin recognized this weakness and avoided it in his commentaries by consciously relegating theological discussion to the *Institutes*, but his sermons inevitably combine the two. The result is that even in Calvin, what purports to be an exposition of certain verses can become more like a thematic study of a particular subject they are touching on and the original context fades into the background.

The preacher who wants to tackle a topic in depth, and not merely deal with it in passing, is therefore forced to decide how he will use the Scriptures to do it. Should he take one or two verses as his starting point and construct the message from there? Or should he be more eclectic, elaborating the subject in a coherent way and citing biblical references only to back up his assertions? For better or worse, the *Homilies* follow the second of these options, thereby running the risk of finding isolated Bible verses to confirm what is being said, whether they really support the case being made or not. Here we have to face the fact that the sixteenth century was more tolerant in its acceptance of the ways in which preachers used the Bible than we are today. They could use (or allude to) texts to support particular arguments in ways that would be inadmissible, or at least controversial, now. Here the *Homilies* cannot be our guide. If historical and textual criticism has achieved anything, it has made us much more sensitive to the ways in which the Bible can legitimately be used.

We understand, better than our ancestors did, how important it is to make sure that what we say is genuinely biblical, and not just superficially so. For example, we may think it a bad idea to let a church building go to ruin, but how do we justify this from the Bible? What passages could we reasonably cite in order to defend our position? There were no church buildings in the NT period, so it is hardly surprising that it does not give us any guidance about how to maintain them. Realizing this, some people may be drawn to the Jerusalem temple as their prototype and defend their position on the basis of God's commands to the kings of Judah to keep it in good repair. The anonymous homilist who wrote on this subject did just that:

> We read in the fourth Book of the Kings, how that King Joas[h], being a godly prince, gave commandment to the priests, to convert certain offerings of the people, towards the reparation and amendment of God's Temple (2 Kings 12:4–5). Like commandment gave that most godly King Josias [Josiah], concerning the reparation and re-edification of God's Temple, which in his time he found in sore decay (2 Kings 22:3–6). It hath pleased Almighty God, that these histories touching the re-edifying and repairing of his holy Temple, should be written at large, to the end we should be taught thereby first, that God is well-pleased, that God is well-pleased that his people should have a convenient place to resort unto, and to come together to praise and magnify God's holy Name. (*Second Book*, third homily)

How legitimate is this interpretation? The temple had a place in Israel's life that no church building can claim today, and reconstructing it was closely tied to the nation's mission, as Jesus demonstrated when he identified himself with it. Interestingly, the anonymous homilist anticipated this objection, and answered it as follows:

> To this may be easily answered, first that our churches are not destitute of promises, forasmuch as our Saviour Christ saith, *Where two or three are gathered together in my name, there am I in the midst of them* (Matthew 18:20). A great number therefore coming to church together, in the name of Christ, have there, that is to say in the church, their God and Saviour Christ Jesus, present among the congregation of his faithful people by his grace, by his favour and godly assistance, according to his most assured and comfortable promises. Why then ought not Christian people to build them temples and churches, having as great promises of the presence of God, as ever had Salomon [*sic*] for the material temple which he did build? (*Second Book*, third homily)

The argument used here is based on biblical principles which at first sight appear to have little to do with the subject under discussion, but which make more sense when seen in the light of Scripture as a whole. First, we are reminded that Jesus promised to be with his people when they worshipped him, and church buildings are the normal venue for that. Secondly, the NT does not abolish the promises made in the Old, but fulfils and enlarges them.

It is hard to see why God would care so much about a building that would eventually become redundant but not bother at all about the way he would be glorified after that had happened. It is by putting these considerations together that we get a picture of how the need to keep church buildings in good repair can be justified on the basis of Scripture and thus answer a question the NT did not address. Today we would probably see no need to go into this particular subject in such detail, but the despoliation of church property by greedy laymen was a serious problem in the late sixteenth century and had to be dealt with. What the homily does is give us a model for arguing a case not clearly stated in Scripture but which can legitimately be derived from it. Our problems today may be very different, but they are no less serious and often demand a similar effort of constructive exegesis. The Bible says nothing about euthanasia, abortion, nuclear weapons or even copyright laws, but the church can hardly avoid these issues simply by claiming that Scripture has nothing to say about them. Of course, particular interpretations may be open to challenge – after all, not everyone thinks it necessary to keep repairing old church buildings – but the principle remains valid and a homily that on the surface seems remote from our everyday concerns may have more to offer us than at first sight appears.

The Bible also shows us how the topics we select for preaching ought to be treated. Everything in our ministry must centre on Jesus Christ and exalt him, so that his people may hear his word and obey it. This is relatively easy to do when we are dealing with a doctrinal subject, but much harder when we are talking about something like gluttony, for example. Of course, Jesus spoke to this issue and the Bible has a great deal to say about eating and drinking, but that is part of the problem. A topical sermon has to range reasonably widely through the scriptural testimony so as not to appear to be lopsided, but at the same time it also has to concentrate on specific things. In a case like this, it would obviously be impossible to deal exhaustively with all the biblical evidence, so selection is imperative. But what do we select? Do we concentrate on principles, such as those laid down in the Sermon on the Mount, or do we find examples of people who ate and drank too much and focus on them? Or should we combine biblical principles with biblical illustrations, in order to make practical applications to our own situations? That is the solution preferred by the homily on the subject, which is further contextualized by being coupled with another sermon outlining the importance and purpose of fasting. As the homilist writes:

Understand ye therefore, that Almighty God, to the end that we might *keep ourselves undefiled* (James 1:27), and *serve him in holiness and righteousness* (Luke 1:74–75), according to his word, hath charged in his Scriptures so many as *look for the glorious appearing of our Saviour Christ, to lead their lives in all sobriety, modesty, and temperance* (Titus 2:12–13). Whereby we may learn how necessary it is, for every Christian that will not be found unready at the coming of our Saviour Christ, to *live soberminded in the present world . . .* (1 Peter 5:8–9). (*Second Book*, fifth homily)

Having established the principle by referring to a wide variety of biblical sources, the homilist goes on to recount the experiences of particular individuals, starting with Adam and Eve and continuing from there to include Noah, Lot and David, not to mention Holophernes (from the apocryphal book of Judith) and Alexander the Great! The sin is an ancient and universal one, and demands vigilance on our part. We live in a fallen world but are meant to shine out in it as lights in a dark place: a maxim that can be widely and constantly applied to the circumstances of everyday life.

The importance of discipline

Mention of gluttony brings us to one of the main themes of the *Homilies* as a whole: the need for discipline in the Christian life. The compilers of the first book thought it important to stress personal sins and failings. They began with rash swearing, something many people today would regard as fairly trivial but which is expressly forbidden by the third commandment because of its great theological significance. To take God's name in vain is to deny or despise his power, and that is the first step that leads to all the other sins. Backsliding, the subject of the next homily, follows naturally from this, because to dishonour God's name is to fall away from him. That in turn leads to an inordinate fear of death, the topic of the next homily, because we are burdened with guilt for what we have done and fear punishment. The only remedy for that is obedience to God and his Word (the next homily), but all too often we fail to see the obvious answer and turn even farther away from him instead. That produces a dysfunctional life, which comes out most clearly in broken relationships: in adultery that destroys the home, and in argumentativeness that destroys society (the last two homilies). In a word, we become insufferable both in and out of doors and the result is self-destruction.

The *Second Book of Homilies* is less carefully structured than the first, but there is still some attempt to group related themes together. The first four sermons deal with public worship and the service of the church, a reminder that our faith can never be privatized but has to be fully and adequately displayed and proclaimed in public. This means our worship must be pure and everything should be done decently and in order. The next area of concentration was on personal self-discipline, particularly in the matters of food and clothing, and there are three homilies devoted to this. Jesus had already taught his disciples not to expend inordinate amounts of energy on such things, but in every generation there are people who live to eat and who will do almost anything to keep up appearances. These are both 'lusts of the flesh', a term that has unfortunately been restricted in modern times to sexual desires. They are particularly serious because they deal with a half-truth: we all have to eat and wear clothing, and if we do not have these basic necessities we will not be free to worship God as we are commanded to. Jesus knew that, and told his disciples that God would take care of them, so that they should not be preoccupied with such things. That is a hard lesson to learn, which may explain why the *Homilies* spend so much time trying to inculcate it.

The next group of sermons deals with prayer and the sacraments, which lie at the heart of our worship. Following them we have a homily devoted to examining the hard parts of Scripture and how we are to use them, along with another on almsgiving. The former of these deals with an obstacle that might prevent us from worshipping God to the full, whereas the latter is an expression of our worship, somewhat sadly represented today by the 'collection' taken up at most services.

From there we move on to the church's year, beginning with Christmas and continuing through Good Friday and Easter, before culminating with Pentecost. The festivals treated are the major ones at which every parishioner was expected to be present. Easter is followed by a sermon on the worthy reception of holy communion, because it was at that feast, more than at the others, that every member of the congregation was expected to communicate. The cycle ends with Rogationtide, when the fields were blessed for the spring sowing. This seems odd to us now, but in a society that was overwhelmingly agricultural, Rogation had a significance scarcely less than that of the great feasts. Its inclusion in the cycle is a reminder to us that the Christian year followed the rhythm of the seasons and was closely connected to everyday life, something that remains of prime importance today. Here is an area of church life where the southern hemisphere (virtually unknown in the sixteenth century) faces a particular challenge, because of the reversal of the seasons. It is impossible to invert the calendar, but there is surely room for some creative thinking about how to rework festivals that were originally designed for exactly the opposite time of year.

Finally, we come to miscellaneous sermons, devoted to important topics but not easily classifiable. Matrimony is of perennial significance, but at no time more than today, when it is under threat from so many different quarters.

Idleness needs to be rethought now that we have so much leisure time and (potentially at least) opportunity for doing things not tied to the bare necessities of survival. Repentance is another matter that is always necessary, and civil rebellion is also a more important topic than many of us might think, particularly at a time when so many people are disenchanted with democracy and seem to believe that freedom allows them to take matters into their own hands. The list of topics covered is not exhaustive – it is already a supplement to the sermons in the *First Book of Homilies* – but it offers us a pattern of what we ought to be looking for and of what we can achieve with the right application of our creative pastoral and liturgical energies.

Conclusion

So how can we reclaim the *Homilies* for today? Preaching them as they stand is hardly a viable option, if only because their style and length are unsuitable for modern congregations. Who, for example, would want to wade through twenty thousand words directed against the 'peril of idolatry and superfluous decking of churches'? Even if we agree with the principles underlying the homily, for a preacher to go on about them at such length today would be a sign that he was mentally unbalanced. Sermons are written to meet the needs of their own time, and we no longer live in a world where such medieval excesses of piety were common. For this reason, it should be no surprise to discover that the doctrinal homilies are the ones most easily adaptable for modern use. Pastoral issues come and go, but the underlying principles remain the same and it is our doctrine that shapes our preaching. The *Homilies* remind us that doctrine comes first and that everything else we say derives from it.

Secondly, the *Homilies* teach us of the necessity of discipline in the Christian life. Believing a set of principles but not putting them into practice is one of the biggest problems the church faces, and it is an open invitation to outsiders to condemn us – rightly – for our hypocrisy. There are many things God wants from us in this life and he deals with no two people in exactly the same way, but some things are common to us all. The *Homilies* concentrate on those things, and rightly so. It is all too easy, particularly in our modern and 'value-judgment free' society, to concentrate on results and ignore the means by which they were obtained. A man who achieves his goals by cutting corners can often be preferred to someone more honest but less effective. Famous people may be excused all sorts of misdeeds if it is thought that their achievements outweigh their defects. Christians cannot accept this approach or be happy with it. We believe that character matters and that whatever we are called to do, whether great or small, must be done in the grace and power of God. It is not the church's job to interfere in politics or business, but to challenge and prepare politicians and businessmen for their respective tasks. Plans and policies may be good or bad, but if those who implement them cannot be trusted, that will not matter much in the end. A Christian preacher may not know much about professional business, but he is not expected to. His job is to concentrate on the moral and spiritual aspects of human life, where the standards and expectations are the same for all. This is what the *Homilies* do so well, and why their priorities are as important for us now as they were when they were first written.

Thirdly, and most important, the goal of all Christian preaching and teaching is to draw us nearer to God. It is no accident that several of the homilies are concerned with prayer and devotion, which are fundamental themes of virtually all of them, one way or another. The call to walk with God has more than one dimension. There is the private side to our devotions, which spiritual writers call the practice of the presence of God. We must commune with him every moment of our lives and dedicate ourselves to his service at all times, remembering that he is present with us and watching over us wherever we may be and whatever we may be doing. There is also the call to public worship, when we participate with others in glorifying God's name and in meditating on what he expects of us as a community. The *Second Book of Homilies* is rightly concerned with this question, which it treats in many of its different aspects. Finally, there is a kind of devotion that involves meditating on the life of Christ and walking with him through the different aspects of his life and ministry. The church has shaped this into an annual cycle, of which Christmas, Easter and Pentecost form the high points. It is a tragic irony of our time that the leisure which past generations were given to contemplate these things has now given way to forms of celebration far removed from what was originally intended, or (in the case of Pentecost) to almost total neglect. Few things are more urgent in the modern church than the need to repossess our festivals and turn them back into occasions that glorify the name of God. By reminding us of these things, the *Homilies* serve to reorient our priorities and to prepare us for a life lived in the true worship and fear of the Lord.

Today the *Homilies* can most obviously be used with profit by theological students preparing for a preaching ministry, because they teach principles, provide examples and illustrate how practical applications of biblical doctrine can be made without sacrificing the integrity of the text or ignoring the needs of the hearers. Being products of their time, they have to be transposed into a modern idiom if their message is to be communicated effectively in the modern world, but that is a useful exercise in itself and basically no different from what we do with the Scriptures in any case. Coming from a key moment in the development of Anglicanism, the *Homilies* give us an insight into the minds of the Reformers that few other documents can match. They put flesh and blood on the skeleton of the Articles of Religion, showing us how those principles were actually applied and communicated. As such, they stand as a witness to the faith of their time and a challenge to ours today. Let us pray that the signs that they are being recovered by a new generation may prove to be the harbinger of a glorious age of preaching, of a kind that can touch hearts and revive the people of God in the way the *Homilies* were originally intended to do.

© Gerald Bray, 2011

12. A MINISTRY OF WORD AND PRAYER: WHAT CAN WE LEARN FROM CHARLES SIMEON TODAY?

Vaughan Roberts

It is a privilege to contribute to this collection of chapters that honours Peter Adam, whose preaching, writing and personal encouragement have meant so much to me and to countless others. I have chosen to write about Charles Simeon, whose ministry impacted the work of the gospel perhaps more than anyone else of his generation, and consider what we can learn today from his teaching and example.[1] As I have been preparing I have been struck by the many similarities between Simeon and Peter Adam, not just as Anglican bachelors but also in the shared priorities of their ministries. Each of the lessons we will learn from Simeon has been modelled superbly by Peter during his long and faithful service.

Charles Simeon was born on 24 September 1759 into a wealthy family in Reading. After his mother died when he was a young child, his father sent him to Eton College at the age of nine, where it seems his only distinction was to have been described as 'the ugliest boy in the school'.[2] It was not a godly place; he told his friend Henry Venn that he should be 'tempted even to murder

---

1. The substance of this chapter was first delivered at the Evangelical Ministry Assembly of the Proclamation Trust, London, June 2009.

2. Charles Smyth, *Simeon and Church Order* (Cambridge: Cambridge University Press, 1940), p. 47.

his son sooner than let him see there what he had seen'.[3] At the time he was something of a dandy with more interest in clothes than in the things of God, but that changed soon after he went up to King's College, Cambridge, when the Provost wrote to all the students to inform them of their obligation to attend a service of Holy Communion in the college chapel. Simeon was horrified, feeling himself unworthy to receive from the Lord's Table and embarked on an intense period of soul searching, which made him ill. Peace came at last when he read a book which explained that in the sacrificial system of the OT the sin of the Israelite was transferred to an animal, which was killed as his substitute. God then opened Simeon's eyes to understand that Christ was the perfect sacrifice who had died in his place on the cross to take the punishment he deserved. He awoke the next day, Easter Sunday 1779, as a new man, rejoicing in the resurrection of Christ and looking forward to attending the service he had previously dreaded so much. He wrote later, 'From that hour peace flowed in rich abundance in my soul and at the Lord's Table in our chapel I had the sweetest access to God through my blessed Saviour.'[4]

Simeon's ambitions changed immediately and he decided to become a clergyman, not, as for many of his generation, simply to take up a respectable profession, but as a means of doing real spiritual good to others. At the time he had not met anyone who shared his theological views, so he did not know how he could possibly find a suitable curacy. At one point he even considered placing the following advertisement in the papers:

That a young clergyman who felt himself an undone sinner, and looked to the Lord Jesus Christ alone for salvation, and desired to live only to make that Saviour known unto others, was persuaded that there must be some persons in the world whose views and feelings on this subject accorded to his own, though he had now lived three years without finding so much as one: and that if there were any minister of that description he would gladly become his curate, and serve him gratis.[5]

In the end he did find a vicar who was prepared to take him on and he began a brief curacy at St Edward's Church in Cambridge. A few months later, in 1783, when he was still only twenty-three, he was given responsibility for the parish of Holy Trinity in the heart of Cambridge, surrounded by university colleges.

---

3. William Carus, *Memoirs of the Life of Charles Simeon, M.A.* (London: Hatchard & Son, 1847), p. 27.

4. H. C. G. Moule, *Charles Simeon* (London: Inter-Varsity Fellowship, 1948), p. 26.

5. Carus, *Memoirs*, p. 22.

He remained in the same post until he died fifty-four years later in 1836, living throughout that period as a bachelor in his rooms in King's College, where he was a fellow. At the start of his ministry Simeon was in a very small minority, but by his death it is estimated that a third of Anglican pulpits were occupied by evangelicals. One recent biographer has traced eleven hundred clergy who were influenced by Simeon at Cambridge and later ministered across the country: from Penzance in the far south to Aberdeen in Scotland, and from Shrewsbury on the Welsh Borders to Lowestoft, the most easterly parish in England.[6] There were many other 'Simeonites', such as Henry Martyn, who travelled abroad to preach the gospel.

Simeon was very much a man of his time but his teaching and example still present an important contemporary challenge to all pastors today. I will focus on eight lessons he teaches us.

1. Let the Bible speak

Simeon made a mark in his pocket Bible next to the words of Jeremiah 20:9, 'his word is in mine heart as a burning fire'. He knew the same experience as the prophet, having been gripped by God's Word since his conversion. His determination as a preacher was to be a faithful steward of Scripture, thus ensuring that he did not communicate his own message but rather served as God's mouthpiece. In a letter to the publisher of his collected sermons he wrote:

> My endeavour is to bring out of Scripture what is there and not to thrust in what
> I think might be there. I have a great jealousy on this head: never to speak more
> or less than I believe to be the mind of the Spirit in the passage I am expounding.[7]

Simeon could be described as the father of modern expository preaching, both exemplifying the practice himself and teaching many others how to do it through his published sermons (2,536 sermon outlines in 21 volumes);[8] his publication of a translation of the Frenchman Jean Claude's 'Essay on the Composition of a Sermon', which had been such a help to him as a young

---

6. Hugh Evan Hopkins, *Charles Simeon, Preacher Extraordinary* (Bramcote: Grove, 1979), p. 33.

7. Moule, *Charles Simeon*, p. 77.

8. *Horae Homileticae*, 21 vols. (London: Holdsworth & Ball, 1832–3).

preacher;[9] and his regular Friday evening sermon classes for undergraduates who were planning to be ordained. He taught his students some rules for the composition of a sermon, summarizing what he had learned from Claude:

1. Take for your subject that which you believe to be the mind of God in the passage before you. (Be careful to understand the passage thoroughly; and regard nothing but the mind of God in it.)

2. Mark the character of the passage. (It may be a declaration, a precept, a promise, a threatening, an invitation, an appeal; or more complex, as a cause and effect; a principle and a consequence; an action and a motive to that action.)

3. Mark the spirit of the passage. Whatever it be, let that be the spirit of your discourse. The soul should be filled with the subject and breathe out the very spirit of it before the people. God himself should be heard in us and through us.[10]

Simeon's fundamental principle for preaching was the vital importance of letting the text shape the sermon rather than imposing a meaning on it from outside, or focusing on a minor point within it. The passage should so govern what the preacher says, 'That no other text in the Bible will suit the discourse'.[11] He urged his students:

Take the subject of the text; illustrate it by the words of the text, but preach always the *subject* of it. Let your sermon come naturally out of your text, like the kernel out of a hazel-nut; and not piecemeal, and, after much trouble to your hearers, like the kernel out of a walnut. Take hold of some point in a text which will give you a handle for the whole. Do not thrust in a handle, but find that which is already in the text. A sermon should be like a telescope: each successive division of it should be as an additional lens to bring the subject of your text nearer, and make it more distinct.[12]

He described his own practice in a letter to the Bishop of St David's:

---

9. Charles Simeon, *Claude's Essay on the Composition of a Sermon* (London: James Cornish, 1844).

10. William Carus, *Extracts from Simeon's Memoirs on the Composition and Delivery of Sermons* (London: Hatchard & Son, 1887), p. 23.

11. William Carus, *Memoirs of the Life of Reverend Charles Simeon, M.A.*, 3rd ed. (London: Hatchard & Son, 1848), p. 505.

12. Abner William Brown, *Recollections of the Conversation Parties of the Rev Charles Simeon* (London: Hamilton, Adams, 1863), p. 183, emphasis original.

> My mode of interpreting Scripture is this: I bring to it no predilections whatever . . . I
> never wish to find any particular truth in any particular passage. I am willing
> that every part of God's blessed word should speak exactly what it was intended
> to speak.[13]

Simeon was determined that what he proclaimed from the pulpit was not his message but God's.

In recent decades there has been a welcome return to an emphasis on the importance of expository preaching. I remember Peter Adam telling me the impact on him of listening to John Stott in Melbourne in the 1960s as he simply explained Scripture and applied it to the contemporary world. Peter had never heard preaching like it and knew immediately that that was what he wanted to do with his life. There must be many young preachers who have in turn been inspired and taught by Peter's own model, not least in England where he has been a much-appreciated contributor at Proclamation Trust conferences. Simeon would surely have approved of the opening line of the Trust's vision statement, 'The fundamental conviction underlying the work of The Proclamation Trust is that when the Bible is taught God himself speaks, and his voice is heard clearly today.'[14]

2. Make sure you get your message across

Simeon had a clear practical aim for all his preaching, inviting the readers of his collected sermons to judge each one according to this test:

> Does it uniformly tend
>
> TO HUMBLE THE SINNER?
> TO EXALT THE SAVIOUR?
> TO PROMOTE HOLINESS?
>
> If in one single instance it lose sight of any of these points, let it be condemned
> without mercy.[15]

---

13. Arthur Bennett, 'Charles Simeon: Prince of Evangelicals', *Churchman* 102 (1988), pp. 122–142.
14. The Proclamation Trust (http://www.proctrust.org.uk).
15. Preface to *Horae Homileticae*, vol. 1, p. xxi.

If a sermon were to achieve the desired result, it had to be comprehensible. Simeon knew it was possible to be faithful as a preacher and yet ineffective because of a failure to communicate the message. Therefore, he stressed the need for clarity, emphasizing the importance of three elements: 'UNITY in the design, PERSPICUITY in the arrangement, SIMPLICITY in diction.'[16]

By 'unity' Simeon meant that each sermon should have one 'big idea': 'Every text, whether long or short, must be reduced to a categorical proposition.'[17] He was convinced that God inspired each passage for a purpose: it was designed to say and do something. The preacher's task was to look beyond the details to discern the thrust of the text as a whole; that thrust should drive the sermon and be the focus of its message.

The first question a preacher should ask, therefore, is, 'What is the principal scope and meaning of the text? . . . Having ascertained this, nothing is to be introduced into any point of the discourse which does not, in some way or other, reflect upon the main subject.'[18]

> The leading point of the whole passage (should) be the point mainly regarded; and the subordinate points only so far noticed, as to throw additional light upon that. If this caution be not attended to, the minds of the people are likely to be distracted with the diversity and incoherence of the matter brought before them. But if an unity of subject be preserved, the discourse will come with ten-fold weight to the minds of the audience.[19]

'Perspicuity in arrangement' referred to the importance of a clear structure. Simeon encouraged preachers to follow Jean Claude's instruction to begin with an introduction, or 'exordium', to draw the listener's attention to the subject of the address. Claude condemned the use of current affairs or 'profane history'[20] in introductions, preferring to begin with theology. Simeon's own practice was to move straight to the topic in hand, as for example in the opening words of his sermon on Galatians 3:19, 'Of all the

---

16. Simeon, preface to *Claude's Essay*, p. vi.

17. Simeon, *Horae Homileticae*, vol. 21, p. 307, in an editorial comment on Claude's essay. The language of a sermon's 'big idea' comes from Haddon W. Robinson, *Expository Preaching* (Leicester: IVP, 1986), p. 31.

18. Simeon, preface to *Claude's Essay*, p. vi.

19. Preface to *Horae Homileticae*, vol. 1, pp. xxv–xxvi.

20. Jean Claude, 'Essay on the Composition of a Sermon', *Horae Homileticae*, vol. 21, p. 406.

subjects connected with religion, there is, perhaps, not one so rarely unfolded to Christian auditories as the law.'[21] It is hard to believe such words would grab a typical twenty-first-century congregation!

After a short introduction, Simeon divided the main body of his sermons into sections with simple headings. These should be clearly stated to assist the listeners: 'The mention of an easy and natural division will relieve their minds, assist their memories, and enable them to inwardly digest the word.'[22] Any more than a few divisions would lead to confusion. Simeon once read a passage in one of Richard Baxter's works that began 'Sixty-fifthly', and was not impressed, commenting, 'As if anyone could remember the sixty-four preceding headings.'[23] His own sermons frequently contained only two points and rarely exceeded three. He took pains to ensure that they all contributed to the basic thrust of the sermon and served the main point.

Simeon stressed 'simplicity of diction' because he was anxious that everyone should be able to receive what the preacher said, as he used accessible language to get the point across. Abner Brown remembered his repeated warnings in sermon classes 'against anything like affectation, mannerism, or grandiloquence'.[24] Recalling his own early years as a preacher, Simeon regretted 'how apt are young Ministers . . . to be talking of that great letter "I"'.[25] He commented, 'The three lessons which a Minister has to learn are – 1. Humility; 2. Humility; 3. Humility.'[26] The pulpit was not a place to show off the extent of his oratory, knowledge or vocabulary: 'Do not preach what you can tell, but what your people can receive,'[27] he pleaded. His curate, William Carus, testified that Simeon himself 'spent much thought to make hard things easy'.[28] The labour involved, both in seeking to be faithful to Scripture and to communicate its message in the simplest possible way, required a great deal of time for every sermon: 'Few cost him less than twelve hours of study, many twice that time, and some several days.'[29] He had no patience with the student

21. *Horae Homileticae*, vol. 17, p. 76.

22. Simeon, preface to *Claude's Essay*, p. ix.

23. Brown, *Recollections*, p. 183.

24. Ibid., p. 51.

25. Ibid., p. 17.

26. Ibid.

27. Ibid., p. 183.

28. Carus, *Extracts*, p. 5.

29. The testimony of Daniel Wilson, Bishop of Calcutta, in Carus, *Memoirs* (1847 ed.), p. 841.

who referred to 'The Son of Amram' instead of Moses in an outline sermon that was presented at one of his sermon classes: 'Who was the son of Amram?' he asked; 'Moses,' the student replied; to which Simeon exclaimed, 'If you meant Moses why did you not say Moses?'[30]

Simeon's instructions to preachers gave much attention not just to the words used but also to the way in which they were delivered. He once lamented that 'It is the want of good and impressive delivery that destroys the usefulness of a great proportion of pious ministers.'[31] He urged his students:

> Never speak from the throat. Get your words easily out of your mouth; the more easily they pass from you, the more easily your audience will take them up. Speak lightly. Speak from your tongue, lips and teeth, not from your chest nor throat.[32]

They should avoid a dull, monotonous delivery, but rather ensure that their words were 'As music and not like a funeral procession'; they should seek to cultivate a natural manner, 'As a father in his family'.[33] Those who spoke in a pompous or quirky manner would be asked to read a passage out loud; Simeon would then read the same words imitating their faults with some exaggeration to show them their defects before giving an example of how he would do it himself.[34]

In his early days as a preacher Simeon preached from a full script, but he felt that this restricted his delivery so he changed his practice as he gained in experience. He still spent hours preparing his text but would then read it 'half a dozen times at least', so that he knew it well enough not to have to rely on reading every word in the pulpit. He recommended a similar practice to others: a middle way between 'extemporaneous effusions and servile adherence to what is written'.[35] Lack of dependence on a full text, he said, 'Gives a minister an opportunity of speaking with far more effect to the hearts of men and of addressing himself to their passions, as well by his looks and gesture as by his words.'[36] This would make it easier for them to express not just the sense of the passage but its spirit as well. However, Simeon never insisted that

---

30. Brown, *Recollections*, p. 51.
31. Carus, *Extracts*, p. 29.
32. Brown, *Recollections*, p. 187.
33. Carus, *Extracts*, pp. 30, 28.
34. Ibid., p. 29.
35. Simeon, preface to *Claude's Essay*, p. xi.
36. Ibid.

all preachers should follow his method, recognizing that 'the talents of men are so various'.[37] He cautioned the inexperienced against preaching extemporaneously for their first three or four years in the pulpit, and, even then, he warned them that 'It takes more time to prepare properly for an extempore sermon than to write one.'[38] A minister, Simeon said, 'Must just preach as his text does – today vehement, tomorrow persuasive. Let him get his text into him in his study, and then get into his text in the pulpit.'[39] 'Be the thing you speak – tender or impassioned – be cast, as it were, into the mould of your sentiment, so as to express in your intonation and action what you mean to convey by your words.'[40]

There is perhaps a danger that in our renewed emphasis on 'getting the Bible right' in some circles, we have not given sufficient attention to 'getting it across', so that our preaching can be somewhat lifeless and dull. Nobody ever laid that charge against Simeon. Although he was concerned not to let his personality get in the way of the message he was preaching, he certainly used it to help get the point across. His former curate and first biographer wrote of him, 'The intense fervour of his feelings he cared not to conceal or restrain; his whole soul was in his subject and he spoke and acted exactly as he felt.'[41] He himself said that he preached not just with his tongue but with his eyes and hands as well; we might also add his heart.[42] One young girl listening to him speak asked her mother, 'O Mama, what is the gentleman in a passion about?'[43] Would anyone ever think of asking such a question of us?

3. Expect opposition

The congregation at Holy Trinity had set their hearts on another pastor being appointed and resented the young Charles Simeon from the moment he

---

37. Ibid.
38. Brown, *Recollections*, pp. 178–179.
39. Ibid., p. 180.
40. Carus, *Extracts*, p. 31.
41. Ibid., p. 12.
42. Joseph John Gurney, *Reminiscences of Chalmers, Simeon, Wilberforce, etc.* (privately published; n.d.), p. 118. Quoted in Michael Eldridge, 'Charles Simeon and the Jewish People: "The Warmest Place in His Heart"', Olive Press Research Paper 5 (2009), p. 4.
43. Brown, *Recollections*, p. 8.

arrived. Church pews were privately rented in those days and the pew holders took the opportunity to register their protest against the new curate by absenting themselves from the church and ensuring that no one sat in their seats by attaching locks to them. Simeon bought chairs and benches at his own expense and placed them in the aisle and at the back of the church, but the wardens threw them into the churchyard, leaving most of the congregation standing for the first ten years of his ministry. His opponents were also able to spite him by choosing another clergyman to give the afternoon lectures in the church. When Simeon took the unusual step of starting an evening service to provide him with another opportunity to preach, the wardens responded by locking the church and carrying off the keys. On the first day this happened he paid a locksmith to open the door and let the congregation in, but felt it wise after that to abandon his experiment. Despite this hostility, and in fact largely because of it, many students began to attend Holy Trinity to hear the young preacher who was causing such a stir. Most came to jeer rather than to hear God's Word; he was often mocked as he left the building to return to his rooms in King's and on one occasion was pelted with rotten eggs.

Simeon was regarded with contempt by most of the chief figures in the university, who believed him to be a dangerous influence on undergraduates and actively discouraged them from going to his church. One college, for example, arranged a compulsory lecture on the Greek NT on Sunday evenings to prevent attendance at Holy Trinity. Students who adopted Simeon's views could expect to face opposition themselves. In one case a candidate for a college prize was placed at the bottom of the list, only to discover later that he had in fact received the most marks; he had been discriminated against because of 'Notorious and obstinate Simeonism'![44] Even Simeon's own college opposed him: the other dons spurned him because of his evangelical views and were careful not to be seen to associate with him. When one colleague walked with him across the college lawns, Simeon remarked on it to a friend as it was such a highly unusual event.

Despite the relentless opposition, Simeon persevered and slowly began to gain the respect of some. After four years it was his turn to preach the University Sermon at Great St Mary's. The church was packed full of students ready to scorn him, but after his address one turned to another and said, 'Well, Simeon is no fool'; his friend replied, 'Fool! Did you ever hear such a sermon before?'[45] Others were similarly impressed and began to attend Holy Trinity

---

44. Moule, *Charles Simeon*, p. 55.

45. Carus, *Memoirs* (1848 ed.), p. 30.

with genuine interest and many were converted, but hostility continued. Simeon was most hurt when a group of forty believers who had previously been close associates of his wrote to the Bishop of Ely complaining about him. It was only after thirty years that internal opposition to his ministry at Holy Trinity finally disappeared.

During the early years the vicious attacks against him distressed Simeon greatly. At a particularly low point he opened his pocket Bible looking for comfort and read the words of Matthew 27:32, 'They found a man of Cyrene, Simon by name; him they compelled to bear his cross.' He noticed the similarity with his own name and made the connection: what a privilege it was to be asked to bear the cross of Christ! He said to the Lord, 'Lay it on me, lay it on me; I will gladly bear the cross for thy sake!'[46]

Most Christians, in the Western world at least, have experienced very little opposition but there are signs that the tide is beginning to turn and that we are likely to face greater hostility from society, the professing church and even the state in the future. The teaching of the Bible and the experience of many great saints throughout history warn us to expect such persecution as part of the normal Christian life. Simeon provides an inspiring model of perseverance and grace in such times. Although by nature prone to a quick temper, he did not respond with anger to those who locked him out of his own church, but rather prayed, 'May God bless them with enlightening, sanctifying and saving grace.'[47]

4. Think strategically

Simeon was diligent in fulfilling his duties within his own parish, yet his vision was never narrowly parochial but encompassed the whole nation. He had a clear sense of his own priorities, saying to the students at one of his conversation parties, 'Let every man see what his line of work is and keep to it. I have, as my work, undertaken to provide ministers for eternal souls.'[48] That goal required him to focus on three tasks: recruiting, training and deploying.

Simeon was well aware of the multiplying effect of his ministry: if a young man he taught was gripped by the gospel and then ordained he could be the means of many others coming to Christ and being discipled. As a student

---

46. Carus, *Memoirs* (1847 ed.), p. 676 (note).
47. Ibid., p. 59.
48. Brown, *Recollections*, p. 126.

entered Holy Trinity he was heard to comment, 'Here come six hundred people.'[49] On another occasion he said:

Many of those who hear me are legions in themselves because they are going forth to preach, or else to fill stations of influence in society. In that view, I look on my position here as the highest and most important in the kingdom, nor would I exchange it for any other.[50]

Ministers in university settings have special opportunities for recruiting a new generation of gospel ministers, but this task should certainly not be left to them alone. Simeon relied heavily on the work carried out by his former disciples who often became vicars in very ordinary settings, as bishops did not trust clergy with evangelical views and would not appoint them to the best jobs. Through their faithful ministry in these backwaters young men were converted and discipled. Simeon and others then established charities to provide funds to enable the most able of them to take a degree in Cambridge so they could be ordained. Henry Venn had pioneered this approach in 1767, establishing what became the Elland Society, with the declared aim of raising 'A fund for the purpose of educating poor pious men for the ministry', especially from the north of England.[51] Simeon was a generous supporter of this fund and later established his own very similar charity, 'The London Clergy Education Society'. In this way many were raised up for gospel ministry from what would then have been regarded as unlikely settings.

Once Simeon spotted converted young men with potential as future gospel ministers he made time to disciple and train them, both one to one and in small groups. In 1792 he began fortnightly sermon classes for fifteen to twenty undergraduates on Sunday evenings after church, which continued for forty years. Later, in 1813, he began weekly Friday evening 'Conversation Parties', as he called them, in which between sixty and eighty students would pack into his rooms. Abner Brown, who attended these meetings as an undergraduate, published his recollections of them in later life, providing us with a vivid picture of the scene and of the range of subjects addressed. Tea would be served at six o'clock from the large, black Wedgewood teapot, which is

---

49. G. Ian F. Thomson, *The Oxford Pastorate* (London: Canterbury, 1946), p. 35.

50. Hugh Evan Hopkins, *Charles Simeon of Cambridge* (London: Hodder & Stoughton, 1977), p. 86.

51. Michael Hennell, *John Venn and the Clapham Sect* (London: Lutterworth, 1958), p. 277.

still preserved at Holy Trinity Church. Students would squeeze into every available space and try to find a seat on chairs, benches, window ledges and, if necessary, the floor. Simeon gave each one a warm welcome, at the same time hoping nervously that none would damage the furniture or leave a mark on his carpets, which were covered with protective mats for the occasion. For a man who was known for his 'scrupulous neatness',[52] these occasions must have been a challenge at times and yet he delighted in the company. On one Friday evening towards the end of his life he said, 'I love to view all my Christian friends as fuel. Having gathered you all together on my hearth, I warm myself at your fire, and find my Christian love burn and glow.'[53] This was an opportunity not just for companionship, but for serious discussion. Once all his guests were settled, Simeon would take his seat and invite questions. The subjects focused on theology and practical ministry, with Simeon's answers providing much needed training for future clergy at a time when there were no seminaries.

Many of those Simeon trained struggled to find suitable jobs as ministers because of their evangelicalism. At the time the right to present a clergyman to a benefice was often held by individuals as a possession and could be sold to another. While disapproving of this unsuitable method of appointing clergy, Simeon determined to do all he could to buy as many as possible of these 'advowsons' so he could ensure the appointment of faithful men. The cost was considerable (£3,000 for the parish of Cheltenham, for example), but the impact has been seen in evangelical ministry that has, in many cases, continued to this day. By the time of his death the Simeon Trust, which still exists, held twenty-one advowsons, to which more were added later.

Simeon's passion to raise up a new generation of gospel ministers should challenge and inspire us. All pastors should be praying 'the other Lord's Prayer' that Jesus instructed his disciples to pray, 'Ask the Lord of the harvest, therefore, to send out workers into his harvest field' (Matt. 9:38).[54] We should also be making ourselves available to the Lord as vehicles for his answering of that prayer as we make time to recruit, train and deploy others. I myself have for some years run a preaching class for those in our congregation who have begun to show potential as teachers of God's Word. There seemed to be only one obvious name for the group: 'Simeons'.

---

52. Brown, *Recollections*, p. 33.

53. Ibid., p. 98.

54. E.g. Christopher Green, 'The Other Lord's Prayer', <http://ninethirtyeight.org/resources/articles/the-other-lords-prayer> (accessed 20 Sept. 2010).

5. Have a global vision

Simeon's passion to be used to raise up workers for the harvest field extended beyond Britain to the ends of the earth. He played an important part in the early days of the modern missionary movement, being a key supporter of the ongoing work of the London Society for Promoting Christianity among the Jews and a driving influence in the formation of the Church Missionary Society.[55] At a meeting of the Eclectic Society in London in 1796, Simeon had proposed the question 'With what propriety and in what mode can a mission be attempted to the heathen from the established church?' No agreement was reached and the matter was not raised again until three years later when Simeon pushed for immediate action, asking his brethren to consider three questions: 'What can we do? When shall we do it? How shall we do it?'[56] On this occasion they all agreed to proceed, and a month later, on 12 April 1799, sixteen clergymen and nine laymen formed 'a society amongst the members of the established church for sending missionaries among the heathen'. It was initially called 'The Society for Missions to Africa and the East', only later changing its name to the Church Missionary Society.

Simeon's greatest impact was seen in India. The East India Company would not allow missionaries in their territories until 1813 so Simeon sought to get round this restriction by recruiting chaplains to serve the British community. Once there they would devote their spare time to learning local languages and translating the Bible into them. Among those who served in this way were two of Simeon's closest friends and former curates: Thomas Thomason and Henry Martyn. Martyn had gained the top first in his year at Cambridge in mathematics and been awarded the university classics prize. He turned his back on a potentially glittering academic career and, having served a brief curacy with Simeon at Holy Trinity, set sail for India at the age of twenty-four. It took him nearly a year to get there and, almost as soon as he arrived, his health deteriorated; he died just seven years later at the age of thirty-one. During that short time he saw only one native converted and yet produced translations of the NT in Urdu, Arabic and Persian, which became the foundation for mission work in that region for years to come.

Two days before Henry Martyn died Simeon travelled to London to receive a portrait of him that had just arrived from India. The old man was overcome

---

55. On the former society, see Eldridge, 'Charles Simeon'.
56. Hopkins, *Charles Simeon of Cambridge*, p. 151 (both quotations).

with emotion as he saw his beloved friend's wasted appearance. He hung the painting in his study and, looking at it, would say to his guests:

> There! See that blessed man! What an expression of countenance! No one looks at me as he does – he never takes his eyes off me; and seems always to be saying, 'Be serious – be in earnest – Don't trifle – don't trifle.' And I won't trifle – I won't trifle.[57]

Simeon would no doubt be envious of how much easier global mission has become, with multitudes from largely unreached countries travelling to our doorsteps and better communications enabling us to visit many such places within a few hours. And yet, would he not also rebuke us for not making the most of these opportunities and for our often half-hearted commitment to cross-cultural mission? Perhaps he would say to us, 'Don't trifle.'

6. Be Bible Christians

There was a clear division among evangelical Christians of Simeon's day between Arminians and Calvinists. He was himself a moderate Calvinist who did not believe in the doctrines of limited atonement or double predestination, but had no doubt that the saved had been chosen by God, acknowledging, 'I knew election must be true for I was forced to admit that, of myself, I should no more have returned to God than a cannon ball would return to its cannon.'[58] However, he refused to let himself be placed in either party and resisted those who so stressed divine sovereignty or human responsibility that they left no room for the other truth. He insisted that 'The truth is not in the middle, and not in one extreme, but in both extremes.'[59]

> When two opposite principles are each clearly contained in the Bible, truth does not lie in taking what is called the golden mean, but in steadily adopting both extremes, and, as a pendulum, oscillating, but not vacillating between the two.[60]

He pleaded with those he trained:

---

57. Ibid., p. 149.

58. Brown, *Recollections*, pp. 70, 274 (quote), 278–279.

59. Moule, *Charles Simeon*, p. 77.

60. Brown, *Recollections*, pp. 74–75.

Never allow yourselves to pit one passage against another . . . opposites may possibly be true especially in Scripture, where we know so little of the mysteries to which passages point. A strong Calvinist looks on statements like that of Paul's possibly becoming a castaway (1 Cor. 9:27) as a dog looks on a hedgehog: he knows not what to do with it. We must be cautious of slighting any passage of Scripture.[61]

'Scripture', he said, 'is hallowed ground. We must be careful not to make it speak more than God has done. God is of no party, and Calvinists and Arminians alike err when they attempt to make the Bible speak their own views.'[62] It is no wonder that Simeon felt he was viewed with suspicion by those from both parties, saying, 'Nobody quite likes me.'[63] He would have approved of the statement of my former vicar, Mark Ruston of the Round Church in Cambridge, who said, 'It is possible to be more logical than biblical.'

Simeon's warnings about the danger of skewing the interpretation of a passage by the imposition of an over-tight system were not limited to Calvinists and Arminians. He cautioned against what he called 'an ultra-Evangelical taste', which sees only the fundamental doctrines of the gospel in passages and fails to give sufficient attention to 'the practical lessons they were intended to convey'.[64] He also ensured, however, that he read each individual text in the light of the teaching of the whole of Scripture, with its focus on Christ and God's redemption through him. Simeon, therefore, certainly did not deny the important role of systematic theology in ensuring that we interpret a text in the light of the whole of the Bible's teaching. In Jim Packer's words, 'The characteristic error of evangelicals then, both Calvinists and Arminians was, to his mind, not neglect of the analogy of faith in their interpreting it, but an over-rigid application of it.'[65] It was to counter such an over-rigid imposition of a doctrinal framework that he stressed, 'God has not revealed his truth in a system; the Bible has no system as such. Lay aside system and fly to the Bible. Be Bible Christians, and not system Christians.'[66]

---

61. Ibid., p. 269.
62. Ibid., p. 212.
63. Ibid., p. 132.
64. Preface to *Horae Homileticae*, vol. 1, p. xxv.
65. J. I. Packer, 'Expository Preaching: Charles Simeon and Ourselves', in Leland Ryken and Todd A. Wilson (eds.), *Preach the Word: Essays on Expository Preaching in Honor of R. Kent Hughes* (Wheaton: Crossway, 2007), pp. 140–154 (quote p. 149).
66. Brown, *Recollections*, p. 269.

We still need to hear that appeal today in case our framework skews our reading of the Bible and prevents us from hearing the authentic word of God. Oliver Barclay's words are timely: Simeon

> was frightened of systematisation . . . because he believed it enabled people to avoid the plain sense of Scripture and to substitute 'doctrine' for the Word of God. I wonder what he would have said if someone had told him with great enthusiasm that they were now preaching the 'doctrines of grace'. I think he would have asked them very searchingly whether they were preaching Christ and expounding Scripture, or were substituting doctrines for Scripture.[67]

7. Maintain a close walk with Christ

Simeon was far from perfect, having a natural tendency to a rather haughty manner and short temper. After he had visited Henry Venn as a young Christian, the old man's daughters commented on his faults. Venn responded by asking them to fetch him a peach from the garden. They thought it was a strange request as it was early summer and all the peaches were still green and unripe. The father then said, 'We must wait; but a little sun and a few more showers and the peach will be ripe and sweet. So it is with Mr Simeon.'[68]

Sure enough, Simeon grew in godliness as he gave himself to the disciplines of Bible-reading, prayer and battling with sin. Despite his busy life he managed to resist a descent into mere professionalism as a minister, but rather ensured that he sustained a vibrant spiritual life. Soon after becoming a Christian he had resolved to pay half a crown to his servant every time he failed to get out of bed early in the morning to read the Bible and pray. This strategy did not work as he began to justify late rising by saying to himself that she was poor and needed some extra money. He then decided on a different penalty, making a promise to himself that he would throw a precious gold sovereign into the river Cam if he failed to rise. This new policy proved effective and helped him establish the discipline that he followed for the rest of his life. He rose each morning at 4 a.m. and devoted the first four hours of the day to prayer and devotional study of Scripture, followed by 'family prayer' with his servant. He rose even earlier

---

67. Oliver R. Barclay, *Charles Simeon and the Evangelical Tradition* (Lewes: Focus Christian Ministries Trust, 1988), p. 12.
68. Moule, *Charles Simeon*, p. 44.

on Sundays that he might have more time for prayer and meditation before he preached; and so when he appeared in the pulpit there was a seriousness and devoutness in his whole aspect and bearing which showed how deeply he felt the gravity of his office, and how much he had been in prayerful communion with his Lord.[69]

Donald Coggan was surely right that his 'costly self-discipline made the preacher. That was primary. The making of the sermon was secondary and derivative.'[70] In his own instructions to others about pastoral ministry, Simeon stressed:

> The whole state of your own soul before God must be the first point to be considered; for if you yourself are not in a truly spiritual state of mind, and actually living upon the truths which you preach or read to others, you will officiate to very little purpose.[71]

No one who knew Simeon could doubt how deeply he himself felt the truths he preached. At the heart of his spirituality was both a profound sense of his own sin and also of God's great love for him in Christ. He had what he called 'The religion of a sinner at the foot of the cross.'[72] At one of his Conversation Parties he was asked what he thought was the principal mark of regeneration. He replied, 'The very first and indispensable sign is self-loathing and abhorrence. Nothing short of this can be admitted as an evidence of real change . . . I want to see more of this humble, contrite, broken spirit among us.'[73] Far from robbing him of joy, his own profound sense of sin made Simeon marvel at the wonder of God's grace. A friend once called on him and

> found him so absorbed in the contemplation of the Son of God, and so overpowered with a display of his mercy to his soul that, full of the animating theme, he was incapable of pronouncing a single word: at length, after an interval, with accents big he exclaimed, 'Glory! Glory! Glory!'[74]

---

69. Carus, *Extracts*, p. 5.
70. Donald Coggan, *Stewards of Grace* (London: Hodder & Stoughton, 1958), p. 32.
71. Carus, *Extracts*, p. 32.
72. Carus, *Memoirs* (1847 ed.), p. 731.
73. Ibid., p. 651.
74. Ibid., p. 100.

Before we become intimidated by what may appear to us an impossibly high standard, we should remember that people went to bed earlier in an age when there was no electric lighting and were consequently able to rise earlier. And Simeon, as a bachelor, with servants catering for all his practical needs, was able to be largely undistracted by much that rightly takes up the time of others. However, his example is still a rebuke to many of us: we may plan to set time aside to prepare sermons and do all we can to ensure that other tasks do not encroach on that important priority. Do we also plan to pray?

8. Stick at it!

Simeon knew that it was not enough to recruit, train and deploy a new generation of gospel ministers if they were then to drift off course as the years went by. He therefore also gave attention to ensuring that they were maintained in faithful ministry. He prayed for his younger disciples and wrote regularly to many of them (copies of over seven thousand letters were found in his rooms after his death). He organized annual summer house parties for clergy for teaching and mutual encouragement and ensured that wives were included, acknowledging their vital importance to their husbands' ministries. He playfully referred to them as 'Ministresses, half-Ministers, often the most important part in your husband's parishes.'[75] He also encouraged clergy to meet regularly in local clerical societies, such as the influential Eclectic Society, which John Newton had founded and to which he belonged.

Simeon himself was an outstanding model of perseverance: despite great opposition for decades he never wavered from the task of preaching the gospel. After twenty years of relentless labour his health deteriorated sharply, so that for many years he was able to preach only once a week and even then often left the pulpit exhausted. Then, suddenly, his energy returned and he was able to take on a greater workload for the final period of his ministry, remaining active and faithful to the very end.

Simeon's last sermon in Holy Trinity was preached on 18 September 1836, on 2 Kings 10:16. Not knowing that his own death was so near he said:

It is not sufficient for any man to run well for a season only. We must endure to the end, if ever we would be saved. Whatever your attainments may be, and whatever you

---

75. Hopkins, *Charles Simeon of Cambridge*, p. 120.

may have done or suffered in the service of your God, you must forget the things that are behind, till you have actually fulfilled your course and obtained the crown.[76]

Shortly afterwards, as he was preparing a university sermon, Simeon went to Ely on a damp day to pay his respects to the new bishop. He got sick on the journey and was forced to take to his bed on his return. He declined rapidly, keeping his eyes fixed firmly on his Lord. 'I am in my Father's hands – all is secure,' he said. 'I cannot have more peace.'[77] In his final hours he was heard to murmur, 'Jesus Christ is my all in all for my soul.'[78] On 13 November 1836, at the age of seventy-seven, as the bells of Great St Mary's were summoning worshippers to the service at which he was to have preached, the great man of God passed into glory. His grateful parishioners placed a plaque in Holy Trinity, which read simply:

In Memory of
THE REV. CHARLES SIMEON, M.A.,
Senior Fellow of King's College,
And fifty-four years vicar of this parish; who,
whether as the ground of his own hopes,
or as the subject of all his ministrations,
determined to know nothing but
JESUS CHRIST AND HIM CRUCIFIED.
1 Cor.II.2.

© Vaughan Roberts, 2011

---

76. Moule, *Charles Simeon*, p. 166.
77. Ibid., p. 172.
78. Ibid., p. 175.

PETER ADAM: A LIFE SERVING GOD'S WORDS

Richard J. Condie

The Revd Canon Dr Peter James Hedderwick Adam has made a deep and lasting impact on the life and health of the church through his careful and intentional leadership and his preaching and teaching ministry, not just in Melbourne but around the globe. The contributors to this volume have all been influenced by Peter in a variety of ways. We hope that this collection will contribute to the ministry of thoughtful biblical preaching, teaching and leadership that has characterized Peter's own ministry.

Peter Adam was born in 1946 and grew up in Melbourne's inner eastern suburbs. He is the youngest of three brothers. He likes to tell that on the occasion of his birth his mother, really hoping for a baby girl, exclaimed, 'Another bloody boy!' A few years later his parents adopted a girl into the family.

During Peter's time at school, one of his teachers used to tell stories to the class about his own father who was a Christian. Even though the teacher himself was not a believer, the stories about his father made a deep impression on the eleven-year-old boy. He was so impressed with the reported quality of the man's life, he thought to himself, 'Whatever he has, I want it.' He went home from school and asked his parents to take him to church. What amazing grace that the witness of a man whom he had never met, from the lips of an unbeliever, would sow a seed that would later flower in faith.

Peter was then hooked on church and music. He had been learning piano from an early age and was smitten with becoming a concert pianist. Sunday by

Sunday his father took him to All Saints' Kooyong, where he went to Sunday school and eventually became one of the organists. He was attracted to the music and culture and the work of the local minister, and, even before he had truly come to faith, thought he might like to enter the ministry. His friends at school called him 'Purey' for his puritanical ways. He was forthrightly moral, and regularly read his Bible at lunchtime.

At the age of sixteen he was invited to fill in for the organist one Sunday at Holy Trinity Williamstown. The vicar, Archdeacon John Moroney, was also away from church that Sunday and the service was led by the Revd Harry Scott-Simmons. Harry, a former precentor of the cathedral and missionary in India, was at the time chaplain to Malvern Grammar. After the service, Harry and Peter travelled back to Malvern and Kooyong respectively on the same train. Harry quickly discerned that Peter was not a believer, and before they parted had issued an invitation to the young man to join him for afternoon tea the following Wednesday, ostensibly to listen to some of Harry's fine music collection.

Peter duly turned up for afternoon tea. The records were never played, but the Bible was opened, and within twenty minutes Peter was kneeling on the carpet and giving his life to Christ. The pattern of the carpet is burned into his memory to this day. Harry then met with him every Wednesday afternoon for the next three years, praying and reading the Bible together. Once Harry began praying for someone, he never stopped. Week by week Harry not only met with Peter but with many other young 'laddies', leading them to Christ. Peter was the preacher at Harry's funeral in 1996, and John Moroney gave the eulogy to this tireless evangelist.

Peter still plays the piano beautifully, and listens to music with careful attention. He once told me he rather dislikes 'background music' because serious music is written to be listened to. Yet the fresh convert turned from his idol of music and his dream of being a concert pianist to serve the living and true God. Almost within an instant he knew he was destined for ministry. He studied music at the University of Melbourne to mark time until he was old enough to begin studying for the ministry. Within a year, Peter's own witness saw his mother soundly converted and beginning active ministry in her local church.

In 1967, at the first opportunity, Peter entered Ridley College to prepare for ordination. He loves to tell stories of his time at Ridley, which usually involve impersonations of the then principal, Revd Dr Leon Morris. Morning Prayer was held in the chapel each morning. Peter was not an early riser and would miss these services with great regularity. He would save up his apologies for the principal, facing him once a week for missing chapel on Monday, Tuesday,

Wednesday, Thursday and Friday. Dr Morris would then ask in his crisp style, 'Have you an effective waking device?' To which Peter would answer, 'Yes, Dr Morris.' To which would come the reply 'Use it!' The same meeting would occur the following week!

Peter graduated from Ridley with a Licentiate in Theology and a Scholar in Theology and was deaconed in St Paul's Cathedral in 1970 by Archbishop Frank Woods. He immediately began his ministry as curate at St James' Ivanhoe, and later at St Andrew's Rosanna. He often tells of the requirement to preach for no more than twelve minutes each Sunday, a discipline that helped develop his clear and pointed exposition of the Bible. Further studies took him to London, where he obtained a Bachelor of Divinity from King's College in 1973, after which he returned to Melbourne in 1974, when his mother died, and worked as curate at St Thomas' Essendon and as a tutor at Ridley.

Peter returned overseas again in 1975 to commence his Master of Theology at King's College London on 1 Peter, which grounded him well in the Scriptures. He then completed his PhD at the University of Durham under the supervision of Professor Stephen Sykes, where he explored the 'Imitation of Christ' in the life of Dietrich Bonhoeffer. The study took him into church history, systematic theology and applied theology. He has frequently said that he draws upon these studies every day of his ministry. Tutorials in Durham forged in Peter a determination to defend his preaching with as much rigour as he used in the classroom.

In 1980, while studying and teaching in Durham, David Boan, an old friend from Ridley, invited Peter to speak at a week-long teaching mission called 'Carlton 80' for the parish of St Jude's in Melbourne. When the Parish became vacant eighteen months later, Peter was invited by the archbishop to take up the ministry there. Peter was very happy in Durham, and did not really want to leave. He speaks of a deep experience of the voice of God assuring him that St Jude's was his gift for Peter, and so he came with joy. Archbishop Robert Dann suggested at the time of his appointment that he 'wouldn't last long' in the Parish. It had a reputation of being a tough post that had been unable to keep its vicars for very long. Peter managed to last for twenty years.

He inherited a highly committed vigorous community at St Jude's, who were well formed in the faith and deeply caring of each other. Members at the time recall him bringing 'a breath of fresh air' to the parish, teaching on the sovereignty of God, the variety of God's people, and the Trinity. His ministry was careful, intentional and methodical as he thought strategically about winning 'Carlton for Christ'.

Under Peter's leadership the parish decided to establish a new congregation in the evening specifically tailored to university students. This grew quite rapidly, and the multiplying of congregations continued, with one on the nearby public housing estate, an evening congregation for workers, and the establishment of a second morning congregation about a month before he finished at St Jude's in 2002. All of these flowed out of his practice of having the parish establish a rolling series of five-year plans.

Peter's preaching ministry was one of the highlights of his time at St Jude's. His style was intellectual and academic, but deeply and warmly pastoral in application. In the early days in Carlton Peter suffered from a serious bout of depression that lasted for a number of years. Yet church members recall these times as Peter's most powerful in the pulpit, even when he was not able to function in other areas. Long sermon series on books like Hebrews and Numbers were a feature of his ministry. In fact, when he left St Jude's, there were only a few books of the Bible that he had not preached from. The Hebrews series became Peter's first major publication as a small commentary called *The Majestic Son: Reading Hebrews Today*.

Peter's great passion for expository preaching had begun around 1965 when John Stott came to Melbourne. Peter had not heard exposition like that before, and became convinced that this was the best way for people to hear the Word of God. He desired that more and more people would serve God's words through exposition, so during his ministry at St Jude's he established The Timothy Institute. This training programme saw many men and women try their hand at preaching and consider full-time ministry of the word. In the 1990s this ministry flourished, and he used the growing interest in preaching to encourage many pastors, teachers and preachers in their work. Many of his insights for preaching appear in his book *Preaching God's Words*.

A feature of his time in Carlton was his strategy to send out many gospel workers from St Jude's, specifically to reform the Anglican Diocese of Melbourne through the provision of preachers and church leaders. Dozens of Melbourne clergy claim significant influence by Peter Adam in their journey towards full-time ministry.

In 2001 the Revd Dr Graham Cole announced that he was moving on as principal of Ridley College to take up a post at Trinity Evangelical Divinity School. In some ways Peter was an obvious replacement. A clearly gifted teacher, thinker, writer and strategist, who since the 1980s had served on the college's Council and taught in a visiting capacity, Peter knew the college and was well suited to the task before him. Initially he was reluctant to apply for the job because of his fruitful ministry at St Jude's. On the morning of the interview God again gave him a real passion for the role, and a confidence about St Jude's, and he was appointed to Ridley in January 2002.

The college had been running on financial deficits for many years, and Peter knew that this needed to be turned around. The radical decision was taken in 2005 to close the part of Ridley that served as a residential college for secular university students and to sell the southern portion of the land, creating an endowment to fund the college's operation. For the first time in decades, under Peter's leadership, the college was financially stable.

In 2007 the Council, in collaboration with the Principal, articulated a new vision. A new name, Ridley Melbourne, signalled a new beginning for the college in a new century as it organized its teaching and formation programmes around learning communities. Peter's drive and thoughtful, intentional leadership was invaluable to the college as it celebrated its hundredth birthday in 2010, the year before Peter celebrates his sixty-fifth. Much of Ridley's history and future prospects are now documented in a centenary volume co-edited by Peter: *Proclaiming Christ: Ridley College Melbourne 1910–2010*. Ridley is in excellent shape as Peter concludes his time as Principal at the beginning of 2012. His contributions to the shape and the life of the college will be sorely missed.

C. H. Spurgeon, speaking of John Bunyan, is quoted as saying, 'Prick him anywhere; and you will find that his blood is Bibline, the very essence of the Bible flows from him.' These words could well have been spoken of the 'Bibline' Peter Adam. He is above anything else a Bible man. His life and ministry have been devoted to preaching it, teaching it, and in equipping and training others to preach and teach it in an invigorating and life-giving way. His sermons and lectures are filled with humour and pathos and vivid application, without diminishing or sidelining the Scriptures themselves. His favourite question for those in ministry whom he has not seen for a while is 'Are you still using the Bible in your ministry?'

This Bible focus is reflected in his book on spirituality, *Hearing God's Words*. It is an exploration of biblical spirituality: what the Bible teaches about relating to God, and the power of God's words in bringing change in the believer's life. So too this Bible focus is reflected in *Written for Us*. He could have ably written a systematic theology text on what theologians have said about the Bible, but the work shows us what the Bible itself says about the Bible.

One of the great themes of Peter's contribution as a teacher and preacher has been his commitment to biblical theology. He grasped this idea in a clear and fresh way during 'Carlton 85' when Peter Jensen was the speaker. Since then he has been painstaking in showing the 'big Bible themes', how the OT is fulfilled in the Lord Jesus Christ, and how the Bible holds together as one story. This emphasis has always been key in his preparation of preachers.

Peter's brand of evangelicalism is genuinely Anglican. He is deeply committed to the Anglican church, working tirelessly for its reform, especially in

Melbourne. He has sought to do this by being as involved in the life of the Diocese as he can be, serving as Archdeacon for Parish Development in the late 1980s, at various times on the Diocesan Council and numerous committees, commissions and task forces, and since 1996 as Canon of St Paul's Cathedral. All the while he has sought to see the Diocese of Melbourne grow in strength of conviction and especially in able evangelical ministries. Literally dozens of men and women are now serving in the Diocese and beyond because of Peter's encouragement of gospel workers.

Peter is a private person. He is most at home in his thoughts and with his own company (with a poodle close at hand of course!). He loves to retreat to his holiday home at the beach where the sand dunes and rock pools of his childhood still beckon him in solitude. Yet he has the amazing discipline and capacity to give himself to others as well. His diary continues to be full of engagements and 'coffees' and meals with many different people. He is a deep encourager of others, regularly meeting with those he prays for, to build them up in ministry and faithfulness.

Peter is also a man at prayer. I do not for a moment think that he finds prayer easy or that it comes naturally, but it is part of his discipline nonetheless. Many of us have received his list of prayer points year after year – including copies of his carefully crafted daily prayers for his own faithfulness, for a long and fruitful ministry, for accepting God's time as a gift, and for protection against moral failure. He is a model for others in his discipline and intentionality.

As we began looking for contributors to this book, our task was both easy and hard. It was easy because there are any number of people who have been influenced by Peter or who admire his ministry enough to want to contribute to the volume. The hard part was limiting the contributors to twelve. There are many people who owe a great debt to this man – many who came to Christ under his faithful ministry, many who have felt moved to offer their lives as gospel workers, Bible teachers and missionaries, and thousands who have been built up as faithful servants of Christ – as a result of his teaching or the teaching of those he has taught. In 2 Timothy 2:2 Paul encourages his young ministry friend with these words: 'what you have heard from me through many witnesses entrust to faithful people who will be able to teach others as well' (NRSV). This is a life of serving God's words, and we are privileged to have Peter Adam among us as one his servants.

© Richard J. Condie, 2011

MAJOR PUBLICATIONS BY PETER ADAM

Compiled by Ruth Millard

Doctoral dissertation

'The Practice of the Imitation of Christ: With Special Reference to the Theology of Dietrich Bonhoeffer' (University of Durham: Department of Theology, 1981).

Books

Hebrews: The Majestic Son: A Message of Encouragement, Reading the Bible Today (Sydney: AIO, 1992; repr. Sydney South: Aquila, 2004).

Speaking God's Words: A Practical Theology of Expository Preaching (Leicester: IVP, 1996; repr. Vancouver: Regent College Publishing, 2004).

Hearing God's Words: Exploring Biblical Spirituality, NSBT 16 (Downers Grove: IVP; Leicester: Apollos, 2004).

Written for Us: Receiving God's Words in the Bible (Nottingham: IVP, 2008).

(Co-edited with Gina Denholm) *Proclaiming Christ: Ridley College Melbourne 1910–2010* (Parkville: Ridley Melbourne, 2010).

Published lectures and booklets

Living the Trinity, Grove Spirituality Series 1 (Bramcote: Grove, 1982).

Guidance, Grove Spirituality Series 27 (Bramcote: Grove, 1988).

Roots of Contemporary Evangelical Spirituality, Grove Spirituality Series 24 (Bramcote: Grove, 1988).

A Church 'Halfly Reformed': The Puritan Dilemma (London: St Antholin's Lectureship Charity Trustees, 1998; repr. in Lee Gatiss [ed.], *Puritans, Warriors, and Servants: Puritan Wisdom for Today's Church* [London: Latimer Trust, 2010], pp. 185–215).

(With Alison Taylor and Richard Treloar) *Making Connections: Theological Leadership and the Australian Church* (Sydney: Anglican General Synod, 2001).

Word and Spirit: The Puritan–Quaker Debate (London: St Antholin's Lectureship Charity Trustees, 2001).

'To Bring Men to Heaven by Preaching': John Donne's Evangelistic Sermons (London: Latimer Trust, 2006).

Australia – Whose Land? A Christian Call for Recompense (Sydney: John Saunders Lecture, 2009). Published in various contexts and formats; e.g. *BriefCACE* 47 (2009), pp. 1–8.

Chapters and major articles

'The Child in the Church?', *Churchman* 91.4 (1977), pp. 318–328.

'Response' (to Peter Jensen, 'Using Scripture'), in Alan Nichols (ed.), *The Bible and Women's Ministry: An Australian Dialogue* (Wanniassa: Acorn, 1990), pp. 17–22.

'The Preacher and the Sufficient Word: Presuppositions of Biblical Preaching', in Christopher Green and David Jackman (eds.), *When God's Voice Is Heard: Essays on Preaching Presented to Dick Lucas* (Leicester: IVP, 1995), pp. 27–42.

'Preaching and Pastoral Ministry', in Melvin Tinker (ed.), *The Anglican Evangelical Crisis* (Fearn: Christian Focus, 1995), pp. 124–143.

'Theological Education in the Diocese of Melbourne', in Brian Porter (ed.), *Melbourne Anglicans: The Diocese of Melbourne 1847–1997* (Melbourne: Joint Board of Christian Education, 1997), pp. 159–178.

'The Trinity and Human Community', in Timothy Bradshaw (ed.), *Grace and Truth in the Secular Age* (Grand Rapids: Eerdmans, 1998), pp. 52–65.

'Preaching and Biblical Theology', in T. Desmond Alexander and Brian S. Rosner (eds.), *New Dictionary of Biblical Theology* (Leicester: IVP; Downers Grove: IVP, 2000), pp. 104–112.

'Communion: Virtue or Vice?', in Robert Tong, Peter G. Bolt and Mark D. Thompson (eds.), *The Faith Once for All Delivered: An Australian Evangelical Response to the Windsor Report* (Camperdown: Australian Church Record, 2005), pp. 71–75.

'Honouring Jesus Christ', *Churchman* 119.1 (2005), pp. 35–50 (repr. in *St Mark's Review* 198 [2005], pp. 11–18).

'The Scriptures Are God's Voice: The Church Is His Echo', in Bruce Kaye (ed.), *'Wonderful and Confessedly Strange': Australian Essays in Anglican Ecclesiology* (Hindmarsh: ATF, 2006), pp. 81–101.

'Arguing for Expository Preaching', *Rutherford Journal of Church and Ministry* 13.1 (2006), pp. 4–7.

'God's Powerful Words: Five Principles of Biblical Spirituality in Isaiah 55', *Southern Baptist Journal of Theology* 10.4 (2006), pp. 28–37.

'Incarnational Theology for a Missionary Church?', *St Mark's Review* 200 (2006), pp. 14–21.

'Morris, Leon Lamb (1914–2006)', in Donald K. McKim (ed.), *Dictionary of Major Biblical Interpreters* (Downers Grove: IVP Academic; Nottingham: IVP, 2007), pp. 751–755.

'Whatever Happened to Preaching?', in Keith Weller (ed.), *Please! No More Boring Sermons: Preaching for Australians: Contemporary Insights and Practical Aspects* (Brunswick East: Acorn, 2007), pp. 13–28.

'Liturgical Preaching', in Keith Weller (ed.), *Please! No More Boring Sermons: Preaching for Australians: Contemporary Insights and Practical Aspects* (Brunswick East: Acorn, 2007), pp. 67–78.

'Power and Authority', *St Mark's Review* 205 (2008), pp. 51–68.

'Preaching of a Lively Kind: Calvin's Engaged Expository Preaching', in Mark D. Thompson (ed.), *Engaging with Calvin: Aspects of the Reformer's Legacy for Today* (Nottingham: Apollos, 2009), pp. 13–41. (Also delivered to and published in *Proceedings of the Uniting Church Historical Society Synod of Victoria & Tasmania* 16.2 [2009], pp. 59–96.)

'Christ and Creation', *St Mark's Review* 212 (2010), pp. 101–115.

'The Founding of Ridley College', in Peter Adam and Gina Denholm (eds.), *Proclaiming Christ: Ridley College Melbourne 1910–2010* (Parkville: Ridley Melbourne, 2010), pp. 13–29.

'Ridley: The Future', in Peter Adam and Gina Denholm (eds.), *Proclaiming Christ: Ridley College Melbourne 1910–2010* (Parkville: Ridley Melbourne, 2010), pp. 177–190.

'Calvin's Preaching and Homiletic: Nine Engagements', *Churchman* 124.3 (2010), pp. 201–215, and following issues.

Speaking God's Words
A practical theology of preaching
Peter Adam

The aim of this book is to provide a robust practical theology of preaching as part of the ministry of the Word in the local congregation: a *theology* of preaching, because only theological arguments are convincing in the long term. To argue that we ought to preach because it works, or that we ought not to preach because preaching is ineffective, is to descend to the realm of the merely pragmatic. We also need a theology of preaching because the practice of preaching suffers nowadays from an uncertain theological base. Changes over recent years in our theology of God's revelation, of the Bible, of Christian formation, of communication, of community and of ecclesiology have tended to undermine preaching. In such a situation it is not wise to continue a ministry without a deep conviction about its sound theological base.

We also need a *practical* theology of preaching because the Bible is practical in its teaching on the ministry of the Word. The key questions of this book are therefore: *What does the Bible teach us about the ministry of the Word? What are the current questions about preaching? What can be said that will have theological substance and be of practical usefulness to those who preach?*

ISBN: 9780851111711 | 176 page paperback | RRP: £12.99

Available from your local Christian bookshop
or via our website at **www.ivpbooks.com**

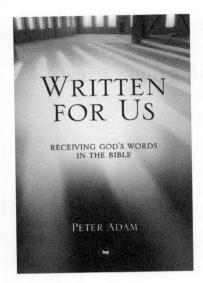

Written for Us

Receiving God's words in the Bible

Peter Adam

Understanding what the Bible teaches about itself is an issue of central importance. However, correct theologies of the Bible can be expressed in non-biblical categories; and it would be foolish to believe of the Bible what it does not claim for itself, whether implicitly or explicitly.

Peter Adam's conviction is that there is a coherent 'biblical theology of the Bible'. In this wide-ranging volume, he searches the Scriptures to find their answer to the question of their identity and use, and expounds the following summary:

- Receiving God's words
- Written for his people
- By his Spirit
- About his Son

This fresh, energetic presentation is a valuable complement to the author's previous works on the function and application of Scripture in Christian life and ministry.

ISBN: 9781844742080 | 272 page paperback | RRP: £14.99

Available from your local Christian bookshop
or via our website at **www.ivpbooks.com**

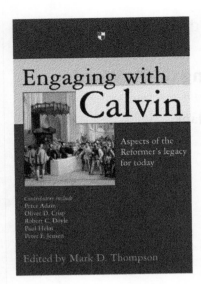

Engaging with Calvin
Aspects of the Reformer's legacy for today

Mark D. Thompson (Editor)

John Calvin was born on 10 July 1509. Five hundred years later, the ideas of this French theologian continue to influence churches all around the world, and Western culture in general. He has also been a victim of caricature and misunderstanding, even within his own lifetime.

The contributors to this stimulating volume, linked with the 2009 Moore College School of Theology, are united by the conviction that Calvin needs to be heard afresh, understood first on his own terms and then drawn on as a theological resource for Christian life and thought today. The essays explore selected aspects of Calvin's contribution and encourage us to read Calvin for ourselves – for to engage with him as he speaks about the knowledge of God the Creator and Redeemer, whom he served with a singular devotion, cannot but mean that we will have our vision of God expanded and our love for him inflamed.

ISBN: 9781844743988 | 352 page paperback | RRP: £19.99

Available from your local Christian bookshop
or via our website at **www.ivpbooks.com**

Printed and bound by CPI Group (UK) Ltd, Croydon, CR0 4YY

13/04/2025